BLOOD
&
BELIEF

BLOOD
&
BELIEF

*Family Survival and Confessional Identity
among the Provincial Huguenot Nobility*

Raymond A. Mentzer, Jr.

Purdue University Press

West Lafayette, Indiana

98 97 96 95 94   5 4 3 2 1

The paper used in this book meets the minimum requirements of American National Standard for Information Sciences—Permanence of Paper for Printed Library Materials, ANSI Z39.48-1984.

Printed in the United States of America
Design by Chiquita Babb

Library of Congress Cataloging-in-Publication Data
Mentzer, Raymond A.
    Blood and belief : family survival and confessional identity among the provincial Huguenot nobility / by Raymond A. Mentzer, Jr.
       p.   cm.
    Includes bibliographical references and index.
    ISBN 1-55753-041-6
    1. Lacger family. 2. Nobility—France—Castres—Biography.
3. Huguenots—France—Castres—Biography. 4. Castres (France)—
Religious life and customs. 5. Castres (France)—Genealogy.
I. Title.
DC801.C287M46 1994
944'.85—dc20   93-25955
                                                   CIP

Contents

Preface

This study of the Lacger, a Huguenot family of the lesser provincial nobility, has evolved and matured over the years. The idea first occurred during a visit to the Château de Navès in May 1976. I was living at Toulouse, completing a year-long research project that focused on the Protestant judicial magistracy. In the process, I had come across an obscure reference to the Lacger family archives. A series of inquiries eventually led me to the ancestral estate outside Castres, where the late François de Lacger was extremely accommodating in making his family's papers available to me. At the time, my interest did not extend beyond some marriage contracts relating to several sixteenth-century judges. Still, I was impressed by the possibilities inherent in this rich collection of documents. Here, neatly shelved and arranged, were the records of one plainly unspectacular, yet representative, family, whose history stretched over more than four hundred years.

A summer stipend from the National Endowment for the Humanities enabled me to return to Castres in 1984 and begin a careful survey of the Lacger archives. Subsequent visits, supported by Montana State University, took place over the next several years and permitted completion of the research at Castres as well as related forays into the archives of Albi, Paris, and Toulouse. A fellowship from the National Endowment for the Humanities, a sabbatical from my home university, and a residential fellowship from the Camargo Foundation at Cassis, France, provided the opportunity to spend the 1989–90 academic year writing a first draft of the book.

The project has, naturally enough, benefited from considerable support and encouragement at every step along the way. Natalie Davis and

Robert Kingdon were, as ever, very helpful, particularly in the initial, defining stages. Elisabeth Labrousse, in a series of lengthy conversations, answered my many questions about the French Reformed community and contributed enormously to the manner whereby I set about framing the study. Later, Miriam Chrisman, Barbara Davis, Mack Holt, Orest Ranum, Ellery Schalk, Paul Solon, and Chris Stocker read and criticized my earliest attempts to interpret the Lacger and their achievement. The resident fellows of the Camargo Foundation offered useful recommendations when I presented a synopsis of the initial chapters at our weekly seminar. At the Purdue University Press, Margaret Hunt has been ever optimistic and cheerful in the complex and deliberate process of seeing a manuscript to press. My wife, Beth, unfailingly took on added family responsibilities during my several summers' absence from home, patiently trudged about France with me for extended periods of time, and assessed with exacting candor every line that I have written about the Lacger. Marriage and the emotional bonds between two people are powerful and sustaining in ways that Lacger daughters and sons would have readily comprehended.

I owe a special thanks to Jacqueline and Geneviève Lavondès, the modern descendants of Guy de Lacger and Jeanne de Carles. While their late uncle, François, first introduced me to the family's papers, they graciously opened their home and archives time and again. Our countless informal chats over coffee or a meal resolved my queries concerning the family's understanding of its own past and helped me appreciate the sense of continuity and tradition implicit in the experience. Their exceptional generosity and kindness to me and my family during our many visits have made this book possible. Theirs is a friendship that I shall always cherish.

ONE

෴

Introduction

Ancestral Archives and Historical Issues

Perspectives

In the late winter of 1756, Marc-Antoine II de Lacger and a stepbrother, twenty years his junior, took over a small, little-used room in the family's town house at Castres and began rummaging through an old chest filled with rat-chewed ancestral documents.[1] The stepbrother was seeking to launch his eldest boy on a military career and needed the legal instruments to reconfirm the family's noblesse. The two men hastily spread the papers and parchments about on chairs, taking those that they regarded as the most important and carelessly trampling others that they had discarded on the floor. More than a decade would pass before one of Marc-Antoine II's own sons, Jean-Jacques-Joseph, noticed several nephews playing with the forgotten papers. Far more appreciative of their historical value than his father and uncle, he gathered the scattered remains with the express idea of preserving them as the proud record of his noble house.

Before embarking on his project, Jean-Jacques-Joseph added to his treasure yet another collection of papers. This second cache of documents came from one of the family's country residences. It had been assembled in the spring of 1758, two years after the first, again by Marc-Antoine II. He had, the previous September, inherited the locally important seigneury of Navès[2] and needed to prove his nobility if he were to be exempted from payment of the *franc-fief,* a fine levied on commoners who came into possession of noble lands.[3] The royal bureaucracy periodically demanded proof from those who claimed noble privileges, such as military commissions or exemption from certain forms of taxation. Forays into the family archives were a regular feature of aristocratic existence during the ancien régime. In part, families assiduously guarded their papers for this reason. Marc-Antoine II's undertaking of 1758, for instance, was made considerably easier by the fact that his grandfather had already gathered and organized many of the more important papers for a *recherche de noblesse* conducted in the area around Castres during the early 1670s. These *recherches,* periodic official investigations, regulated nobility by requiring families to establish their noble status legally. The Lacger house, to cite the obvious, was in January 1671 "maintained in its nobility and recognized as *noble de race.*"[4] The commissions accepted only legal documents, and families had to prove that they had been living nobly for at least three generations.[5]

In the second half of the eighteenth century, when Jean-Jacques-Joseph, the self-appointed genealogist and family historian, began arranging and copying the materials, he had before him the letters, estate and household accounts, marriage contracts, testaments, legal judgments, property leases, cadastral surveys, and inventories of possessions that constituted his family's history since the early sixteenth century.[6] Far larger and more detailed than the popular *livres de raison,* this was not just a family journal or domestic memoir.[7] It was an immense, yet systematic, collection of documents. Jean-Jacques-Joseph began the project in July 1769 and worked for a little more than five years. In the process, he filled five volumes, accounting for 2,231 folios. The first volume alone occupied him for nearly three years. Upon its completion, his elder brother François, by this time the family patriarch, composed a few brief verses that he then affixed to the frame below Jean-Jacques-Joseph's portrait in the family gallery.[8]

Cest autheur était toujours dans son cabinet
à déchifrer dates, beaux titres en secret.
Trois ans de lacture, trois ans d'atantion
fut le temps qu'il mit à la composition
de toute sa généalogie, l'histoire
qui randit son nom très digne de mémoire.[9]

[This author was always in his study
deciphering dates and handsome titles in seclusion.
Three years of reading, three years of attentiveness
was the time that he devoted to the composition
of his entire genealogy, the history
that rendered his name deserving of remembrance.]

Jean-Jacques-Joseph's purpose, fully if not quite lyrically expressed in these lines, went beyond the legal requirements and social objectives that had propelled his father and great-grandfather. He sought to validate Lacger honor, merit, and position by reference to ancestral heritage. It was as much a matter of pride as proof. The emphasis was upon lineage, blood ties, and the hereditary qualities associated with the idea of *race* and "good stock."[10] The family genealogy and history, moreover, dignified its very memory and, of course, its continuing experience. Every house found distinction in the antiquity and luster of its name, the prominence and virtue of its men and women, even the valor and esteem of other families to which it was connected by bonds of marriage and friendship. Within a year of the completion of Jean-Jacques-Joseph's endeavor, the family published at its own expense a *Généalogie historique de la maison de Lacger* complete with *pièces justificatives* attesting to its fame and accomplishment. It was a proud testimonial addressed to a wider public audience.[11] On the other hand, Jean-Jacques-Joseph could scarcely have appreciated, or even imagined, the possibilities that historians two centuries later would find in his genteel and youthful achievement.

The papers themselves survived into the eighteenth century for sound practical reasons. They were invaluable legal documents, hopefully incontrovertible proof, that confirmed aristocratic families in their political power, economic position, and social privilege.[12] The historical record of Lacger ancestry also furthered the family's reputation by conferring the place and prestige of an ancient lineage. Genealogy, this preoccupation with family and descent, was a matter of special pride among nobles and contributed to their sense of distinctive character.[13] Honor and heredity were inescapably bound together. It was, after all, a world in which rank was bequeathed largely by birth. On the other hand, modern historians, alive to a different set of interests, view such assemblages of family papers[14] as valuable opportunities to test various hypotheses surrounding such matters as family structure, kinship relationships, gender roles, marriage patterns, power elites, and religious ideology. There are, however, obvious limitations. While the Lacger family archives are extremely informative of the principal Protestant line, they reveal less about collateral, especially Catholic, relatives. In addition, the papers have a heavy patriarchal orientation toward the public and more masculine aspects of family life.

The ability of upper-class families such as the Lacger to formulate and effect long-range strategies for success has become a commonplace among historians of early modern Europe. Yet the studies that have appeared typically concentrate on great houses and are frequently set in an urban world. They focus on social mobility as well as the accumulation of wealth and power, and with few exceptions, they tend to analyze the attempts by elite families to achieve regional and national prominence amid a relatively stagnant economy and fixed social hierarchy.[15] Though these volumes have made a substantial contribution toward understanding the ancien régime, little attention has been given those families that fell by the wayside or, perhaps more commonly, barely managed to sustain kith and kin in the rural hinterland. The Lacger, whose influence and estates were and still are in and around the town of Castres in southern France, are one modern survivor among the many also-rans. The family's history is, to be sure, highly instructive in understanding the dynamics of economic achievement, political empowerment, social advancement, and assimilation into the nobility. These matters weigh heavily in any examination of early modern elites, and the study at hand is no exception. Yet the fundamental focus of the present exploration is the question of family endurance and resilience as well as the related matter of Protestant identity.

The Lacger's accomplishment—their long-term survival—was made all the more remarkable by the fact that they converted to Protestantism in the late 1550s and early 1560s. The family subsequently withstood the violence of the Wars of Religion, weathered the pressure of Richelieu's armies during the 1620s, adjusted to Louis XIV and his revocation of the Edict of Nantes,[16] and persevered through the general proscription of Protestantism that followed. What explains this extraordinary tenacity? Did the Lacger, like the more famous aristocratic houses examined by other historians, demonstrate a capacity to conceive and implement far-sighted social relationships and economic arrangements, reaching out over generations? At the same time, what weight ought to be assigned to the role of religious ideology and confessional identity relative to the commonly considered factors, such as wealth, social position, and blood relationships? Simply put, did the Lacger draw their strength and dura-bility from unshakable conviction in the face of religious oppression? Or is their survival best attributed to shrewd business sense, well-conceived family alliances, and sustaining kinship networks?

Circumstances

In order to understand better the context for discussing these questions and to appreciate fully the value of this rich collection of family papers, let us begin by identifying the Lacger more specifically. They were mem-bers of the provincial nobility and, as such, formed a part of the social, political, and economic elite of ancien régime France. The family was rela-tively new, not especially wealthy, and heavily dependent upon royal officeholding. The Lacger were judges who belonged to the nobility of the robe, so designated by virtue of their judicial garb. These royal func-tionaries were distinct from the older nobility of the sword, an obvious reference to the aristocracy's cherished military role.[17] The Lacger wielded no independent military power and never controlled castles or fortified garrisons.[18] They, like many lesser provincial houses, found their situation ambiguous and sometimes precarious.[19] Even the Lacger asser-tion of nobility in the *recherche* of 1671, for example, was not a foregone conclusion. Although the family successfully pressed its case, the royal commissioners were only too willing to challenge such claims.[20]

Perhaps the single most distinctive feature of the Lacger was their Protestantism. When the religious wars drew to a close at the end of the sixteenth century, French Calvinists were no more than 6 or 7 percent of the population—1.2 million people, perhaps slightly more. Their numbers, however, were concentrated; more than four-fifths lived in western and, above all, southern France, the area known as the Midi.[21] The southern provinces were home to numerous Huguenot families of the petty nobility like the Lacger. They were scattered throughout the rural hinterland as well as the small and medium-sized towns of the region. Castres, the Lacger's particular residence, was a middling, powerfully Protestant community that, along with several other southern towns such as Montauban and Nîmes, played a decisive role in the Protestant movement during and after the sixteenth century. Under the terms of the Edict of Nantes of 1598, Castres became a fortified *place de sûreté*. Huguenots could freely worship in a surety town, and they controlled the garrison as well.

Situated astride the Agout River and about seventy kilometers east of Toulouse in the western half of the province of Languedoc, Castres was the principal urban agglomeration in a relatively poor, compact mountainous district that took its name from the town and was known accordingly as the Castrais. Whatever unity existed was more political than geographical and resulted mainly from the creation of the county of Castres during the Middle Ages. The town was the administrative center for the feudal territory and the site of a lesser bishopric. The surrounding Castrais was a traditional agricultural area, where most people cultivated cereal crops in a subsistence system typical of early modern France. The richer alluvial deposits of the valley of the Agout were suitable for the production of wheat. The uplands, notably south toward the Montagne Noire, possessed far thinner soils and were largely restricted to the pasturing of sheep and the cultivation of hardier cereals such as rye. Oats, destined chiefly for livestock, and barley were decidedly secondary; although vineyards existed, they were not widespread. Industry, principally the manufacture of woolens and leather goods, was mostly limited to the town of Castres and wholly framed by the larger rural peasant world.

The Lacger could be found occupying judicial and administrative posts at Castres and several other smaller settlements in the immediate vicinity beginning in the 1530s. Emerging from obscurity, they gradually entered the nobility, the roughly 2 to 3 percent of the population that formed the hereditary elite. The Lacger sent their sons to the university and subsequently placed them in the law courts associated with the county or the provincial parlement. Later, in the seventeenth century, the army held an increasing allure as more than a dozen young men took military commissions and thereby sought to enhance the family's reputation and simultaneously seal its assimilation into the noble ranks. Warfare was, after all, the acknowledged vocation of the aristocracy, and the ideal of the "warrior" held the imagination of noble and nonnoble alike.[22] The crown's demand for religious conformity after 1685 inevitably weighed heavily upon these Protestant judicial magistrates and military officers. They were men of public affairs and civic participation for whom such service represented a political, social, and economic opportunity. Their situation was crucially linked to a state that demanded obedience. Lacking the independent status of the older feudal nobility, some chose to cooperate with the governing authority and become at least nominally Catholic. Those within this Huguenot house who resisted best, but passively even then, were those favored by landed wealth, which brought a practical measure of autonomy.

The acquisition of real property, some urban town houses but mostly rural agricultural estates, was another key component in the establishment of Lacger fortunes. The most prominent of these so-called *métairies* were those of Clot, la Planesié, and Navès. The family acquired the first two during the sixteenth century and the latter in the early eighteenth century. All were hard by Castres to the southeast, where the smaller Thoré River flows into the Agout. The three were contiguous, thereby offering a tight, coherent set of properties. The tenures further benefited from the fertile soils of the low-lying plains along the looping Agout and Thoré. This landed wealth was, to be sure, unevenly distributed within the family.

Legal customs and practice in southern France encouraged preferential treatment of the eldest male child as principal heir, which resulted in a dramatically unequal division of the ancestral patrimony. Shares varied according to gender and the order of birth. The Lacger bequeathed the oldest son as much as two-thirds of the family's wealth.[23] Among younger siblings, brothers had progressively diminished interest in the inheritance, and sisters normally received no more than a marriage portion. Favoring the eldest male had the practical effect of transmitting the family's economic resources more or less intact and retaining them under the control of a series of patriarchs. The practice obviated excessive and ruinous divisions of wealth among numerous heirs and thereby assisted in the survival of the family, even if it severely disadvantaged many family members.

Marriage, along with the panoply of arrangements tied to it, is arguably the most fundamental element in any family study. Under the ancien régime, it provided the structure for continuation in the basic sense. Marriage was the legal institution for the procreation and nurturing of children. It further provided the context for transmitting assets from one generation to the next. The family and its name flourished through its progeny. Here the Lacger had a distinct advantage in that they regularly possessed medium-sized families, averaging five children per family over eight generations from the early 1500s through the late 1700s. They achieved, however unintentionally, a balance between too few children and too many. Families needed enough offspring to carry on the line but not so many as to drain and exhaust patrimonial resources. Most Lacger children survived into adulthood and many had extraordinarily long lives, thus contributing to the family's well-being and the conservation of its property.

Reproduction was not, of course, the sole consideration in marriage. Marital unions were also an opportunity to consolidate and extend resources. Lacger males, particularly in the sixteenth and early seventeenth centuries, found marriage a useful way to add to the family's wealth. Brides often brought attractive dowries and inheritances—above all, real property. Moreover, as the house flourished and its honor increased, marriages were a ready device to initiate as well as strengthen friendships and political alliances. The marriage pattern among daughters and sons was highly endogamous within a regional Protestant elite. They took spouses from among the provincial judicial magistracy, the petty nobility, and exceptionally, older families of the feudal aristocracy, but always within the confines of confessional affinity.

The Lacger house probably achieved its greatest brilliance in the second and third quarters of the seventeenth century, a period of considerable accomplishment for Protestants throughout France. Its women married into some of the most distinguished Protestant houses of Languedoc, including that of Toulouse-Lautrec. Three of its men were judges in the special Protestant chamber of the Parlement of Toulouse, the highest royal court in Languedoc. Two others left Castres for Paris and service in the ever-burgeoning royal bureaucracy. Another briefly served the Queen of Sweden; wrote a lengthy, if undistinguished, series of madrigals and sonnets; and eventually was among the founders of a literary academy at Castres. Yet these achievements and their promise were cut short by growing royal animosity toward Protestants. The crown's attempts at elimination of the Reformed Churches of France had a lethal effect.

Adherence to Protestantism permeated, molded, and modified Lacger designs and stratagems. Their influential position within the community assured them considerable authority in the religious sphere, yet they rarely demonstrated a direct interest in ecclesiastical matters proper. None ever trained for the pastorate, and only once did a family member join the governing ecclesiastical circle of the local Reformed church: Jacques was an elder on the consistory for the 1674 term. Every local church had a consistory made up of one or more pastors and ten to twelve lay persons serving as elders and deacons. The members, who met weekly, exercised responsibility for ecclesiastical administration, social welfare, and morals control. Above the individual church and its consistory, there was a highly structured presbyterian-synodal organization. A pastor and elder from each of a dozen or so local churches gathered biannually in the colloquy. Similar delegations from the churches within each of the sixteen ecclesiastical provinces of France met once a year in the provincial synod. The provinces, in turn, appointed two pastors and two elders to attend the national synod, which convened annually at first, but irregularly as time wore on. These colloquies and synods settled both administrative and theological matters. They fixed policy, developed comprehensive ecclesiastical regulations, clarified belief, and resolved a variety of disputes.

The Lacger, like many other elite families, preferred to participate in the Huguenot political assemblies, which united the Protestant nobility in organizing the cause financially, militarily, and constitutionally. This role suited Lacger notions of social place and political importance in the Protestant world. Pierre, the reigning family patriarch after 1600, attended an entire series of these political assemblies during the second and third decades of the seventeenth century. Like his father and uncles in the previous century, he strove to reduce the seemingly endless conflict between Protestants and the crown. On the whole, the Lacger adopted a moderate position on the religious question, viewing it largely as a private matter. This practical stance found reinforcement in the fact that they were royal magistrates who wished no quarrel with their Catholic sovereign. Many more-passionate Huguenots had no sympathy for what they regarded as a compromising approach and classed the Lacger among the "party of the *escambarlats*," Protestants who behaved like toadies in their obsequious obedience to the crown.

If the Lacger's particular approach to religion led to certain difficulties with members of their own church, their Protestantism created a far graver set of general problems. The family discovered that its faith severely curtailed ambitions. Although four generations of Lacger males held royal judicial office, none ever attained national prominence. Most were subalternate judges at Castres or, at best, members of the *chambre de l'Edit,* a special bipartisan court for the judgment of Protestant litigation. The chamber had a divided bench staffed with proportionate numbers of Protestant and Catholic magistrates, and while theoretically a part of the Parlement of Toulouse, it had its permanent seat at Castres. For Protestant families such as the Lacger whose aspirations were tied to service in the royal magistracy, ambitions frequently ended at this Protestant tribunal at Castres. Even when Lacger sons migrated from the Midi to Paris—as did two brothers in the early 1600s—the next generation returned to Castres and the chamber. Even this tightly circumscribed opportunity had closed by the last quarter of the seventeenth century when, as part of its general assault on Protestantism, the crown abolished the *chambre de l'Edit* and further required that all royal officers make attestations of Catholicity.

Another sort of royal service, increasingly popular among Lacger males beginning in the 1660s, involved military commissions in one or another of the king's regiments. Buckling on the sword was, understandably enough, extremely attractive to young men from recently ennobled houses who were anxious to imitate the ancient feudal aristocracy, and Louis XIV provided a long series of bellicose ventures toward satisfying this craving for battle and its glory. Military exploits denoted family reputation and personal merit in a way which early modern society took to be fundamental. The Lacger, lacking great wealth, contented themselves with infantry commissions rather than those in the more glamorous cavalry regiments, and most officers from the house never rose above the rank of lieutenant or captain. Exceptionally, several family members became battalion commanders and lieutenant colonels, while another ended his long military career as a *brigadier des armées*. These grades, however, speak to achievement and effort rather than wealth and influential lineage. They represent the reward for continued diligent service and not the purchase of authority and position as was possible, say, for the rich families of the older aristocracy, whose members were proprietary colonels in command of entire regiments.

The Lacger favored the Regiment of Auvergne; ten of its men served it from the beginning of Louis XIV's personal rule until the end of the ancien régime. This particular regiment, recruited in part from the rural Calvinist world of the Cévennes Mountains and the province of Languedoc, had a reputation for Protestantism.[24] By 1685, these Reformed soldiers and their officers confronted an official demand for adherence to Catholicism. Men in the ranks could usually get by with prudent reserve and occasional dissimulation. Commissioned officers were a bit more hard-pressed. The Lacger who were in the military effectively faced a choice between retirement and conversion. Those who possessed other assets, principally land, opted to relinquish their commissions. The less well-off submitted to the royal will, although it was plainly a matter of expediency for one or two—they had the fewest of other resources and could ill afford to repudiate the military career on which they had already set their course. Their newfound Catholicism did not always easily suit them, and they occasionally found ways to assist—especially financially—those cousins who had maintained greater constancy in the commitment to Protestant beliefs.

Those within the Lacger house who were best equipped to resist Louis XIV and Louis XV's persecution of Protestants were the inheritors of landed wealth. Secure in their economic wherewithal, they could, in most respects, maintain a confessional privacy that allowed them to retain their Protestant views so long as they in no way publicly contradicted or opposed the official Catholicism demanded by the state. This posture—officially Catholic, while privately Protestant—naturally exacted a price. It delimited economic, political, social, and cultural boundaries with painful austerity and precision. Careers in government or law were curtailed or, in some cases, were no longer a possibility; regional political influence slipped from Lacger hands; marriages became ever more endogamous within an immediate Protestant community; and everyone was subject to a cultural offensive directed by the agents of Versailles. The landholders among the Lacger held out, but they remained inextricably tied to the locality. They lived in a tight and contained world. On the other hand, their religious position did not prevent and likely promoted family solidarity. The confessional oppression fired them with a will to endure and, in the process, contributed significantly to their continued existence into the eighteenth century and beyond.

Comparisons

The Lacger draw our attention because of their meticulously documented past. They were, to be sure, participants in a general process. The specifics may vary somewhat, but other petty noble houses whose histories are rarely so well recorded underwent similar sorts of experiences and often responded in similar ways. Residing in the lesser towns and rural world of the Midi, these families typically established themselves by the early sixteenth century in mercantile pursuits or the legal profession, then used their wealth to purchase offices in the financial and judicial bureaucracies. They sought simultaneously to acquire land and to embark upon the process of ennoblement. Such families were frequently in the vanguard of the Protestant movement, where, as members of the elite, they soon assumed direction over political and administrative affairs within the Reformed community. Huguenot military leadership, on the other hand, fell to the older feudal aristocracy. Later, after the close of the religious wars, the lesser provincial nobles remained the mainstay of Protestantism throughout southern France. They suffered the revocation of the Edict of Nantes and endured the prolonged persecution that ended only with the Edict of Toleration in 1787.

The Escorbiac (or Scorbiac) house of Montauban was remarkably similar to the Lacger in its historical development. As such, it too tells us much about the political position, social status, and religious ideology of the provincial Protestant magistracy. Like the Lacger, the Escorbiac made their appearance at a moderately sized town—in this instance, Montauban

—during the first decades of the sixteenth century and set their initial roots in the legal profession. The early family members were notaries who, in turn, sent their sons to the law school at Toulouse. Received into the ranks of Montauban's attorneys in his mid-twenties, Guichard d'Escorbiac, for instance, embarked upon a civic career. He participated in municipal politics by serving as a councilman, and in 1560, though not yet thirty-five years old, represented Montauban at the meeting of the Estates General. When the Escorbiac joined the Reformed Church during the early 1560s, the family was able to sustain its traditional ambitions within the civic elite and explore new roles that opened as the result of the commitment to Protestantism. Again, Guichard was active at several of the many Huguenot political assemblies that met in southern France during the mid-1570s. These highly independent representative assemblies occupy an important niche in the history of political resistance and, as such, offered an unusual opportunity for the exercise of legislative power by the various delegates, especially those from strongly Calvinist towns such as Montauban or Castres. The development has prompted at least one modern historian to dub the system a sort of "United Provinces of the Midi."[25]

Another opportunity for social and economic advancement that was linked to Protestantism came through the patronage of the major Huguenot princes, such as Condé or Henry of Navarre. These national leaders cemented ties of devotion and continuing support among their clients by offering political offices or positions in their households and on their many feudal holdings.[26] Following the Peace of Bergerac in 1577, Henry of Navarre rewarded the loyal Guichard d'Escorbiac with the office of *maître des requêtes,* a remunerative administrative post in his household government. Nonetheless, it was access to the highest levels of the provincial magistracy—seats on the parlement—that families such as the Escorbiac and Lacger ultimately sought and received.

Since the initial burst of religious violence in 1562, Protestants had been effectively barred from the Parlement of Toulouse. Only in the final quarter of the century, with the creation of the *chambre de l'Edit,* did offices on the sovereign court open to Protestants. The aspiring Huguenot houses immediately set about securing these royal positions for themselves and their heirs. As might be expected, once acquired, the offices were rarely relinquished. The Escorbiac first achieved the rank of associate judge in 1579 at the tentative beginnings of the judicial venture. Though there were some interruptions in service, Guichard d'Escorbiac, his son Samuel, and his grandson Thomas sat on the court until its last days. This tenacious grip on parlementary positions can be explained as a trait shared by many economically and socially ambitious families of the ancien régime. Yet for the Protestant magistracy of the Midi, there was added significance. By the early decades of the seventeenth century, it was clear that there would be little opportunity for advancement beyond royal judicial offices, particularly those in the *chambre de l'Edit* that sat at Castres. To a degree, the situation resembles the allotment of political privilege and civil-service positions among the religious and ethnic minorities of some contemporary modern nations. For the Protestant families of the Midi, aspirations were closely tied to the king's court and, in any event, rarely went further than the *chambre* at Castres. Those who arrived first held on, usually until extinction of the lineage.

The sense of dependency that permeated this particular level of Protestant society can be illustrated with reference to attitudes at the time of Rohan's rebellion in the 1620s. Whereas Guichard d'Escorbiac was instrumental in securing the gates of Montauban for Condé's party in 1562, his son Samuel fought the tide of popular enthusiasm for war during the second and third decades of the seventeenth century. He attempted in vain to maintain the town in obedience to the crown. Finally, the Rohan faction drove him from Montauban. During the subsequent and famous siege, Samuel watched from a nearby château, where the king had graciously installed him. When the ill-fated strife ended, the king repaid Samuel's fidelity by allowing him to exchange his civil and criminal judgeship on the seneschal's court at Montauban for a seat on the *chambre de l'Edit*. Unfortunately, his service to the crown was not complete. In 1632, during the twilight of his career, he received the onerous chore of reshaping Montauban's consular government into a bipartisan structure. A municipal council that had been exclusively Huguenot since 1560 was now to be *mi-parti*. Its six seats would henceforth be divided equally among Catholics and Calvinists. Samuel d'Escorbiac worked closely with and for the crown but at the cost of having become the anti-hero among many of his coreligionists.[27]

The Nautonier family of the Castrais offers another ready comparative example. The house appears to have risen to wealth and power through commercial activity, perhaps in the textile or pastel (a blue dye) trades. By the early sixteenth century, however, its members aspired to the ranks of noble landholders, having become seigneurs of Castelfranc, northeast of Castres. Yet they had not wholly forsaken commercial and financial pursuits. Pierre de Nautonier, for example, was active in the provincial tax administration during the 1520s. Pierre's son, like so many of his generation and status, converted to Protestantism, probably in the late 1550s. He subsequently became an energetic participant in various regional political assemblies of the Huguenot faction. At the Protestant delegates' meetings at Pierreségade and Réalmont in 1572 and 1573, respectively, he was even appointed treasurer for the "cause." On the other hand, the several generations that followed possessed decidedly more theological and intellectual interests.

Guillaume de Nautonier, Pierre's grandson, studied for the ministry at Lausanne during the 1580s and, upon returning to his native Languedoc, served for nearly thirty years as pastor at Vénès and Montredon. Both were rural churches near the family estates at Castelfranc, where Guillaume, head of the Nautonier family, was the local seigneur. The combination surely lent him a heady measure of political, economic, religious, and social ascendancy in the immediate area. His position and intellectual formation naturally insured a flourishing ecclesiastical career. Guillaume was, among other things, part of the team that engaged a Jesuit controversialist in public debate at Castres in 1599. During the next decade, he served as provincial delegate to the national synod of the French Reformed Churches and was even drawn, albeit tangentially, into the preliminaries of the famous dispute surrounding the apostate pastor Jérémie Ferrier of Nîmes.[28] These contributions notwithstanding, Guillaume de Nautonier's best-known and most original achievement came in the realm of mathematics and science when, in 1603, he published his *Mécrométrie de l'eymant*. This brief navigational treatise improved upon existing techniques for determining longitude and latitude by using tables of declinations and inclinations of a magnetic needle.

The children and grandchildren of Guillaume de Nautonier retained a staunch, if not defiant, commitment to Protestantism. His two sons—one of them a pastor—were enthusiastic followers of the duc de Rohan and the ill-fated Protestant rebellion of the 1620s. Such zeal inevitably led to anguish as Huguenot military and political fortunes declined. Rohan's defeat, for instance, resulted in the razing of the greater part of the family château at Castelfranc in 1628. As the century wore on, the persecution became more intense, and with the revocation of the Edict of Nantes, the choices were few and unpleasant. Adrien de Nautonier, Guillaume's grandson and yet another pastor, was in grave danger after 1685. Like all Huguenot ministers, he faced the distasteful choice between abjuration and banishment—the latter carrying the additional, severe requirement that he leave behind all children older than seven. Adrien elected exile on his own terms—at first, internal and, afterward, abroad.

Adrien eventually fled to London, reluctantly abandoning twelve children; his spouse had apparently died earlier. Of the offspring he left behind, the three older ones immediately abjured. Jean, the eldest son and an infantry officer, apparently converted to Catholicism as an "official" act designed to protect the investment in his royal military commission and the family property that he stood to inherit. A second son also abjured and remained in France awhile, until he too could safely emigrate to Protestant England. A daughter who converted was confined to a convent and probably died shortly thereafter. The nine youngest children, all minors, were held in protective detention, a clumsy attempt to scare the offspring of this Reformed minister into renouncing their faith. The seven girls were soon released into the custody of Genevan relatives and made their way from there to England. The two remaining boys were sent to hard labor in the French Antilles, where British sailors eventually rescued them and escorted them safely to England.

A cadet branch of the house was far less stubborn and, as such, illustrates another, perhaps more common, strategy adopted by the Protestant *hobereaux* of the Midi in reaction to the Revocation. The members of this junior line, much like many other Huguenots, eschewed exile and opted instead for legal compliance with Catholic religious demands. These "new converts" or "new Catholics" performed the obligatory gestures but often no more. Such conventions were sometimes sufficient to preserve position and wealth. Yet the outward conformity frequently masked an enduring private commitment to Reformed beliefs.[29] As time wore on, more and more "new Catholics," including many prominent members of the community, began to risk attendance at clandestine religious assemblies. Catholic and royal officials sometimes ignored these meetings "in the wilderness" (*au Désert*); on other occasions, they reacted harshly. In July 1754, another Guillaume de Nautonier was part of a group arrested for participating in Protestant services held at night in the woods near Castelfranc. Despite Guillaume's advanced age—he was over sixty—the authorities sentenced him to work in the hospital attached to the prison galleys at Toulon, where he remained for three years. They also confiscated his property, though this penalty seems to have been lessened later. At about the same time, Guillaume's only child, a daughter named Jeanne, was also caught attending illicit Huguenot services. In consequence, she spent several years in a Catholic convent, her release coming only on the occasion of her marriage to an "old Catholic." The arrangement was meant to insure her continued good behavior.[30]

The parallels between the Lacger and Nautonier are at once distinct and illuminating. Emerging from obscurity in the first years of the sixteenth century, they soon entered the government bureaucracy—one into the judiciary, the other into the fiscal administration. They also insinuated themselves into the local elite, acquiring land and titles. Here the advent of Protestantism offered an additional opportunity. Both as laypersons and as members of the ordained ministry, they wielded ecclesiastical power and political authority within Reformed circles in a direct and far-reaching fashion that simply was not open to such families during the Middle Ages.[31] While the Lacger never took so close a theological interest as the Nautonier, concentrating instead on Protestant political activism, their common confessional stance eventually led them to encounter analogous difficulties.

On the other hand, responses to the Edict of Fontainebleau, which repealed the Nantes proclamation in 1685, varied. Because of the Nautonier's association with the Calvinist pastorate, some family members emigrated along with more than 200,000 fellow Huguenots. Others reacted like the Lacger, staying in France and playing a double game. They married and baptized their children in the Catholic church but otherwise refrained from active participation, unless forced to do so by administrative or military pressure.

Still other families of the Castrais parallel the Lacger in their immediate postfeudal emergence, social ambition, lengthy religious ordeal, and fundamental endurance. The shadowy figures of Benoît de Calvairac and his son Bernard can first be found at Espérausses in the mountainous terrain east of Castres shortly after 1500. From the outset, they affected a noble style. Family tradition saw the father Benoît as the "village *gentilhomme*" with "sword in hand," while the son, by the time of his marriage in 1560, had assumed the title of sieur de Calmels. This latter personage undoubtedly led the family into the Reformed Church. The evidence is wholly indirect but nonetheless convincing. His son and grandson, for example, bore forceful biblical names such as Samuel and Jacob, the indelible mark of many early French Calvinists.

Jacob de Calvairac purchased the noble estate of la Tourrette in 1618, and his son made at least four additional strategic purchases of land over the next decades. These estates remained within the family into the nineteenth century. The next generation, now suitably endowed with land and title, embarked upon military careers. The brothers Marquis and Cézar de Calvairac secured commissions as lieutenants during the early 1670s, yet neither remained long in the army. After several years, Marquis, the older brother, who was now further dignified as a retired officer, returned to Espérausses and assumed control over the family seigneury of la Tourrette. Among the leading local Protestant notables, Marquis de Calvairac also served the Reformed church of Espérausses as an elder seated in the consistory. It was in this capacity that he presided over the official and peaceful dissolution of the local church when Mathieu Barbara, subdelegate at Castres for the intendant of Languedoc, arrived in March 1686 and confiscated whatever ecclesiastical records and meager possessions remained. The temple, as French Protestants styled their building for public worship, for its part, had already been pulled down several years earlier.

Marquis de Calvairac now entered the domain of the "new Catholics." Not surprisingly, the Catholic authorities regarded his conversion as insincere. A report to the intendant of Languedoc lists Calvairac as *"mal converti,"* insolent and given to agitation. The religious assimilation of Protestants in these rural environs was, at best, an uncertain affair; and Marquis de Calvairac provides additional, less direct evidence of an abiding, albeit private, religious fidelity. The opening lines of his testament avoided obvious and elaborate Catholic phraseology—neither the Virgin nor the saints are mentioned. Favored instead is a plain and laconic crypto-Protestant formula whereby the testator simply commends his soul to "God—Father, Son and Holy Spirit."[32]

Another Protestant house, the Espérandieu of Uzès and Castres, more closely resembles the Lacger by virtue of the fact that its fortunes rested on judicial officeholding. Family members were among the leading bour-geois of the town of Uzès in eastern Languedoc during the fifteenth and sixteenth centuries. Several were initially active in the municipal consulate, and their descendants entered the judicial magistracy after 1500. Gilles d'Espérandieu was *juge mage,* the principal judge, for the seneschalsy of Uzès by the 1530s. His son Jean, in turn, succeeded to the position. The judgeship, in an altogether familiar process, had rapidly become a family "possession" and would remain so for at least another generation.

Jean d'Espérandieu was a spirited associate of the Huguenot party. Representatives from the Reformed Churches of Bas-Languedoc, meeting at Nîmes in 1581, delegated him to express their position regarding the recently concluded treaty of Fleix (November 1580) to the prince of Condé and Henry of Navarre. The following year, he undertook another diplomatic mission, acting on behalf of the inhabitants of Uzès in voicing their concerns to the duc de Montmorency-Damville, governor of Languedoc. Henry of Navarre, leader of the Protestant faction, eventually rewarded Jean's "loyalty, faithfulness . . . and diligence" during the mid-1580s. Like Guichard d'Escorbiac several years earlier, he received an appointment as a *maître des requêtes* in Navarre's household administration. Navarre's patronage also helped him secure a position as *avocat,* or barris-ter, at the newly created *chambre de l'Edit,* the special Protestant tribunal attached to the Parlement of Toulouse but seated at Castres. Jean d'Espérandieu remained at Castres, practicing before the court until his death in 1626. At this point, the family split into two branches: one at Uzès, another at Castres.

Jean's eldest son, Louis, headed the family fortunes at Uzès. In fact, he had already assumed his father's judicial post there in 1609. Uzès was one in a series of Protestant strongholds in eastern Languedoc. The Reformers had organized a church there as early as 1559, and the Huguenot party wrested exclusive political control over the town by 1573. With the proclamation of the Edict of Nantes at the end of the century, it became a *place de sûreté*, where Protestants enjoyed the protection of a Huguenot garrison. Louis d'Espérandieu himself assumed a prominent public role in the Reformed community, serving, for instance, as a member of the delegation from the ecclesiastical province of Bas-Languedoc to the Huguenot political assembly at Grenoble in 1615.

This branch of the Espérandieu family answered the proscription of Protestantism after 1685 with a mixed voice. Louis died without male issue. His eventual heir, nephew Jean-Louis d'Espérandieu, demonstrated a remarkable religious constancy after 1685 and consequently spent eight years in prison, finally dying there in 1694. Jean-Louis's children, however, were more circumspect. A daughter, Claire, converted to Catholicism but appears to have remained secretly Protestant—the Catholic authorities, at any rate, voiced grave doubts concerning the sincerity of her conversion. A son, on the other hand, openly embraced the king's religion and often acted as the family's public spokesman in various attempts to shield, for example, his much distrusted sister. This sort of assistance and protection willingly accorded crypto-Protestants by their more fully converted relatives was once again a theme common to eighteenth-century France.[33]

The Castres branch of the family, descended from Guillaume, a younger son of Jean d'Espérandieu, was probably wealthier, more fully immersed in politics, and equally, if not more, attentive to developments in the religious sphere. Guillaume, like his father before him and several descendants who followed, had a flourishing legal career as a barrister at the *chambre de l'Edit*. He also maintained the family interest in civic matters. He was a municipal officer, having been elected first consul at Castres in 1615. The town council immediately dispatched him to Paris when rumors circulated that the crown might transfer the *chambre de l'Edit* elsewhere. Later in the same year, he and Pierre de Lacger, the judge, served as delegates from the Reformed Churches of Haut-Languedoc to the Huguenot political assembly at Grenoble.[34]

Guillaume d'Espérandieu was initially a warm supporter of the duc de Rohan. During the initial campaign of 1621–22, Rohan displayed an appreciation for Guillaume's talents and selected him to be a chief fiscal administrator within the region. When hostilities erupted anew in 1625, however, Espérandieu was distinctly less enthusiastic. At first, he prudently absented himself from Castres on the pretext that his brother, the *juge mage* of Uzès, required his assistance. Like so many in the same position—at once Protestant and tied to royal officeholding—Guillaume needed to tread warily. In the eyes of less cautious southern French Protestants, he had become yet another ingratiating self-seeker with a foot in each camp. With the fall of La Rochelle in October 1628 and the unmistakable signs of general Huguenot defeat, Guillaume d'Espérandieu quietly withdrew to his recently purchased seigneury at Aiguefonde in the mountains south of Castres.

Guillaume's two sons benefited from the comparatively peaceful conditions that prevailed at Castres and elsewhere between the Peace of Alès, which ended Rohan's uprising in 1629, and the intensification of persecution during the late 1670s and early 1680s. Deprived of their own "party," Protestants were politically weakened. Yet the absence of factional strife and rivalries allowed the faithful a normal existence and, in the short run, offered considerable security. For their part, the Espérandieu brothers enjoyed the social and economic assurance that came with the possession of seigneurial lands. They were closely tied to the community of lawyers and judges associated with the *chambre de l'Edit* at Castres and were locally renowned for their literary talents. The two men, along with Jacques de Lacger and others, were vigorous participants in the Academy of Castres, a literary society of the sort that had become enormously popular in the French provincial world of the mid-seventeenth century. The brothers were reputed to be eminent Latinists and fine poets. Both died by the early 1670s and were thereby spared the confessional ambiguities suffered by their descendants.

The royal intendant of Languedoc, in the aftermath of the Revocation, distrusted the Espérandieu of Castres as "doubtful Catholics." One member of the house, Louis, eventually followed in the footsteps of his cousin Jean-Louis d'Espérandieu at Uzès and went to prison for his faith. If others of the family opted for a less strident existence, their commitment was just as resolute. During the early 1760s, the then-patriarch of the Castres branch, another Jean-Louis, was forced to flee abroad after one of his daughters was discovered drowned in a well. She evidently suffered from severe mental depression following a lengthy internment in a Catholic convent. In a series of events reminiscent of the famous Calas case, the authorities immediately accused the father of murdering the young woman to prevent her conversion to Catholicism. It was only through the pressure of public opinion and the efforts of Voltaire and others that the courts rehabilitated this falsely accused crypto-Protestant and permitted his return from exile.[35]

Finally, in this rough survey of the petty Protestant nobility of southern France, there are the Baudan of eastern Languedoc. A large family with a wider geographic range and more diverse interests than those observed thus far, its members occupied civic offices at Nîmes, Montpellier, and Alès. They also held positions in the judicial magistracy, financial administration, army, and church. The different branches of the family eventually came to possess nearly a dozen seigneuries of varying size and importance in the countryside around Alès, Uzès, Nîmes, and Montpellier.

Described originally as bourgeois and well-to-do landowners, the Baudan were well situated at Nîmes by the 1550s and sufficiently prominent to enter municipal service. Jean Baudan, a moderate Catholic, was among the four consuls elected at Nîmes in 1557 and again ten years later. His second term corresponded with the single most violent episode in Nîmes's religious history, the so-called Michelade, a wholesale massacre of Catholics by Protestants on the feast of Saint Michael in 1567. The incident began with the hotly contested consular elections for that year and the Catholic refusal to seat a bipartisan consulate—two Catholics and two Protestants—as proposed by the latter faction. The Reformed delegates then stormed out of the municipal assembly and the Catholics elected four of their own, including Jean Baudan. The Calvinists protested the election but to no avail. When warfare broke out at the national level several months later, in the early autumn of 1567, the confessional tensions and resentment that had been building at Nîmes exploded. On 29 September, the Huguenots massacred a hundred or so priests and prominent Catholic laymen. They spared Jean Baudan, a hint perhaps that he was not looked upon as a religious extremist. On the other hand, the Protestants replaced him and the other Catholic consuls with men from their own party. Finally, some fragmentary evidence suggests that toward the end of his life, Jean may have switched sides and joined the Reformers' ranks.

Pierre Baudan, Jean's younger sibling, was squarely in the Protestant camp. He had a vital role within Calvinist ecclesiastical and political circles but seems also to have been a moderating force. He declared for the Reformed Church at an early stage, served on its consistory, and with the Protestant rise to political power, regularly participated in the sessions of Nîmes's ordinary council (*conseil ordinaire*), an advisory body to the four-man consulate. Pierre did not, however, take part in the Michelade and, in the immediate wake of the Saint Bartholomew's Day Massacre of 1572, collaborated with his elder Catholic brother on a select bipartisan commission designed to maintain peace at Nîmes.

The children of these two men were very much members of the regional Protestant elite. Jean Baudan's eldest son became *maître des oeuvres du roi,* the royal supervisor of public works for the seneschalsy of Beaucaire-Nîmes. Of Pierre Baudan's several sons, Jacques became, through marriage, coseigneur of Vestric, a morseled fief south of Nîmes. He nonetheless remained close to civic affairs and was elected first consul at Nîmes in the mid-1580s. Another of Pierre's sons, Maurice, trained in the law and became seigneur of Saint-Denis as well as a regional comptroller, a fiscal officer associated, in this instance, with the administration of the *gabelle,* the famous royal salt tax. He was also an elder of the Protestant consistory on at least one occasion.

The close of the religious wars of the sixteenth century brought new opportunities for the Baudan house. Family members quickly entered careers cherished by the socially ascendant. They became judicial magistrates at Nîmes and, more commonly, financial administrators. The latter were initially affiliated with the salt taxes as comptrollers and *grenetiers,* and later occupied positions as treasurers, accountants, and tax judges in the complex fiscal system of the ancien régime.[36] As the seventeenth century wore on, the Baudan took an increasing interest in military service. The sword, martial leadership, and battlefield command were the ancient prerogatives of the nobility. Recently ennobled families naturally aspired to this most aristocratic of vocations. In addition, the size and professional character of the king's army was growing during the period, as was its active employ in glorious foreign campaigns, particularly during the reign of Louis XIV. Families whose sons had once been bureaucrats sought careers as officers, and the Baudan proved no exception. In the century and a half between 1635 and 1785, a dozen of its sons obtained commissions in various royal infantry and cavalry regiments. The majority never advanced beyond the level of captain, but the accomplishment sufficed to bolster familial honor and authority.

During this same period, the religious situation presented the familiar challenges. In and around Nîmes, the duc de Rohan aroused the ardor of Protestant artisans and ordinary workers throughout the 1620s. The notables, however, were decidedly more circumspect and generally struck a far less bellicose posture.[37] The Baudan, in any event, were royal officeholders who could ill afford fierce confrontation with the Catholic crown. Among them, furthermore, a steady confessional hemorrhage soon developed.

The oldest son of Jacques Baudan inherited the family's seigneury of Vestric and was, by profession, a judicial magistrate in the seneschalsy of Beaucaire-Nîmes. He appears to have been firm, if quiet, in his Protestantism. The succeeding generations, however, were pulled in opposing directions. At least four members of the family became Protestant pastors. One even headed a short-lived religious riot peopled mainly by Huguenot artisans at Nîmes in the mid-seventeenth century. Understandably, these ministers left France after 1685, emigrating to Germany and Holland. On the other hand, Louis Baudan, born in 1644 and eventual heir to the lands at Vestric, was a youthful convert to Catholicism. His religious conversion was not an isolated event. It took place within the massive Catholic counteroffensive spearheaded at Nîmes by the bishop and the Society of Jesus. Several of his cousins, moreover, had entered the Catholic fold at an even earlier date, long before the frightful pressures that attended the Revocation.

The immediate descendants of Maurice Baudan, seigneur of Saint-Denis and fiscal comptroller at Nîmes, were hard-pressed to remain Protestant. Pierre Baudan, for example, succeeded his father as comptroller and then, in the early seventeenth century, entered the *chambre des comptes* at Montpellier. The chamber, and several others like it within the kingdom, was a sovereign fiscal tribunal that handled litigation between the crown and tax officials. Pierre was at first a chief accountant and eventually rose to become one of the presidents in the court. An abandonment of Protestantism accompanied his success. Such religious conversion was certainly not mandatory, but it measurably reduced the many obstacles that frequently impeded and sometimes blocked Protestant advancement in the royal bureaucracy. This process, combined with the constant pressure of the Counter-Reformation, had a marked impact on the Calvinist notables.

By the second decade of the eighteenth century, most family members who remained in France were Catholic. Their confessional position, moreover, was not merely an expedient precaution or judicious dissimulation. The Baudan sons and daughters, now sincere and steadfast Catholics, christened their infants with characteristically Counter-Reformation names such as François-Xavier, married in the "Catholic, Apostolic and Roman Church," sought the intercession of "the Holy Virgin Mary and all the Saints of Paradise," were ordained into the priesthood, and took religious vows as members, for instance, of the Ursuline order of nuns.[38]

When these family histories[39] are considered together, certain consistent patterns emerge. To begin, there is the sixteenth-century conjuncture of royal officeholding, land acquisition, and the embrace of Protestantism. The advance of numerous families during this period and their simultaneous attraction to the Reformation has long been acknowledged.[40] Following the disruptive Wars of Religion and the equally threatening insurrection of the 1620s, these Huguenots of the provincial nobility enjoyed a half century of relative stability and achievement. They continued to be active in the judicial realm, gradually joined the ranks of royal military officers, and even turned to poetry and other literary endeavors. By the final quarter of the century, however, the Catholic monarchy imposed ever-tighter restrictions on the Protestants and eventually forbade Reformed practice. Some Huguenots found themselves forced to flee France, some converted more or less facilely to preserve their position and wealth, and still others conformed outwardly while retaining an inner Protestant identity. This latter group is, in many ways, the heart of the present study. Who endured? Who were the survivors, first of the religious violence of the sixteenth and early seventeenth centuries and then of the proscription and persecution after 1685? What were the processes and techniques for resilience and perseverance? And how does the matter of religious resolve relate to the more general issue of family survival? It is with these and related questions in mind that we concentrate on the Lacger, a family that has left a remarkably detailed record of its own ordinary and unexceptional, hence representative, and informative past. This microhistorical focus on the experience of this particular family, its associates, and its universe serves, in turn, to disclose and portray a wider historical experience.

T W O

∾

Rudimentary Ambitions and
the Conversion to Protestantism

Examination of the Lacger necessarily begins with a portrait of the first several generations. How did the family go about setting its roots and what were the major obstacles as it struggled through the religious turmoil of the sixteenth and early seventeenth centuries? In many respects, the Lacger were hardly different from other aspiring families throughout the provincial world of early modern France. Like their countless competitors, they possessed the determination, aptitude, and desire that were critical to any family's success and endurance. These elements combined as the Lacger set out to enlarge and improve their social status, political power, and economic fortunes. This period also witnessed the beginnings of their commitment to Protestantism—the one factor that, in the long run, distinguished them from many other families that historians have thus far studied, particularly for the areas outside southern France.

Despite later genealogical claims that the Lacger—or Latger, as the name was occasionally spelled during the ancien régime—had originated in the region of the Forez near Lyon during the thirteenth or fourteenth century, the earliest reliable information comes with the last will and testament that Pierre de Lacger drew up and deposited with his notary in March 1523.[1] Pierre and his spouse, Guilhalme, resided at Puylaurens, a small settlement fifty kilometers east of Toulouse. The site's very name, derived in part from *puy,* or peak, suggests the topography of this hill town that dominates a landscape of low ridges and fertile valleys. It had long guarded a regional crossroads and, since the Middle Ages, had been home to a fortified garrison and a weekly market.[2]

Pierre de Lacger seems to have belonged to the aspiring bourgeoisie. Though he called himself a "noble person" (*nobilis vir* or *noble homme*), the designation did not in itself signify noble status.[3] It is unlikely that Pierre and his family fulfilled the proper legal requirements for nobility. He possessed no noble fief, held no ennobling office, and neither he nor his descendants ever produced royal letters patent of ennoblement. Rather, the terminology hints at the beginnings of a familiar evolutionary process whereby families informally usurped a claim to nobility. The gradual assumption of noble status—ennoblement by prescription—was by no means uncommon.[4] Pierre's pretensions were bolstered, if only in his own view, by virtue of the fact that he was the self-styled sieur of Lagene,[5] an apparently undistinguished parcel of land that has left few traces. Again, the assumption of titles such as "sieur" by ambitious members of the bourgeoisie was widespread. Only long after Pierre's death would the progressive acquisition of ennobling judicial positions by his descendants lend the clan a firmer claim to noblesse.

Even the family's notability, quite apart from any claim of nobility, was qualified. Nonetheless, the Lacger were, already at this early date, part of a local economic and social elite. Family members had for some time resided at Puylaurens or at least claimed the prestige and presumably the leadership that were the legacy of a distinguished local ancestry. Pierre, for example, requested that he be buried in the "tomb of his predecessors" at the parish church. The phrase, however formal or commonplace, suggests the family's sense of its own importance and place within the community. The allusion to Lacger ascendants also reinforced a perception of family sentiment and continuity. Indeed, some of Pierre's collateral relatives, chiefly landholders and merchants, continued to live at Puylaurens well into the seventeenth century. The heart of the substantial Lacger property at and near Puylaurens in the years around 1500 were two town houses whose interior furnishings and silver plate were a matter of special pride. The family also owned three outlying *métairies,* a term that, in the Midi, generally referred to a fairly unified and compact, but frequently small, rural tenure with appropriate buildings and livestock, and worked by someone other than the owner. Tenants were known variously as *métayers* and *bordiers.* They worked the land under a sharecropping arrangement and divided the harvest with the owner according to prearranged terms, ordinarily "half and half" for cereal crops.[6] Other Lacger patrimonial assets at Puylaurens included a mill, a vineyard, and a dozen pairs of oxen to till the arable. Altogether, the property belonging to this branch of the house had an estimated value of approximately forty-five thousand livres during the early sixteenth century.[7]

Guilhalme, Pierre's wife, was also from locally prominent stock, and she too assumed the title "noble." The circumstances surrounding the drafting of Pierre's testament suggest that his spouse came from Lautrec, a small town less than a day's journey north of Puylaurens. Pierre took ill there while visiting his brother-in-law, the sieur de Peyrole. The will, which he dictated from this distant sickbed, mentions two sons, despite later external evidence that indicates one or more additional sons and perhaps a daughter. The elder, Antoine, was the principal heir; a younger son, Guy, described as a law student, possibly at the University of Toulouse, received a settlement of three thousand livres. Nothing is known of Antoine's fate; Guy, on the other hand, established the essential base upon which the Lacger future would be constructed.

Having completed his legal studies by 1526, Guy de Lacger entered the world of royal officers and secured a minor judicial post at Puylaurens. The community fell under the jurisdiction of the royal judge of Villelongue, who, in turn, depended upon the seneschalsy of Toulouse. Guy became the judge's *lieutenant principal* at Puylaurens and, as such, exercised in his stead judicial authority over the town and several dozen surrounding villages.[8] The next major advancement occurred about five years later when Guy abandoned Puylaurens for Castres, a substantially larger community some twenty kilometers to the east. He did so in conjunction with his marriage and the acquisition of a more prestigious and lucrative position in the complex hierarchy of royal courts.

Castres may have possessed a population as large as 6,000 or 7,000 when Guy de Lacger established residence there in the early 1530s; that its inhabitants numbered about 10,500 by the end of the seventeenth century seems a far surer estimate.[9] The town had long been the cultural, political, and economic focus of the region. A medieval settlement had developed around the abbey of Saint-Benoît by the early ninth century. Following the Carolingian decline, the site became fortified, and it was this sense of a *castrum,* or protective stronghold, that lent its name to the location. The papacy transformed the abbey into a bishopric in 1317, and accordingly, Castres was the headquarters for a modest diocese. A century earlier, in the aftermath of the Albigensian Crusade, it had become the seat of a feudal seigneury with extensive administrative, judicial, and military responsibilities. The crown reconstituted the seigneury into the county of Castres in 1356 and, by the early sixteenth century, reunited it to the crown. Although the king was now count, the law courts associated with the county continued to function and, in some ways, increased in importance. Finally, by the later Middle Ages, the commercial production of leather goods and a thriving enterprise in the manufacture and export of woolen textiles developed alongside a traditional artisan economy and subsistence agriculture.[10] These different activities attracted a steady trickle of immigrants, and Guy de Lacger's move there was within a migration pattern shared by a diverse group of people in mercantile affairs, the legal professions, and the various crafts and trades.

The union of Guy de Lacger and Jeanne de Carles in 1531 was typical of marital arrangements among upwardly mobile families of the age. She was the daughter and sole heir of a thriving bourgeois merchant from Castres. The family was socially undistinguished, having only recently emerged from artisan origins. Jeanne de Carles's grandfather, who had laid the foundation for their wealth, was no more than a carpenter or joiner, even if a prosperous one. On the other hand, the bride's dowry and inheritance delivered considerable property: a house in town, a grange and garden near the municipal walls, a small vineyard, a meadow, and the fertile *métairie* of Clot immediately outside Castres at la Caze. The land attached to the *métairie* of Clot was by local standards not insignificant, totaling nearly twenty-six hectares (about sixty-four acres).[11] Together with the house in town, it formed the nucleus around which successive generations ordered and augmented the patrimonial property. During their lifetimes, Guy and his wife made gradual but substantial additions to the family's landed wealth. They bought and sold a number of parcels in the immediate vicinity and had more than doubled the value of their property holdings by the early 1550s, on the eve of Jeanne de Carles's death.[12]

The Lacger combined the acquisition of land with investment in administrative offices—above all, judicial posts. Shortly after his marriage, Guy purchased the office of *juge d'appeaux,* a superior civil and criminal magistrate for the county of Castres. A royal judge, he heard appeals from inferior jurisdictions such as the *vicomté* of Lautrec or the *baronnie* of Lombers. His actions were, in turn, subject to review by the court of the seneschal and the Parlement of Toulouse. Although Guy hardly commanded the great esteem and far-reaching authority of magistrates seated in these higher jurisdictions, he was nonetheless an influential local figure. His appellate judgeship was among several powerful and prestigious judicial offices associated with the county of Castres, and the Lacger counted it among their chief assets. The position meant much more than the exercise of legal authority; it also conferred civic distinction and lent the incumbent considerable political and moral clout within the community. Then, in 1575, the family exchanged the post for that of *juge ordinaire,* a similar yet more powerful royal judgeship. In all, three successive generations possessed important offices within the local royal court system. The tradition did not end until the death of Guy's grandson, Pierre de Lacger, in 1655. Three years after his demise, Pierre's heirs finally sold his office to an outsider.[13]

The extent to which the family invested in *rentes,* particularly during the early stages of its emergence in the sixteenth century, is unclear. Placing money in *rentes,* or annuities, was an increasingly familiar facet of noble wealth. The *rente* was, in fact, a device for raising capital and was popularly utilized by both private persons and the government. There were two types: the *rente foncière* and the *rente constituée.* The first evolved during the later Middle Ages and provided a perpetual annuity secured through the alienation of real property, such as a house or parcel of land. The individual who acquired the property became the legal owner, and the former proprietor received, in exchange, a perpetual annual income based on some percentage of the value of the property alienated. The *rente constituée,* in place by the sixteenth century, extended the concept by producing a perpetual annual income in exchange for the alienation of a sum of money. It proved attractive to private borrowers and a cash-starved state as a ready means of raising money; the investors, chiefly members of the nobility and upper bourgeoisie, viewed these sorts of bonds as attractive, stable financial ventures.[14]

The Lacger, for their part, seem to have had limited initial interest in *rentes,* although greater investment occurred in the seventeenth and eighteenth centuries. Samuel de Lacger, an attorney who spent his adult life at Paris, had about one third of his assets in government and private bonds at the time of his death in 1652. François de Lacger, in the following century, also invested in public and private *rentes;* they accounted for nearly 50 percent of his total worth. Toward the end of the eighteenth century, François's younger cousins invested a somewhat more modest proportion of their assets in this fashion.[15] During the sixteenth century, however, *rentes* did not represent a substantial portion of the family's assets. It may be that economic development was comparatively slow in the remote, rural, and Protestant Castrais. Moreover, the use of *rentes* as a public instrument of royal credit had only gotten under way at Paris in 1522 during the reign of Francis I. In any event, for the first several generations, Lacger wealth, income, political power, and social position rested primarily upon investment in land and offices—above all, posts in the hierarchy of royal tribunals.[16] These, in turn, depended upon ties of affinity and consanguinity, or to be more specific, upon well-managed and strategic systems of marriage and inheritance.

Guy de Lacger and Jeanne de Carles had five sons, who by mid-century had dispersed throughout the western reaches of Languedoc in near-Rothschildian fashion. Acting in accordance with the standards of the age, Guy and, to a lesser extent, his wife, exercised considerable parental and familial authority in the selection and advancement of their sons' careers. Three of the five took law degrees, undoubtedly at the University of Toulouse, then wrangled royal judgeships. The eldest, Antoine I de Lacger, served initially as *juge ordinaire*—a generic appellation, which, in this instance, denoted a seigneurial magistrate—at nearby Brassac. Not long afterward, in July 1554, he secured a cherished appointment to the Parlement of Toulouse. It was the highest sovereign court in southern France, and the Lacger entry into the ranks of the parlement's judges was a major step toward provincial and hopefully national prominence. Antoine I's subsequent conversion to Protestantism, however, made the full exercise of the office difficult, particularly after the eruption of religious warfare in 1562.[17]

At about the time that the elder Antoine I entered the parlement, a younger sibling, Jean de Lacger, established himself as *juge ordinaire* of Castelnaudary, a subalternate magistracy within the county of Lauragais. Jean's move southwest from the mountainous terrain of the Castrais onto the flatter and more fertile Lauragais carried him beyond the Lacger's traditional range, yet he left behind none of the family's characteristic ambition. When the crown suppressed the office of *juge ordinaire* in the early 1560s, Jean de Lacger immediately exchanged it for the profitable new post of *lieutenant particulier,* the second-ranking judge in the royal presidial court associated with the seneschalsy of Lauragais. Like his older brother, Antoine I, Jean joined the Reformed camp and was, at least initially, an ardent supporter.[18] A third Protestant brother, a younger Antoine—generally referred to as Antoine II—succeeded their father as *juge d'appeaux* at Castres in April 1560. Guy probably died not long afterward, and Antoine II then presided over the family's growing assets and influence in the vicinity of Castres.[19]

Guy de Lacger's two remaining sons, both Catholics, made their way in commercial and ecclesiastical affairs. Adrian was a successful merchant at the large, conservative, and Catholic city of Toulouse. He most likely specialized in the pastel exchange. Trade in the blue dye, one of the few commercial crops in the region, reached its height during the middle decades of the sixteenth century. The plant was cultivated in the area around Toulouse, the headquarters for its processing and export. Adrian evidently shared in this prosperity. He married into the commercial elite of Toulouse and, upon his death in the mid-1570s, left a reasonably large estate, of which the single greatest item was 312 bales of pastel warehoused at Bordeaux and valued at 10,500 livres.[20]

Sébastien, probably the youngest of the brothers, held several clerical appointments associated with the collegial church of Saint Pierre at Burlats, a village neighboring Castres. The family had nurtured these ecclesiastical interests since the later 1530s, when Guy de Lacger and his wife acquired agricultural property and a house at Burlats. Several years later, one of

Guy's brothers followed loosely in the footsteps of his older sibling. Upon finishing a law degree at Toulouse, he left the family residence at Puylaurens for Castres. This younger brother, another Jean de Lacger, entered the church, undoubtedly with financial support from Guy. Jean held, as early as 1535, the chaplaincy of Galèye, a minor appointment attached to the cathedral of Castres. Then, in the early 1540s, he became canon and later dean of the chapter at Burlats. Sébastien, following his ordination in 1559, joined this paternal uncle, first as preceptor, then as canon, and by the early 1570s, as dean of the chapter. During the same period, the family acquired an additional, more modest church benefice in the form of a vicarage at Vielmur, a small community just west of Castres. Again, it passed from uncle to nephew.[21] Thus, this first clutch of eager brothers, the sons of Guy de Lacger and Jeanne de Carles, entered the time-honored realms of judicial administration, commerce, and the church. They did so at Castres, at several adjacent towns, and at the major urban center of Toulouse, with its prestigious university, powerful courts, and lucrative business opportunities.

The Lacger, like all ambitious houses of early modern Europe, never forgot that the acquisition and careful conservation of landed property was essential for long-term survival. They lived, after all, in a predominantly agrarian world where land remained the chief measure of wealth and position. For example, Antoine II de Lacger, judge of Castres, amassed considerable real estate, much of it arable farmland. As we shall see, most land came to him through marriage and inheritance, traditional avenues for first assembling and then retaining intact the patrimony. On some occasions, however, he made strategic purchases of his own, as when he bought the productive *métairie* of la Planesié for four thousand livres in April 1575. The estate adjoined the *métairie* of Clot, itself a middling agricultural property brought to the family by Jeanne de Carles, Antoine II's mother. Each was a typical rural holding with fields and pastures, a principal dwelling or house, and specialized agricultural buildings—eventually to include a *pigeonnier,* or dovecote, that most visible of aristocratic distinctions. From a legal perspective, both were nonnoble tenures (*terres roturières*) rather than fiefs and, taken together, were the Lacger's most valuable landed assets at Castres through the early eighteenth century.[22] In all, Antoine II had, by the time of his death in September 1591, assembled real property valued at close to thirty-seven thousand livres. It included five substantial farms, or *métairies;* a similar number of smaller ones; five vineyards; two meadows; and a house and garden in town.[23]

A goodly share of the family fortune derived from astute marriages. The Lacger were active and successful within the regional marriage market; they used it to evident advantage. Although the canon Sébastien obviously did not wed, Adrian's widow, Antoinette de Baillot, subsequently married a merchant who had risen to the rank of municipal councilman (*capitoul*) at Toulouse, a detail that suggests her background was one of money, social prominence, and Catholicity. The three other brothers tended to marry widows and to take successive spouses. These traits, common for the time, related closely to the opportunity for economic and social advancement as well as family survival in a basic biological sense.[24] Antoine I married Gabrielle de Marion, a widow whose first husband had been a judge on the Parlement of Toulouse. It was his very office to which Antoine I succeeded. He married the widow only after he had purchased the office. She, moreover, had a son by her first marriage, who presumably received the major portion of the proceeds from the sale of his father's judicial post. On the other hand, the subsequent union of Antoine I and Gabrielle de Marion concentrated the couple's professional interests and social rank, and may have even achieved some consolidation of their financial affairs.[25]

When considering marriage in the late 1550s, Jean de Lacger, judge of Castelnaudary, revealed the criteria in a letter to his father at Castres. Ought he to marry into the Meynuiguet house? The proposed match was with a sister of the criminal judge for the seneschalsy of Carcassonne. Women of this family usually brought a dowry of three thousand livres. In this case, it would be a third less, but he could eventually expect to receive the remunerative judicial office from her brother. In the end, this particularly profitable marriage project failed to materialize, but Jean did marry—twice, in fact, and, in both instances, to widows. Almost nothing is known of his first wife, Germaine de Capdeboeuf; the second was Claire de Trégoin, widow of Raymond de Marion, who had been fiscal comptroller for the Queen Mother Catherine de Medici in the county of Lauragais. The Protestant Marion had died when a Catholic mob attacked Reformed worshipers at Castelnaudary in March 1562.[26]

Antoine II also married twice. The first time was in June 1561 when he wed Jeanne de Coras, daughter of Jean de Coras, the celebrated juris-consult and *parlementaire* at Toulouse.[27] While the marriage produced a dowry of no more than middling size—only seventeen hundred livres and some minor personal property—it signaled the Lacger admission into a Huguenot nobility of the robe. The marriage contract, signed in Coras's house, was witnessed by no less than four Protestant judicial officials— three judges and a *maître des requêtes de l'hôtel,* all associated with the Parlement of Toulouse.[28] The union was an expression of the ideological and professional bonds that united the regional Protestant magistracy. These men later cooperated in active support of the Huguenot party, establishing, for example, a Protestant court system. Moreover, several of them, including Antoine I de Lacger and Jean de Coras, shared death in early October 1572 in the Toulousain reverberations of the Saint Bartholomew's Day Massacre.

Jeanne de Coras, for her part, died by the mid-1570s, and not long afterward, Antoine II married Jeanne de Perrin, widow of the seigneur de Fiac.[29] This time, the dowry was more substantial, amounting to three thousand livres and consisting of a house in Castres, a modest vineyard, and some personal property. These assets, said to have been left to Perrin by her first husband, represent the recaptured dowry from that previous childless marriage as well as the widow's *augment,* a supplement to the dowry. The terms of the marriage contract normally established both the dowry and the *augment.* The latter increment to the dowry, technically a donation, was a benefit of survivorship established by the husband for his spouse should he predecease her. It was drawn on the property of the deceased husband and, in the region of Toulouse, was customarily 50 per-cent of the bride's dowry. Jeanne de Perrin's first marriage involved a dowry of two thousand livres, or the equivalent, and an *augment* of one thousand livres; and because the dissolved marriage was childless, she was entitled to both restoration of the dowry and payment of the *augment.*[30] Meanwhile, the obvious benefits of serial monogamy had not escaped Lacger attention. These successive marriages established external alliances, provided access to career opportunities, and offered the accumulation of property through attractive dowries and eventual inheritances.[31]

Another element in this account of the Lacger's initial establishment and stabilization was the degree to which succession patterns, both lineal and collateral (or vertical and horizontal), consciously organized and concentrated resources. The regional laws and practices surrounding inheritance were different from the customary law of Paris, for example, which maintained a traditional equality among siblings.[32] Instead, following the legal customs of the Midi, where the influence of Roman law ran strong, successive generations of family patriarchs consistently favored the eldest son. This system of the *préciput* invested considerable power in the father, permitting him to advantage one child to the detriment of the others. Typically, the oldest male received a favored and disproportionate share of the family's property, especially land, prior to any apportionment of the estate among the remaining brothers and sisters. Younger brothers inherited vastly unequal amounts; sisters, though in receipt of marriage portions, frequently lost all claim to a share in the inheritance. By this device, the family property remained, to a great extent, impartible and flowed relatively intact from one generation to the next, if not from one patriarch to the next.[33]

Accordingly, when Antoine II de Lacger died in 1591, he bequeathed his judicial office and 40 percent of the family's landed wealth to his eldest son. The three remaining sons received much less important offices and progressively smaller shares of landed property, amounting to 25, 20, and 15 percent of the total. For each of his four daughters, Antoine II assigned marriage portions of three thousand livres, intended for dowries that would secure advantageous matches for the young women within the local Protestant aristocracy. The allocation excluded the endowed daughter from subsequent inheritance and, in particular, a share in the family's lands. Nearly a half century later, the next generation of Lacger exercised similar paternal power in the continuing attempt to prevent fragmentation and dismemberment of the patrimony, to keep it in the lineage. Under the terms of his 1655 testament, Pierre de Lacger accorded his eldest son a generous preferential legacy valued at slightly less than 65 percent of the entire estate, while the three remaining children had to be content with shares of less than one-eighth each.

A related trait, especially pronounced among the sons of Guy de Lacger in the sixteenth century, was the assemblage of collateral inheritances. Here again, the Lacger, like other early modern houses, were anxious to preserve the lineage properties (*propres*) that individuals received from their parents and that were meant to pass intact to their nearest blood relatives. *Propres*—"immovables" (*immeubles*), such as real property, as well as fictive immovables, such as royal offices and *rentes*—went to a person's children or, in the absence thereof, returned to the line whence they came. There were, in addition, those properties that a husband and wife acquired in common during the course of their marriage, known accordingly as *acquêts*. They too were immovables, as opposed to personal property or "movables" (*meubles*), and naturally became *propres* when transmitted to the next generation. In practice, however, these distinctions could be difficult and confusing, especially when the succession involved collateral heirs. Not surprisingly, the result was a substantial body of law, along with considerable litigation.

Antoine II proved especially adept and vigorous in husbanding the wealth of his deceased brothers. He shared in the inheritance of the older and childless Antoine I following the latter's execution for heresy by the Parlement of Toulouse in 1572. A year later, after the assassination of Sébastien by Huguenot militants in the course of an iconoclastic riot, Antoine II successfully pressed a claim to be this brother's sole heir. Finally, when Adrian, merchant of Toulouse, died childless, Antoine II and Jean, by this time the only surviving brothers, divided his estate between themselves.

On each of these three occasions, Antoine II was more than willing to engage in vigorous legal battles to secure what he evidently regarded as his patrilineal due. So much so that by the mid-1580s, Antoine II and, to a lesser extent, his brother Jean, judge of Castelnaudary, successfully collected and consolidated the inheritances of their three deceased siblings. Under the terms of an agreement signed in June 1584, Antoine II acquired the family property in the proximity of Castres, while Jean received a large cash settlement and some land near Toulouse.[34] There are good reasons to believe that these two brothers shared in the estate of their uncle, the older canon Jean de Lacger, too. In the end, Antoine II amassed a generous amount of real property: ten different farms, five vineyards, the paternal house in town, and so forth. Although ensuing generations inevitably fragmented to some extent Antoine II's grand patrimonial creation, the essential strategy was plain and unambiguous. The succession was not simply a matter of family possessions passing vertically from one generation to the next. Upon the death of collateral relatives, especially brothers and uncles, the Lacger stood ready to press their inheritance rights with an eye to a practical economic solidarity among kinfolk. The pattern would be repeated, though on a smaller scale, throughout the seventeenth and eighteenth centuries.

Intertwined in this intricate family history was, of course, the religious issue. The Reformation had early and strong support at Castres. A growing Protestant community organized a church there around 1560 and, within two years, took political and military control of the town. Apart from issues of confessional discontent, religious conversion, and personal commitment, Protestantism in many medium-sized and smaller towns of the Midi benefited from a lengthy medieval heritage of municipal privilege. The establishment of Reformed churches and Huguenot political regimes at Castres, Montauban, Nîmes, and elsewhere reinforced established mechanisms of self-governance and strengthened the local elite's control over its own affairs. At Castres, moreover, civic authorities and royal officers, acting in concert with Reformed Church officials, now filled the vacuum left by the absence of the major ecclesiastical and political powers. The bishop had long been nonresident, and since 1519, the count was the distant figure of the king. Castres eventually became a *place de sûreté,* one of fifty-one towns garrisoned by Huguenot troops paid by the king under a system initiated during the 1570s and subsequently confirmed and extended under the terms of the Edict of Nantes in 1598. The town was also the seat for the *chambre de l'Edit* of Languedoc, which provided equitable justice for Protestants.

The Lacger found the Reformed position extremely attractive, yet they nearly always acted in moderate fashion. This restraint manifested itself in the ideological attitude of each of Guy de Lacger's five sons. Understandably, Sébastien, the canon, remained Catholic. He even died at the hands of the Huguenots in the course of the Reformation conflict when, in early October 1573, a band of Protestant extremists from Castres surprised the Catholics, who, at that time, held the small town of Burlats. The attackers, upon capturing the hamlet, took vengeance, pillaging Catholic residences and the Chapter of Saint-Pierre; they massacred a number of inhabitants, including Sébastien, who was dean of the chapter. He was, by one account, "inhumanely shot." Another witness testified that Sébastien died while guarding the family house at Burlats. No matter.

Antoine II was enraged by the death of his brother; he was reported to have "never forgiven" the Huguenot captain who led the attack.[35] Sébastien was clearly on good terms with his Protestant brothers and may have even sympathized with the reformers. Nonetheless, he held officially to Catholicism, if for no other reason than to retain ecclesiastical office and the revenues attached thereto.

Sébastien's religious position may well have been akin to that of his uncle and fellow canon Jean de Lacger, who neither broke with Catholicism nor opposed the reform. In 1574, several Catholic farmers, tenants on the lands attached to his chaplaincy at Galèye, complained that the mass was no longer said there. They argued, in a suit brought before the seneschal of Carcassonne, that Jean ought to be stripped of his chaplaincy. The prospect of gaining control of the chaplaincy for themselves partially fueled the tenants' accusation. Jean countered that he had held the benefice for nearly forty years and only in the last several had trouble arisen. True, mass was no longer celebrated. This turn of events was due to a singular absence of priests and the fact that Catholic services were effectively banned in the region. Everyone—even the provost of the chapter, the archdeacons, and the canons—had been forced to attend Protestant worship. Naturally, Jean attended, but "he did not practice the Reformed religion except to hear the pastors."[36] This position, at once cautious and restrained, reveals a singular lack of enthusiasm for the zealots of either camp. Though some Catholics suspected Jean of Protestantism, they had little hard evidence. He and his nephew Sébastien, even if they sympathized with the Calvinists, were not likely to make an ardent public demonstration of belief. In addition to some very real economic concerns on their part, the religious issue only destabilized the community, endangering the political and social order. The chaos threatened the elite and those who aspired to the elite. Lacger appreciation of how seriously these ideological questions polarized society and undermined the public weal was brutally reinforced by their own suffering and loss of life.

Adrian, the merchant who ran his pastel business from ultra-Catholic Toulouse, conducted himself according to the traditions of an unreformed Christianity. That he was able to maintain an uneventful existence amid the religious strife and Catholic zeal that gripped Toulouse in the 1560s and 1570s suggests as much. And there are other clues. The concluding phrase of his last will and testament, for example, sought the intercession of the "glorious Virgin Mary and all the saints of paradise." Although these words were no more than a wooden notarial formula, nothing in Adrian's life suggests a Nicodemite struggling to survive in a hostile environment.[37]

Antoine I was, by contrast, a celebrated Protestant martyr. His conversion was no doubt a gradual process. A judge on the Parlement of Toulouse by the mid-1550s, he was increasingly critical of the court's harsh treatment of Protestants and eventually forged close ties to the handful of other judges who were attracted to the reform. Though a committed Calvinist by about 1559, Antoine I maintained a discreet public silence, if only to protect himself from his zealous Catholic colleagues on the parlement, a bastion of conservative anti-Protestantism.[38] The outbreak of religious hostilities at Toulouse in May 1562 ended in the massacre of many Huguenots and the flight of countless others. The parlement then purged its own ranks of more than a dozen suspected Protestants, including Antoine I. He and others fled to safety elsewhere. Although reintegrated the following year, these Reformed jurists never again exercised the full power and influence of their offices. The high court expelled its Protestant magistrats once more in 1567 and 1568. More than a half dozen Huguenot judges, Antoine I among them, then took refuge at or near Castres, where they attempted to establish a Huguenot counterpart to the parlement. Acting under commission from the prince of Condé, they organized a sovereign court for Languedoc. The fact that the participating magistrats held royal office conferred an aura of constitutionality upon the effort. The court's geographic jurisdiction corresponded to that of the Parlement of Toulouse, and it was empowered to adjudicate both civil and criminal cases involving Protestants. Although the notion of separate tribunals for Huguenot litigants would eventually lead to the creation of a special chamber within the parlement (the *chambre de l'Edit*), this early venture at Castres was predictably short-lived.

Forcibly kept from the performance as well as the financial rewards of his judicial office, Antoine I found some small measure of recompense when, in late 1569, the principal Huguenot leader, Henry of Navarre, appointed him *intendant des finances*[39] at Millau in the Rouergue, a poor yet strategic mountainous region northeast of Castres. Such patronage was typical, and Huguenot jurists such as Antoine I de Lacger were obviously not without political interests. Jean de Coras, also expelled from the Parlement of Toulouse, became chancellor for Jeanne d'Albret, the Protestant queen of Navarre. The final and fateful return of these and other Huguenot judges to Toulouse occurred during the months following the Peace of Saint-Germain of August 1570. Lacger, Coras, and a third Protestant *parlementaire,* François de Ferrières, then found themselves trapped at Toulouse in the late summer of 1572. Municipal authorities, acting in concert with the parlement, imprisoned the trio on 3 September as part of a general arrest of Toulousain Protestants following the Saint Bartholomew's Day Massacre at Paris. A month later, they and several hundred other followers of the Reformed Church were systematically executed. Antoine I and his two judicial companions, dressed in their crimson robes—the unmistakable sign of honor and privilege, office and rank[40]—were hanged in the square in front of the parlement.[41]

The religious posture of the fourth brother, Jean, had a less dramatic, albeit equally instructive, evolution. He joined the Protestant cause promptly and energetically; he was even wounded defending his fellow Protestants at Castelnaudary in March 1562. And this strong support continued for a time. A half dozen years later, when Huguenot leaders from the region assembled at Castres to plan their strategy against the Catholic enemy, they selected Jean and another to serve as treasurers for the confederation. The two men's chief task was to confiscate the revenues belonging to absent Catholics and divert the money for support of the prince of Condé's Protestant army. After more than ten years of violent struggle, however, Jean's ardor and dedication waned and he returned to Catholicism. A desire to retain his judicial office as the prospect of Protestant success in the Lauragais diminished may well have prompted the action—Castelnaudary came, in the end, under firm Catholic control. An equal, if not stronger, possibility is that he finally despaired of the chaos engendered by the religious conflict and sought refuge and stability in adherence to the king's faith.

Jean witnessed two brothers suffer violent death in quick succession: Catholics killed the first, Antoine I, in 1572; Huguenots the other, the canon Sébastien, some thirteen months later. Jean found the second assassination especially discouraging—members of his own "party" had murdered his brother. The bloody episodes led him to reconsider his stance and the hope of achieving a more secure and reliable resolution to the seemingly endless warfare. Following the deadly events of 1572–73, Jean turned to Catholicism. He was not alone in the decision. The massacres of 1572 marked a turning point for Calvinist strength in France. Protestant numbers dropped dramatically thereafter. In the gruesome confusion, Jean, ever the trained lawyer and royal judge, must have found the Catholicism professed by his monarch an attractive, immediate, and trustworthy recourse. By the mid-1580s, he could report that his sons were studying at one of the *collèges* at ultra-Catholic Toulouse, while his daughters' training had been entrusted to a community of nuns. They and his other descendants, mostly jurists and ecclesiastical officials at Castelnaudary and Toulouse, remained steadfastly Catholic.[42]

Antoine II was unequivocally Protestant. To be sure, this constancy and clarity of purpose benefited considerably from the fact that he lived in the staunchly Calvinist community of Castres. Yet he never adopted a militant posture. He was, by temperament, a negotiator and pacifier who might best be described as a Protestant loyalist. He did not actively participate in the Huguenot assumption of power at Castres in May 1562 and may not have publicly declared his Reformed faith for another two years. In the course of the incessant military campaigns that followed, Antoine II was seldom a supporter of armed belligerency. His role in the provincial aftershocks of Saint Bartholomew's Day offers ample testimony for his temperate and mediating stance. News of the events at Paris prompted the vicomte de Joyeuse—lieutenant of the duc de Montmorency-Damville, governor of Languedoc—to order, among other things, the military occupation of Castres. The intention was to avert bloodshed and, on 3 September 1572, the sieur de Lacrouzette and two companies of soldiers entered the town without resistance. He offered safe-conduct to those who wished to leave, and many militant Huguenots did so. He simultaneously resisted pressure from the crown and Parlement of Toulouse to slaughter the town's Calvinists. Lacrouzette formed a council from among the less-strident Protestant leaders who remained at Castres to assist in his governance of the town; its membership included Antoine II. The latter's principal contribution came when he served as emissary to the heavily fortified Huguenot town of Réalmont and unsuccessfully urged its citizens to follow Castres's peaceful example. Antoine II's selection for this unproductive mission was due, in part, to the fact that his wife, Jeanne de Coras, and her family were from this small but militant Protestant settlement immediately north of Castres.[43]

Even the assassination of his older brother and father-in-law at Toulouse a month later did not dissuade Antoine II from encouraging restraint. He continued to work with Lacrouzette and the rapidly emerging *politique* group.[44] The more aggressive Huguenots, not unexpectedly, assailed him for pursuing what they considered a policy of accommodation and perhaps betrayal. They even held him ransom for a brief period after they reestablished control over Castres in August 1574.[45] On the other hand, as cooler heads began to look for ways to find an effective reconciliation and bring the warfare to a close after the mid-1580s, Antoine II emerged as a prominent member of Castres's Protestant community. He was consistently one of the half dozen or so political confidants called upon in the town's dealings with the Huguenot chief, King Henry of Navarre and later of France, and the *politique* faction led by the duc de Montmorency-Damville. Antoine II's actions point toward a fundamental agreement with the *politique* acceptance of royal authority and emphasis upon political unity rather than confessional uniformity.

When Henry of Navarre and Montmorency-Damville conferred at Castres in March 1585, Antoine II was among the principal hosts. Later in the same year, he was involved in the process that led to Montmorency-Damville's selection of the count of Montgomery as governor of Castres. The newly appointed governor, in turn, named Antoine II and five other moderates to an advisory council; Antoine II seems to have remained part of the close circle of local persons from whom Montgomery sought counsel. Even after Montgomery's departure from Castres, Antoine II's overall influence in civic and religious affairs continued. For example, in late 1589, the Huguenot assembly for the ecclesiastical province of Haut-Languedoc, meeting at Castres, delegated him and the sieur de Sénégats to congratulate the new king Henry IV upon his succession to the throne.[46] Later, in the early seventeenth century, Antoine II's son Pierre assumed a similar political role and shared his father's desire for order and stability—essentials which, in their view, only the monarchy provided. He actively participated in religious and political affairs, yet carefully avoided any sign of disloyalty toward the crown and never showed himself to be extreme in his Protestantism. Pierre repeatedly served as royal commissioner to meetings of the Protestant synod of Languedoc and vigorously opposed Rohan's adventurous schemes. Like his father before him, he frequently acted as a go-between in the friction between the crown and the local Protestant community.[47]

Nothing here suggests a band of ideological opportunists, taking advantage of the religious issue for little more than personal gain. Although the Reformed faith was ultimately a barrier to aspirations beyond the region of Castres, the Lacger chose, with certain exceptions, not to abandon it. They simultaneously avoided becoming overzealous. The religious question rarely put them at odds with the monarchy and was never permitted to split or injure the family. The two brothers, Jean and Antoine II, maintained a close cooperative relationship despite the religious differences that had emerged by the mid-1570s. Throughout their regular and considerable correspondence—there was an average of one letter per month—the occasional quip about one or another's "party" does not appear to have lessened the amiable bonds between them. They possessed a powerful sense of family interdependency and worked together for their mutual advantage. The ties of kinship and sociability overcame religious division.[48]

Perhaps the most dramatic instance of this solidarity occurred in 1575. The death of Charles de La Roche the previous year had left vacant the office of *juge ordinaire* at Castres. The crown, according to custom, would have selected a successor from a list of three nominees prepared by the municipal consulate. Owing to the chaos attending the religious wars, however, the consuls requested the duc de Montmorency-Damville to confirm their choice, Jean de Rotolp, sieur de Lescout, at least until the peaceful stabilization of the region. Montmorency-Damville agreed. Jean de Lacger, now in the Catholic camp and a distant protégé of Catherine de Medici, then went to Paris and petitioned directly on behalf of his brother, Antoine II. The royal authorities received the appeal favorably, largely because of the perception that while both candidates were Huguenots, Antoine II was the "more accommodating spirit." In the end, the crown installed him rather than Rotolp as the new *juge ordinaire* for the city and county of Castres on 27 October 1575. Security and prosperity as well as its planning, execution, and achievement were then a mutual and cooperative familial affair. Kin, particularly in troubled times, depended upon and supported one another in providing assistance, protection, and advantage.

Jean, in the years that followed, continued to watch over his Protestant brother's interests at Toulouse and Paris, where his Catholicism allowed greater freedom of movement. He understood these interests to be matters of joint and shared concern. "Our affairs" was a favorite phrase. It was Jean, for instance, who directed the legal maneuvering at Toulouse as the two brothers set about in the early 1580s establishing claim to the inheritance of their childless brother Adrian. It is more difficult to know precisely how Antoine II may have looked after the Catholic Jean's interests at Castres. He no doubt did. Unfortunately, the only letters in their exchange that have survived in the Lacger family archives are those received by Antoine II; he did not keep copies of those that he sent.[49]

Their practical approach to the issue of religious conflict derived, in part, from the fact that the Lacger were royal officeholders. Continued strife and instability only served to hamper the ambitions of advancing families, especially those attempting to progress through the judicial magistracy. At the same time, the Lacger's religious position was of a distinctly private or personal nature and, in this sense, modern. Belief tended to be an important yet individual matter. If anything, the Lacger downplayed many of the traditional public aspects of religion.

The Lacger were unquestionably determined to get ahead. Judicial officeholding, progressive purchase of lands, strategic marriage alliances, and consolidation of economic assets through inheritance represented a broadly conceived, long-term traditional effort. Yet the desire to succeed socially and economically must be balanced against the family's adherence to Protestantism. Furthermore, as we explore Lacger survival in the sixteenth century and thereafter, we cannot help but notice the strongly patriarchal structure and patrilineal sense of family typical of the ancien régime.[50] Its presence was unmistakable from the beginning. The emphasis was on agnatic lineage, the male line of descent, as economic assets and social position passed from one generation to the next; there was, in addition, a repeated and precise utilization of marriage alliances to enhance and secure the family's position; and the preferential inheritance by the eldest male as well as the assemblage of collateral wealth served as a means of maintaining the indivisibility of the patrimony. A strong sense of cooperation and interdependence marked the family. Its members counted upon one another. All of these elements combined to support the family, to lend it longevity. The Lacger set great store by family ties and valued close blood kin enormously. In so doing, they insured their continued existence.

THREE

∾

The Patrimony

Land, *Rentes,* and Offices

The Lacger patrimony rested upon a broad foundation of landed estates, *rentes,* and royal offices. The three intertwined and complemented one another in a symbiotic relationship. Together they offered stability as well as mobility and satisfied the needs of both tradition and ambition. Real property provided durability, permanence, and continuity. Once acquired, it almost never passed from the family. Not until the years immediately preceding World War I did the family divest itself of significant parcels of land that it had obtained as early as the 1530s. Even today, it retains the château and estate of Navès, the most economically significant and socially distinguished of its real property holdings under the ancien régime.

While the Lacger's investment in bonds and annuities, or *rentes,* was sizable in some instances, they never matched the family's landed assets in meaning or function. Their focus was more properly economic. *Rentes* offered, above all, secure investment opportunities. On the other hand, while *rentes* may not have conveyed power and prestige in the same way or to the same degree as real property, they were hardly devoid of such consequences. Some annuities were essentially personal loans that reinforced and sustained a network of business and social exchanges among the Protestant elite. Other *rentes* were royal and municipal government bonds that attested to a sense of civic obligation and community responsibility that went beyond financial acumen.

The family's offices in both the judiciary and the military were generally linked to political advantage and social betterment. Possessed of a more fluid history than the patrimonial estates, they were bought and sold within and without the family, exchanged for more prestigious and lucrative posts, and finally almost completely abandoned by the eighteenth century with the long persecution of Protestants. If landed wealth offers an opportunity to view the abiding features of family strategies, the Lacger's various offices and, to a lesser extent, investment in *rentes* provide indications of the median range of fluctuations, adjustments, successes, and failures.

Land

The principal Lacger properties were the *métairies* of Clot, la Planesié and Navès. The family acquired the first two during the sixteenth century— Clot by marriage in the 1530s, la Planesié through purchase some forty years afterward. Navès was also purchased, but not until much later, in 1724. The three were immediately southeast of Castres, straddling the Thoré River and bordering the left bank of the Agout. They adjoined one another directly and formed a compact, manageable set of holdings.

Clot, whose nomenclature suggests bottomland, lay immediately adjacent to the Agout. La Planesié, which was higher up and beyond, likely took its name from the Planès brothers, who held and worked the land during the late fifteenth and early sixteenth centuries. Both were non-noble agricultural tenures and, though not large, were complete with grain barns, stables for livestock, various sheds, and perhaps an oven and bakehouse. Each had a house, too, though the one at la Planesié was evidently modest. The dwelling at Clot seems by comparison to have been substantial. It sat prominently on the left bank of the Agout and faced the river. Antoine II de Lacger began construction of a new manor house there in 1590, just a few years prior to his death. His heirs renovated it and the adjoining buildings extensively during the 1640s. At about the same time, the family patriarch began to style himself the sieur de Clot,[1] despite the fact that the holding was not a feudal seigneury. The development hints at the beginnings of the process whereby the Lacger made a gradual transition from the urban magistracy to the world of rural proprietors and the petty nobility. Clot remained the family's chief country residence until the acquisition of Navès in the following century. Even then, a cadet line lived there till shortly before the property's sale in the early 1900s.[2]

By way of agricultural production, the estates of Clot and la Planesié were mainly devoted to the pasturing of sheep and the cultivation of cereals. In November 1655, the date of a rare but precise inventory, the two *métairies* had a combined total of 104 sheep: 14 rams, 37 lambs, and 54 ewes. The textile manufacturers at Castres were undoubtedly a convenient and reliable market for the fleece. Among the other animals were three valuable sows and ten piglets as well as some cattle, including three cows and calves, several heifers, and two bulls. There were also three pairs of oxen—two at Clot and one at la Planesié. Each pair was complete with yoke, harness, and wheeled plough reinforced with iron strapping. The animals and ploughs were held "in common" by the landlord—in this particular instance, Pierre de Lacger—and the tenants. Each *métairie,* incidentally, had but a single tenant.[3]

Harvest records detailing cereal production are, unfortunately, extremely spotty and fragmentary. An unwieldy *livre de récoltes*[4] for 1582 provides a crude proportional notion of the crops harvested on the Lacger estates: roughly 71 percent wheat, 22 percent rye, and 7 percent oats. The predominance of wheat suggests relatively fertile soil and, most likely, correspondingly good yields. More accurate and detailed estate accounts have survived for the several years immediately following Antoine II's death in 1591; they confirm the earlier data. Antoine II's widow, Jeanne de Perrin, acted as guardian for the minor children and their share in the patrimonial possessions.[5] She made an annual administrative report to a family council composed of her stepson, brother-in-law, and brother.

During the first year of her stewardship, for example, the total grain harvest was 372 *setiers,* 6 *mégères,* 2 *bois,* or approximately 404 hectoliters—nearly 1,150 bushels. Of this, not quite two-thirds was wheat, especially *moussole,* a grain regionally prized for grinding into fine flour. Another quarter was rye, and a bit more than 5 percent was oats. The small remainder of the harvest was legumes—nitrogen-fixers such as beans and vetch that may have been sown in the fallow—and minuscule amounts of barley and millet. Following a prearranged division with its tenants, presumably the customary 50 percent, the family retained twenty *setiers* each of wheat and rye for its own purposes, then sold the rest at market.[6]

Other than arable farmland and the adjacent meadows, the most conspicuous agricultural lands were vineyards. Small and never very valuable, they were typically estimated at about one-twentieth or less of the worth of *métairies* such as Clot or la Planesié. Toward the end of the sixteenth century, Antoine II's real-estate possessions included five vineyards, yet their combined worth was only 3 percent of all his property. Vineyards, to be sure, had a practical value. A family needed wine for its own table and could always sell the remainder at market. Vines were not, however, a major source of income in the Castrais, nor were they viewed as a particularly attractive investment. Estates sometimes had vineyards attached to them, and families who could afford vineyards saw them as a necessity much like a house or barn. A special taste or particular fondness for the wine of a certain vineyard may have even developed over time. Some plots, such as the vineyard of Peyroux, remained in the Lacger family for five or more generations.[7]

The largest, richest, and most important property in the Lacger patrimony was the estate of Navès. The designation derived from the ancient Gallo-Roman *nava,* meaning boat, trough, or valley. It alluded to the deep hollow formed by the Thoré River where it empties into the Agout. The estimated value of the estate at the end of the eighteenth century was double the combined worth of Clot and la Planesié. The tract of land associated directly with Navès was extensive; and two additional noble estates—the *métairies* of Malzac and Le Gua—as well as several ancillary parcels completed this ample holding. The entire complex amounted to approximately 198 hectares, or nearly 487 acres, of which the lands associated with Navès proper accounted for two-thirds. It was enormous compared to la Planesié, which was slightly less than 48 hectares, or about 119 acres, and Clot with only 26 hectares, roughly 64 acres.[8] Navès, in addition, possessed a large manor house, or château; farm buildings; a mill along the Thoré with three grindstones for milling grain;[9] extensive arable farmland; pasturelands; meadows; woods; and vineyards. Perhaps most significantly, since the mid-thirteenth century it had been a noble property dependent upon the abbey and later the cathedral chapter of Saint-Benoît at Castres. As such, it conferred coveted aristocratic privilege upon its possessor. The seigneur had the legal right to hunt and fish, to maintain pigeons and rabbits, and even to dispense "high, middle and low" justice. By the eighteenth century, the latter prerogative meant the nomination of a seigneurial judge, typically an experienced attorney from Castres. This magistrate's jurisdiction extended over the estate and the dozen or so families who lived in the tiny hamlet associated with Navès.[10]

As noted previously, the Navès parcel was a late addition to the ancestral patrimony. François de Lacger purchased it in the early 1720s, several years prior to his retirement from the army. He had had a long, distinguished, and successful military career beginning in the mid-1680s. François advanced steadily over more than forty years, retiring as lieutenant colonel and brevet brigadier in 1728 and, along the way, accumulating salary, allowances, and pensions. His service coincided with the Sun King's many wars. The Regiment of Auvergne, of which François was a principal officer, fought in the German Palatinate during the early 1690s and throughout northern Italy and Spain a decade later. During these many years of fighting abroad, François profited from extra campaign pay, quicker promotion, and perhaps less readily defined financial rewards, what might loosely be called the "gains of war."[11] In any event, he returned to Castres an extremely wealthy man, paying 56,000 livres for the estates at Navès, including the *métairies* of Malzac and Le Gua. He spent 6,550 livres for several additional parcels in the decade that followed; purchased a town house in Castres for 3,000 livres; invested over 45,000 livres in bonds with the province of Languedoc and another 30,000 livres in an annuity at Paris; and was still able to proceed with reconstruction of the château of Navès at a cost of more than 17,000 livres.[12]

The original château, dating from the Middle Ages, had been altered and added to over the centuries; it was sturdy, if severe in appearance.

Even today it is used for agricultural storage as well as for the grounds keeper's quarters. François, upon taking possession of his seigneury, however, appears to have wished for something less spartan and more in keeping with the tastes of the age. He constructed a new, costly residence and surrounded it with a stately garden or perhaps more a park. It certainly complemented the major economic advance achieved by this royal military officer. Marc-Antoine II de Lacger, François's much younger cousin who inherited Navès in 1758, made further renovations, repairing the floors and ceilings of the medieval structure. He also cleared some of the nearby woodland. Thereafter, in the nineteenth century, the family added to the newer château extensively, nearly doubling its size. It was the family seat throughout the eighteenth century and remains so down to the present. Modern descendants even built a textile mill on the grounds in the later nineteenth century. The factory operated from 1878 until 1923 and, at its height, employed about fifty people.[13]

The Lacger naturally enough possessed other agricultural tenures. These tended to be scattered throughout the area around Castres. There were two *métairies,* some vineyards, and one or more houses at Burlats.[14] They had originally been held by Sébastien de Lacger and, upon his death in the mid-sixteenth century, passed to his brother Antoine II. Again, these particular lands remained within the family for several generations. Some property, however, occasionally found its way into collateral lines and thereby fell outside family proprietorship. For example, Jean de Lacger, the eldest son of Antoine II, inherited two valuable *métairies*[15] along with several minor parcels upon his father's death in 1591. Jean, a magistrate of the *chambre de l'Edit,* eventually acquired the even richer seigneurial properties of Massuguiès and Arifat. They lay north toward Albi, and his property interests shifted accordingly from the orbit of Castres. However, Jean retained his two *métairies* at Castres and bequeathed them to his son, Hercule. When the latter, in turn, died childless in 1652, they went to Hercule's mother and three sisters and thus passed entirely from Lacger patrilineal control.[16] The process confirmed the general belief among these elite families that land left to daughters left the family. Not surprisingly, most clans sought to avoid such losses.

Besides these country estates and sundry other plots of land, the Lacger maintained one or more residences in town and had done so since Guy de Lacger's move from Puylaurens in the 1530s. At the time, his wife, Jeanne de Carles, provided, as part of her dowry and inheritance, a house on the rue dels Pradals, not far from the cathedral.[17] This residence served the next generation as well. Antoine II listed it in his testament of 1591 as the "paternal house" with an assessed value of two thousand livres; it was among the property he left to his eldest son, Jean. The record then becomes ambiguous, but it would appear that Jean or his heirs ultimately sold the house.

Pierre, Jean's younger half-brother who succeeded their father as judge of Castres, owned a town house, too. Given Pierre's vigorous role in Castres's political affairs, it served as his principal residence. The house was probably that which his mother, Jeanne de Perrin, brought to the family as part of her dowry. Located near the town hall, it was a two-story affair with eight or more rooms. They included the usual living, sleeping, and cooking areas in addition to a study or office for Pierre. The latter contained a small library; in an adjoining room, Pierre kept family papers as well as documents pertaining to his judicial office. Finally, the house had two granaries and a cellar. The family repaired and improved the house during the 1660s, and it remained under Lacger ownership until the 1720s.[18] The acquisition, again through marriage, of another and finer house likely prompted its sale at this point.

The new residence sat along the Agout next to the Pont Neuf, the town's primary bridge, and looked across a tree-lined square toward the cathedral and episcopal palace. The location had greater distinction than that of the previous residence, and the property was worth about half again as much. Still, it was about this time that the family obtained the seigneury and château of Navès, substantially altering its economic and social focus. After the mid-eighteenth century, the two eldest males of the Protestant line abandoned the city in favor of the countryside. One resided at Navès, the other at Clot, leaving the town house for use by an older married sister and her family.[19] The change generally reflects the family's withdrawal from its previous role as part of an urban judicial magistracy that was deeply involved in municipal affairs. The pattern was by no means unusual. Families who had risen to wealth and social prominence through royal officeholding frequently purchased seigneuries and, once ensconced, abandoned their posts in the judicial or financial administration. For Protestants families, there were additional considerations after the Revocation. Their members found it impossible to serve as royal officials without formal conversion to Catholicism. As a result, retreat to a rural world and the management of country estates held great appeal. When viewed in the light of religious fidelity and economic survival, they found the move more palatable than public repudiation of Protestantism.

Not all the Lacger, however, deserted the town. For some, it was never an option. This was particularly true of those sons who had pursued military careers or who were cadets and therefore economically disadvantaged. They had more limited choices, usually lacked landed wealth, and could be heavily dependent upon royal patronage for success. The combination often led to confessional lapses after 1685 and continued existence within a circle of urban officeholders and civic leaders. The branch of the family to which the brigadier François de Lacger belonged possessed very little real property. Accordingly, he and three brothers secured military commissions, and they adopted Catholicism officially and unavoidably in order to perpetuate their careers. As previously noted, upon retirement François invested heavily in land and the construction of a château at Navès. He also bought a respectable residence in Castres. It was in a neighborhood of stately town houses built over the course of the seventeenth century by Protestant judges and attorneys attached to the *chambre de l'Edit*. François's civic standing was such that in 1723 he became governor of the town of Castres, a largely ceremonial municipal post created some thirty years earlier.[20]

His house was just across from the ornately baroque church of Notre-Dame de la Platé. Ruined over the course of the religious wars and only reconstructed during the first half of the eighteenth century, the church symbolized better than any other edifice in Castres the religious practice that the royal government and Catholic hierarchy had forced upon the Protestant populace of the region. François spent his last days at this residence, dying there in January 1758 at the age of ninety-seven. A younger brother, Louis, sieur de Saint-Laurens, lived there with him during these final years. Louis, too, had had a career of some forty years in the Regiment of Auvergne, albeit not so profitable and successful as his older sibling's. Like François, he had converted to protect his livelihood, risen to the grade of battalion commander, and in the end, returned to Castres, where he spent the next twenty years in modest retirement. Louis died in

October 1757, just four months earlier than François. Both men were solemnly interred in the church of la Platé.[21]

These two brothers had a cousin whose experience was very similar. Jean-Jacques, known as the chevalier de Lacger, joined the Regiment of Auvergne in 1693; campaigned through Italy, Spain, and the Empire; rose to the grade of lieutenant colonel; and finally retired in 1743 after more than fifty years in the army. He had, of course, converted to Catholicism and even received a small royal pension in consideration thereof. Jean-Jacques spent his last three years at Castres, where a Protestant niece looked after him. They lived, together with her husband and children, in the town house belonging to her equally Protestant brother (and his nephew) along the river near the Pont Neuf. Jean-Jacques died there in 1746 and was buried in the parish cemetery of Notre-Dame de la Platé.[22]

A far more striking case of continuance within a traditional urban context involved a junior line that originated in the early eighteenth century. Marc-Antoine I, head of the fifth generation of the Lacger at Castres, had married twice, initially in 1694 and again in 1716. His first wife bore seven children; the second and much younger spouse, but one. The two older sons from the first marriage fared well. They eventually inherited the estates of Navès and Clot, respectively. But their younger half-brother, Jean-Jacques-Joseph, who was only an infant when their father died suddenly in 1720, had few prospects. Cadets, especially if the issue of a second marriage, traditionally faced a severe disadvantage; the fact that he came from a crypto-Protestant family merely compounded the problem. He took a military commission in the Regiment of Auvergne and there had modest success, no doubt aided to some extent in consideration of his three older relatives who had long served the same regiment. Despite this, Jean-Jacques-Joseph only remained in the army about a dozen years. His fortunes improved dramatically upon receipt of some land and capital, inheritances from two uncles—one maternal, the other paternal. He then returned to Castres and married Marguerite de Roux, the daughter and heiress of a wealthy and extremely Catholic family from Toulouse. He offered, at the time of the marriage in 1747, a public profession of Catholicism.

Through his spouse, Jean-Jacques-Joseph acquired additional financial security and social position; in particular, her family provided the seigneury of la Trinque. He and his wife had as their principal residence, on the other hand, an attractive seventeenth-century town house at Castres. It sat diagonally across the intersection from François's residence. The family, in subsequent years, sold this house and purchased the so-called Hôtel de Lacger across the street and next to the church of la Platé. Jean-Jacques-Joseph, even more than François, immersed himself in the civic affairs of Castres. He took an active role in the deliberations of the city council and was elected first consul in 1768. These interests continued when, several years later, he received a commission as *lieutenant des maréchaux de France* for the region of Castres. This judicial office, which Jean-Jacques-Joseph quickly passed to his son Honoré-Joseph, had been created in the early eighteenth century and had military overtones. The crown empowered the lieutenants to resolve disputes between *gentils-hommes* who bore arms and those who simply "lived nobly."[23]

Honoré-Joseph also married a rich heiress, the only daughter of the wealthy proprietor of a royal manufactory at Montoulieu. This enterprise alone was valued at 140,000 livres.[24] In the end, this Catholic branch became reasonably affluent, almost entirely the result of the dowries and inheritances that came through two successive marriages to wealthy women. On the eve of the Revolution in the mid-1780s, the estimate of its worth stood at more than 436,000 livres. These Catholic cadets remained fairly prominent in the municipal and Catholic ecclesiastical circles of Castres until a few years after the close of World War II. The family then sold the *hôtel* and moved to Paris, where the current head, Antoine, baron de Lacger, resides.[25]

The Lacger had occasionally, even in the centuries prior to the eighteenth, moved in divergent directions. These early splits resulted mainly from geographic separation. After all, Guy, the family's founder, left Puylaurens for Castres; one of his sons, Jean, had, upon moving to Castelnaudary in the 1550s, established a branch in the Lauragais. Half a century later, another Jean, magistrate on the *chambre de l'Edit,* took up principal residence nearer Albi at the seigneury of Massuguiès. Only in the case of the Lauragais branch was there a religious cleavage as well, and even then it took time to unfold. In contrast, the fissures of the eighteenth century developed not along geographic lines but according to a religious and professional-economic axis. After the Revocation, those with land and other real property gradually drifted onto their rural estates and there quietly and privately clung to a Protestant heritage. Younger sons and individuals dependent upon royal offices and military commissions for a livelihood confronted a more difficult situation, tending out of necessity to become Catholic and to remain within an urban orbit. In fact, this segment of the Lacger family formed a tight knot in the fashionable neighborhood surrounding Notre-Dame de la Platé at Castres. The family's bifurcation into a rural Protestant and urban Catholic branch was, at heart, the result of the religious situation; while the division never led to internal family antagonisms, it bespoke a harsh reality.

Rentes

Another component of the Lacger patrimony was investment in a variety of private and public interest-bearing obligations. These bonds, or *rentes constituées,* paid a fixed percentage of the capital in perpetuity and were popular, secure financial opportunities for wealthy families of the nobility and bourgeoisie.[26] The purchaser (the lender) made over to the seller (the borrower) a capital sum. The borrower could be a private individual or a public institution, such as a town government or the monarchy and its various agencies. The purchaser received in return an established annual income. Though the borrower could theoretically repay the principal at any time, the lender could not obligate him to do so. Indeed, the chief advantage to the borrower was that he did not have to reimburse the loan at a fixed date. Technically and legally, the *rente* was not even a loan but a sale of property rights. Investors, for their part, found that these constituted *rentes* generally offered competitive rates of return and long-term security.[27]

The Lacger appear to have been active in purchasing such annuities on a limited scale by the second half of the sixteenth century. Many of the private bonds were arranged within a close circle of Protestant jurists and legal officers.[28] Yet information is far too fragmentary to permit an exact calculation of the range and importance of these early investments by the Lacger. Only by the mid-seventeenth century do the contours begin to emerge distinctly.

Slightly more than 33 percent of Samuel de Lacger's assets, for example, were in *rentes* upon his demise in 1652. Through this device, he extended private loans, several of them for relatively large sums, to a half dozen or more persons. Samuel was an attorney and a minor legal official. Most of the borrowers were judges and other lesser judicial officers from the same professional and social milieu.[29] His older brother, Pierre, possessed somewhat greater resources and far more land. Still, he, too, held a number of public and private bonds. Pierre had over 8,000 livres in public *rentes* with seven different municipalities in the immediate area of Castres and another 33,000 livres in *rentes* with ten different private individuals. Altogether, they constituted about 44 percent of his wealth. The rate of return of these investments varied widely, from less than 2 percent to more than 10 percent, though most hovered between 4 and 6 percent. The single largest borrower was his nephew Jacques, who also benefited from most favorable terms—Pierre had lent him 18,069 livres at 1.8 percent.[30]

François de Lacger, in the following century, placed approximately one-half of his considerable riches in these sorts of investments. His obvious preference was for government bonds. He held five different annuities secured by the provincial estates of Languedoc. Their combined worth was 45,725 livres, and the interest rates varied between 1 and 5 percent. François also placed 30,000 livres in what was apparently an unsecured annuity at Paris. Finally, he invested in four private bonds totaling 19,847 livres. Typical of these private *rentes* was the 10,000 livres that he advanced to Joseph Dulac, a retired lieutenant colonel, in return for an "annual and perpetual" payment of 500 livres—an interest rate of 5 percent. The borrower for his part used the money to help purchase the seigneurial tenure of Labrugière.[31]

François's cousins invested capital in similar fashion, but the ventures invariably represented a smaller portion of their overall financial worth. Marc-Antoine I had 15,700 livres, roughly 40 percent of his assets, in annuities during the first decades of the eighteenth century. His son, in mid-century, had 28,304 livres, a mere 15 percent of his estimated wealth, in various financial contracts.[32] These investments, especially the government annuities, offered a reasonably high but by no means exceptional rate of return—5 percent seems to have been common. Their greater advantage, much like the investment in land or offices, was stability. Moreover, loans to local municipalities and private individuals served to foster family prestige and extend its influence; those to kin assisted directly and symbiotically, as family members were heavily dependent upon one another and, accordingly, tended to prosper or suffer together.

Judicial Offices

The Protestant Lacger can only have turned away from royal office-holding—positions that conveyed status, public power, and financial benefit—with reluctance in the late seventeenth and early eighteenth centuries. While some Lacger entered military service in the mid-seventeenth century, aspiring to the prestigious nobility of the sword, the family initially and primarily achieved its stature through offices in the judicial administration. The men of the family had, for nearly two centuries, been among the most esteemed and influential magistrates of the Castrais. Three generations, from the 1530s until the 1650s, were the principal subalternate royal judges for the city and county of Castres; and four individuals, over an even longer span of time, were successive magistrates on the Parlement of Toulouse and *chambre de l'Edit* of Languedoc.

These royal judges distinguished the family name, played a leading role in regional political affairs, and accumulated significant wealth, all the while establishing a tenure in office that made it possible to secure the family as part of the nobility of the robe. Many royal offices and certainly the higher judicial positions, such as judge (*conseiller*) on the parlement, gradually ennobled. Their continued possession—the general rule was three generations—conferred noble status, not merely on the office-holder but upon his offspring as well. Henceforth, nobility would be the legal right of the entire family.[33] Thus, while Guy de Lacger or his father before him in the early sixteenth century could offer no more than a highly tenuous claim to "live nobly," crown commissioners officially confirmed the house's noble standing in a *recherche de noblesse* of 1671. Family members had held ennobling offices for the requisite length of time, which, in conjunction with an acculturation process involving the acquisition of landed estates and the appropriation of a noble way of life, established the necessary basis for the claim of nobility. The Lacger were not alone in combining the device of ennobling offices with elements of a less formal prescriptive procedure for ennoblement. They fulfilled the legal requirements through officeholding and, at the same time, gradually assumed noble values, manners, and attributes.[34]

Beyond the status that they offered, judicial offices were property and, as such, were part of the patrimonial wealth. Like land, they were purchasable and hereditary. Once acquired, these offices became lineage property (*propres*), in this instance "fictive immovables," and therefore part of the family heritage. Within the Lacger, they passed from father to son, between siblings, and occasionally among collateral relatives. These positions were venal, or, as one historian recently put it, "legally available by purchase."[35] Nonetheless, the sixteenth-century officeholder and his family ran a risk of losing this sizable financial expenditure through unexpected death. Unless the holder sold the office during his lifetime or resigned in favor of a relative at least forty days prior to his own passing, the office reverted to the crown. Fortunately for those families whose position and power rested on venal offices, the introduction of the *paulette* in 1604 secured the investment by making offices hereditary and, in this way, transforming them into an assured family possession.[36] The office could be conveyed to descendants as part of the succession, alienated for a different office with higher status, or sold outright if there was no suitable heir upon whom to settle it.

Guy de Lacger's purchase of the office of *juge d'appeaux* for the county of Castres occurred in the mid-1530s. He had earlier held a lesser judicial post at Puylaurens but relinquished it for this more desirable position. This process of advancement through the hierarchy of royal offices, from lower to higher, was common to the farsighted plans of families bent upon improving their status through officeholding. Guy's new office, an appellate judgeship for both civil and criminal matters, was one of the more desirable and influential in the vicinity. Shortly before his death, in 1560, Guy resigned the office in favor of one of his younger sons, Antoine II, who exchanged it fifteen years later for the office of royal *juge ordinaire* for the city and county of Castres. The new judgeship then went in succession to Antoine II's two older sons, first Jean and later Pierre. Jean held the office for ten years, then ceded it in 1601 to Pierre in order to join the more illustrious magistrates of the *chambre de l'Edit*. For his part, Pierre enjoyed an extraordinarily long tenure as judge of Castres, only giving up the position with his death in 1655. Neither of Pierre's sons was, at that point, willing or perhaps capable of continuing. The older, though trained in the law, preferred a commission in a cavalry regiment, and the younger seems to have lacked ambition and was perhaps a trifle irresolute. The family finally sold the office in 1658 for twelve thousand livres.[37]

Ascent to the next level of royal judicial offices, those associated with the sovereign court of the parlement, was wholly in keeping with the political and social appetites of upwardly mobile families. Here the Lacger moved rapidly and aggressively, joining the *parlementaires* at Toulouse about twenty-five years after Guy's arrival at Castres. Antoine I, Guy's eldest son, purchased an appointment on the high court by the middle 1550s. Yet the divisive violence and chronic destructiveness of the Reformation prevented the family from consolidating this quick breakthrough. Antoine I and several other Protestant judges were assassinated in 1572; and Huguenots generally had few opportunities to reenter the Parlement of Toulouse until the organization of the *chambre de l'Edit* toward the end of the century.

The *chambre* itself had a tumultuous history. Huguenot demands for a separate sovereign court and equitable treatment coincided with the explosion of chaos and bloodshed in 1562. The prospect of trial before Catholic-controlled tribunals terrified Protestant litigants. In addition, the reactionary Parlement of Toulouse repeatedly and brutally purged itself of Calvinist magistrates. As a result, the Huguenot judicial leadership attempted several times, once in the late 1560s and again in 1575, to set up its own sovereign court at Castres. Several Huguenot political assemblies meeting at Montauban and Nîmes in 1574 and 1575 echoed the call for reasonable access to justice under "peaceful and safe" conditions. These abortive ventures and continuing petitions ultimately led to provisions for *chambres mi-parties,* bipartisan tribunals for the judgment of suits involving Protestants. Commonly called *chambres de l'Edit* by virtue of the Edict of Beaulieu, which in 1576 first envisaged their creation, they were to be attached to each of the eight sovereign parlements and staffed at least partly by Protestant judges. Though the arrangement was never fully realized, several of the special courts eventually flourished, notably for the parlements of Bordeaux, Grenoble, Toulouse, and, in a more limited way, Paris and Rouen. Confirmed by subsequent legislation, including the Edict of Nantes in 1598, they were empowered to settle any dispute, civil or criminal, in which one of the parties litigant was Protestant.[38]

The chamber for Languedoc, attached to the Parlement of Toulouse, was especially vigorous. Because Toulouse was so fanatically Catholic, the Huguenots balked at meeting there. The tribunal convened in two brief initial sessions, 1579–80 and 1583–85, at Lisle, a neutral site midway between Toulouse and Albi. Later, when Henry IV reopened the court in 1595, it was held at Protestant Castres, where a bipartisan assemblage of Catholic and Protestant judges—two presidents and sixteen associate magistrates drawn equally from each faith—met in annual sessions. Of the several *chambres de l'Edit* throughout the kingdom, this was the only one that was truly *mi-partie,* with a bench evenly divided between the two faiths.

Despite the fact that it dealt with tens of thousands of cases before its dissolution in 1679, the chamber at Castres was constantly plagued by problems. The Catholic *parlementaires* were, on the whole, less than enthusiastic about the project and always reluctant to travel to the Protestant town of Castres. While the Protestant magistrates sat continuously and permanently, the Catholic judges from the Parlement of Toulouse wished to avoid any appearance of durable commitment and accordingly dispatched a new group of magistrates each year. Then Rohan's revolt disrupted the chamber for over a decade. At the onset of conflict in 1621, the Catholic judges, with probable justification, fled Castres. Following an interruption of two years, the crown reestablished the chamber at Béziers. The parlement reluctantly agreed to the renewed venture, even though it would have preferred to unite the chamber directly with the high court at Toulouse. Toward the end of the 1620s, the special tribunal again embarked on a peripatetic existence. The 1629 session opened at Puylaurens; the following year, the chamber sat at Revel, and in 1631 and 1632, it met at nearby Saint-Félix-Lauragais. Only in March 1632 did it return to Castres, where it remained for nearly two generations. The parlement's incessant clamoring for integration of the chamber or at least its relocation to a less Protestant site finally led to its transfer to the Catholic town of Castelnaudary by 1671. Eight years later, the monarchy suppressed the *chambre de l'Edit* of Languedoc, as it did those elsewhere in France, and incorporated the Protestant *parlementaires* into the Parlement at Toulouse.[39]

Three different Lacger males sat successively and continuously on the chamber during this turbulent period. They followed, in this respect, the general tendency among *parlementaire* families to advance one child per generation to the court.[40] Jean, Antoine II's eldest son, first purchased the office in 1600. Following Jean's unexpected and possibly suspicious death while the chamber was in session at Béziers in 1624, the judgeship went to his son, Hercule. When, thirty years afterward, Hercule died without issue, the heirs sold the office to a cousin, Jacques de Lacger, who endured the rigors of the chamber's dissolution and integration into the Parlement at Toulouse and even converted to Catholicism in order to salvage the office as well as to protect at least a portion of the economic and social investment that it represented. When Jacques died at Toulouse in 1688 and was buried there in the cathedral cloister, none of his sons chose to assume the office. The four younger ones, among them the future brigadier François, were well on their way to careers in the army; the eldest, though an attorney, appears to have had no desire to ascend to the bench. Perhaps he could not bring himself to make the public profession of Catholicism that it would have required. Three years after his passing, Jacques's widow and children finally sold the office at a considerable loss. They received only thirty-nine thousand livres, a price of less than half the eighty thousand livres that his family had originally paid for it in 1652.[41]

These figures visibly point up the financial havoc wreaked upon Protestant *parlementaire* families by the dissolution of the *chambre de l'Edit* and the integration of the Reformed magistrates into the Parlement at Toulouse. The limited number of Protestant judicial offices on the chamber at Castres during the mid-seventeenth century had likely inflated their value. Once these Protestant judges had been incorporated into the Parlement of Toulouse toward the end of the century, the worth of their positions tumbled to the much lower levels that offices there commanded.[42] The Revocation of 1685 merely exacerbated the situation. In the end, the families that reckoned these positions as part of their patrimony suffered accordingly.

Naturally, other Lacger offspring held a variety of posts in and out of the royal bureaucracy. Antoine I was, for a time, *juge ordinaire* at Brassac, and for a brief interval he held a post in financial administration. Henry of Navarre commissioned him *intendant des finances* for the Rouergue in the late 1560s. His younger sibling Jean was *juge ordinaire* at Castelnaudary and later *lieutenant particulier* of the seneschal of Lauragais. At the beginning of the seventeenth century, Antoine II's two youngest sons, Jacques and Samuel, secured positions at Paris. The first purchased an office as *secrétaire du roi;* the latter became an *avocat au conseil privé du roi.*

The *secrétaires du roi* prepared, sealed, and dispatched the great mass of documents issued from the various royal chancelleries. There were, however, far more *secrétaires* than could be usefully employed, and this venal office became, in time, a title without real function. It was, however, an office that ennobled in relatively easy fashion and, as such, was highly prized. If the purchaser held the post for twenty years or died while serving, he and his posterity became noble. Besides the privilege that it conferred, the office also represented a financial investment. The Lacger purchased the post of *secrétaire* in 1606 for 11,700 livres and sold it some fifty years later for 20,000 livres. The office also had a salary (*gages*) attached to it, and successive Lacger holders—Jacques and, after his death, Samuel—had collected this income over the years. The *gages* in the mid-1600s, for example, offered an annual return of about 5 percent on the office's sale price, roughly equivalent to the average yield on an investment in annuities or bonds. An appointment as *avocat au conseil* was even more ceremonial and, from an economic viewpoint, worth far less. When Samuel passed away in 1652, his office of *avocat au conseil* sold for 4,500 livres, less than one-fourth the value of the office of *secrétaire.*[43] Altogether, these positions were not lacking in prestige or value, yet they did not compare by way of power and influence with the cluster of family posts at Castres. They were patently subordinate to offices in the *chambre de l'Edit* and, lacking authority as well as the continuity of possession over several generations, never empowered the family in the same manner as did positions in the local magistracy of the Castrais. They played, at best, a supporting role.

The pattern of preparation for entry into the royal judiciary typically involved university training in the law followed by some practical experience—a short spell as a minor, perhaps seigneurial judge, or several years' tenure as a barrister, pleading before one of the subalternate tribunals or the *chambre de l'Edit*. Formal education among noble or would-be noble houses possessed more than a functional or technical character. Academic instruction was viewed within the framework of an aristocratic ideal. It was necessary for the proper formation of the gentleman, a step toward the development of the spirit. It would, in turn, complement physical attributes.[44] Guy de Lacger studied at Toulouse, perhaps at one of the *collèges* and certainly at the law school associated with the university. He then served as a lesser judge at Puylaurens before becoming *juge d'appeaux* at Castres.[45] Those of his children who became magistrates observed similar stepping-stones. Antoine I, for example, received a law degree, probably from the university at Toulouse; subsequently served as *juge ordinaire* at Brassac; and finally bought an office on the parlement.[46]

The next generation, Protestant from birth and living amid the religious wars, was less inclined to attend school at Catholic Toulouse. These young men—for this educational and officeholding milieu was gender exclusive—increasingly entered the newly founded municipal *collèges* at Protestant towns for their primary and secondary schooling. Jean, the eldest son of Antoine II, studied for a year or so during the mid-1580s at Poitiers. Accompanied by his stepmother's brother, he may have been there to begin his education in the law. Yet only several years later did he complete his university degree and then at the well-known law faculty at Montpellier, a city with a large Protestant community. At the time of his father's death in 1591, Jean was practicing law before the court of the seneschal of Carcassonne. The choice of Carcassonne was again the partial result of familial ties; a paternal uncle was a judicial lieutenant of the seneschalsy at nearby Castelnaudary. Antoine II's passing naturally occasioned the transfer of the family's judgeship at Castres to this oldest male.[47]

Two younger siblings, Pierre and Jacques, traveled first to the *collège* of Nîmes, undoubtedly the most famous of the Protestant schools in southern France.[48] After four years there under the tutelage of the esteemed master Anne Rulman, they went in 1594 to Toulouse, perhaps in the company of their Catholic cousins, the children of the uncle who was judge at Castelnaudary. Pierre apparently stayed at Toulouse to finish his legal training, while Jacques went to Montpellier. Pierre finally returned to Castres in 1598, was admitted to practice before the *chambre de l'Edit,* and within three years, succeeded his older half-brother as judge of

Castres. Jacques, on the other hand, turned north to Paris, where he became a *secrétaire du roi* and, to the extent possible, looked after family affairs within the royal bureaucracy. A fourth and final brother, Samuel, went to the Protestant college at Montauban about 1600.[49] He remained there at least six years and afterward took a law degree, though it is unclear where. Samuel, too, moved to Paris, where he established what appears to have been a flourishing legal practice. He also secured a post as an *avocat au conseil privé du roi* and later succeeded his brother Jacques as *secrétaire du roi*. Only upon Samuel's death in the mid-seventeenth century and the extinction of this Parisian offshoot did the family sell the two offices: that of *avocat au conseil* for forty-five hundred livres, that of *secrétaire* for twenty thousand livres.[50]

Beyond the established judicial duties, the Lacger's standing as royal jurists furnished them with semiofficial, and often wholly unofficial but nonetheless real, public authority. Antoine II and his sons were an integral part of the community's foremost leadership. They worked closely, for instance, with Castres's city consuls and the officers of the Reformed Church during the Wars of Religion and the subsequent insurrection of the 1620s. Antoine II joined forces with municipal officers throughout the 1570s and 1580s in an often frustrating effort to bring a semblance of peace and order to Castres. Pierre and to a lesser extent his older brother, Jean, relished this conjuncture of position and power even more than their father. An informed contemporary characterized the pair as exceptionally "powerful" within the town and the district.[51] In particular, Pierre's tenure as *juge ordinaire* during the uncertainty, instability, and confusion of the early seventeenth century offers a ready context for assessing the depth and breadth of civic influence exercised by the Protestant judicial magistracy.

The office of *juge ordinaire* carried sufficient prestige that its occupant and the "first" of the four municipal consuls were Castres's preeminent citizens. Pierre together with the first consul represented the town when the prince of Condé made his entry into Toulouse in May 1611. The same pair extended an official greeting to the duc de Montmorency when he passed through the province the following summer. These necessary, but largely ceremonial missions soon gave way to far graver responsibilities requiring genuine diplomacy. Pierre; the first consul, Guillaume d'Espérandieu; and perhaps the pastor Benoît Balarand were Castres's delegates to the tense Huguenot political assembly that convened at Grenoble in 1615. Disturbed by the anti-Protestant policy and actions of Louis XIII, many deputies called for a military response. In opposition were partisans of the La Trémoille family, a distinguished noble house that formed part of the Huguenot national leadership. The Lacger had, by this time, become clients of the La Trémoille family through Jacques, who was now living in Paris. François de Nets, Jacques's father-in-law, had been appointed a household official for the duchesse de La Trémoille and her son. Jacques, in turn, loyally urged his brother Pierre to support La Trémoille's delegates and their notion of "reasonable accommodation" at the Grenoble assembly. This fraternal counsel coincided with Pierre's own views. He cautioned against resort to war and consistently opposed the duc de Rohan's bellicose partisans. The efforts, however, were for naught. In the end, other delegates threatened Pierre at gunpoint, and he departed the meeting early.[52]

Pierre had for some time taken an interest in the political-religious affairs of the Reformed Churches. Besides attending the national political assembly at Grenoble in 1615, he served as a delegate to various provincial political assemblies, the provincial synod, and the local colloquy. For several years beginning in 1611, he participated in the provincial assemblies and regional colloquies that gathered at Castres, Mauvezin, Pamiers, Réalmont, Revel, and Roquecourbe. He was also present for the synodal meetings at Réalmont and Saint-Affrique during the middle years of the next decade. By this time, however, Pierre's capacity had changed. He had become the royal commissioner to the Protestant synods and reported on their activities to the crown.[53] This particular development, Pierre's assumption of a role as the king's agent—perhaps more accurately his client—within the Huguenot community of the Castrais had its roots in the series of crises that unfolded after 1620.

The Lacger, along with most Protestant jurists and especially those who were members of the *chambre de l'Edit,* understood all too well the convergence between their own needs and the more general royal interests. They numbered among the so-called prudent Huguenots who sought to win the king's affection or, at a minimum, avoid his wrath by demonstrating their loyalty and obedience. In addition, dependent as they were upon royal judicial offices, they dared not challenge the monarchy too forcefully and thereby endanger the source of their political power, social prestige, and economic sustenance.[54]

Throughout the decade of Rohan's rebellion, these magistrates had an altogether ambivalent relationship with the larger Protestant community. A nostalgia for its diminishing military capacity likely fired the older petty landed nobility in their support of the uprising. Many artisans, fervent in their religious convictions, joined them in the initial enthusiasm. The middling bourgeoisie, on the other hand, soon became the nucleus of a growing peace party at both Castres and Montauban. The merchants and bourgeois did not, however, go over to the royal camp in the fashion of some royal magistrates who could ill afford to oppose the crown and became servile in the attempt to maintain the bonds of fidelity.

When the first serious rumors of war circulated about Castres in 1621, Pierre along with his brothers Jean, judge on the *chambre de l'Edit,* and Jacques, royal *secrétaire* at Paris, joined with other jurists of the chamber and the leading members of the consulate in seeking to avert bloodshed and maintain obedience to the king. Jacques, for example, openly criticized Huguenot political and religious leaders who preyed on popular imagination and exploited common fears. He thought it a "strange blindness to risk forever losing the security and liberty that we have in France for so useless an undertaking."[55] He agreed with his influential political patron, the duc de La Trémoille, who had no desire to fight and who generally opposed Rohan's adventurism. The Lacger retained this conciliatory posture throughout the Rohan rebellion.

By May 1621, the Catholic judges associated with the chamber as well as the bishop and other Catholic clergymen at Castres feared for their own safety. Pierre had a major hand in an attempt to offer safeguards and dissuade them from bolting. Their flight, it was argued, would only weaken the position of the moderates in the face of the war party. When this logic failed to convince, the moderate Protestant jurists and the municipal council accepted defeat and provided the Catholic officials a protective escort well beyond the city walls.[56]

With the effective suspension of the *chambre de l'Edit,* Jean withdrew to his estates at Massuguiès, while remaining in contact with his brothers by letter. Pierre, though he stayed at Castres, appears to have become discouraged and briefly considered resigning his judicial office in favor of the youngest brother, Samuel. Jacques, for his part, had been following developments at Paris closely and reporting to the family in the Castrais. Unfortunately, in September 1621, Rohan's followers intercepted a letter from Jacques to Jean at Massuguiès. The note, partially written in a crude code,[57] contained incriminating details concerning secret negotiations with the duc d'Angoulême, Catholic commander of the royal forces in the region. If the intention had been to spare Castres, the plan's discovery gave the duc de Rohan and his backers an opportunity to take complete control of the town. While artisans rioted and physically menaced those who would "betray" their community to the hated Catholics, Rohan and his soldiers entered in force and arrested Pierre as well as the first and second consuls. Pierre spent the next month in prison. It did not help that he and his brother Jacques were clients of the duc de La Trémoille, a rival Huguenot aristocrat who, despite his Protestant roots, opposed Rohan and preferred not to challenge the king. Upon release from confinement, Pierre prudently retreated to his older brother Jean's château at Massuguiès, remaining there until the temporary cessation of hostilities the following November.[58]

The so-called peace of late 1622 proved to be no more than a short truce. Dissatisfaction surfaced quickly, and the advocates of war continued to have their way. When the town of La Rochelle reopened the fight, a new hawkish municipal council at Castres voted its support in April 1625, despite the vigorous opposition of Pierre, the pastor Josion, and several others. Over the next four years, until the Peace of Alès in June 1629, Pierre attempted a difficult course. He and the other Protestant royal officers were anxious to maintain calm—the more so since the rebellion against the crown threatened their very station—and repeatedly counseled peace.[59] Pierre's actions, however, went beyond an effort to find some middle ground or encompassing compromise in the need for both confessional integrity and political stability.

During the final stages of the Rohan revolt, in May 1626, Louis XIII awarded Pierre an annual pension of six hundred livres "in consideration of the services that he had rendered" to His Majesty during these difficult times and to repay Pierre for "the great losses and damages that he had suffered" as a result. The practical effect was to bind Pierre for the near future as the king's factor in the Castrais. He attended and reported to Paris on the regional synods of the Reformed Churches. Throughout the crucial period of 1626–27, he made regular accounts to the royal court on the public mood and state of affairs at Castres. A stunning expression of Pierre's understanding and perception of royal power came in a letter that the magistrates and consuls of Castres sent to their colleagues at Nîmes in September 1627. The missive, whose composition and editing Pierre seems to have carefully directed, warned the Huguenot leaders at Nîmes against rebellion. Their best interests lay in obedience to the crown. The power of the royal officers and ministers descended from the king and the heavens. It would be criminal to oppose them for "any cause, pretext or reason whatsoever."[60]

The conduct of Pierre de Lacger and his brothers during these troubled times deeply angered many Protestants. The more extreme Huguenots by no means shared the views of the Lacger and resented what they regarded as compromising and traitorous actions. Two unpleasant episodes occurred as early as 1615. Political enemies "spitefully" burned the small *métairie* of la Fontesie and the vineyard of la Fosse, both belonging to Jacques, in June. Less than two months later, some local residents, one of them described as a merchant, "maliciously" set fire to Pierre's estates at Clot and la Planesié. Nearly a decade later, in June 1624, the sudden death of Jean occasioned an autopsy on the suspicion that his passing had not been from natural causes. While the apprehensions expressed in this particular incident may have been unfounded and exaggerated, the family felt imperiled and justifiably feared reprisal from its opponents. In January 1629, their fears were realized when some of Rohan's troops took lodging in Pierre's house at Castres and threatened to demolish it until his sister Marie paid them more than four hundred livres.[61]

The social position, economic rewards, and political power attending juridical office were enormous. The Lacger readily understood the central juxtaposition of family and state, and keenly appreciated the opportunity inherent in service to the aristocratic, yet bureaucratic, government.[62] The family ascended to and cemented noble status through their royal offices, found them a profitable livelihood, and used the station implicit therein to influence the governance and conduct of the community. Yet adherence to Protestantism sharply curtailed access to offices and set effective regional limits for families such as the Lacger. Huguenot office-holders also felt the deep tension between the demands and requirements of the Reformed community in which they lived and those of the crown that they served.[63] Far from diminishing, the distress only deepened and sharpened, particularly as the end of the seventeenth century approached.

Military Commissions

A related, albeit later, feature of royal service among the Lacger was progressive attention to opportunities in the military. A commission in the army, even as a lieutenant or captain, carried distinctive aristocratic dignity. While not hereditary and sometimes not even venal in the same manner as a royal judicial office, it bestowed authority and the right of command, both ancient noble prerogatives. Under Louis XIV, many sons of noble houses from legal and administrative backgrounds realized honorable military careers. Besides prestige, the army offered the petty nobility an advantage in that its position could be established as much on merit as on birth and wealth. A great number of Lacger men eventually held military commissions, far more than had been magistrates. They entered the army in impressive numbers beginning in the 1660s, and while not all remained for lengthy careers, the development dramatically underscored a shift in the focus of the family's interests. With the death of the *parlementaire* Jacques de Lacger in 1688, the family no longer held any judicial posts. Its men ceased to train in the law and they dissociated themselves from the administration of justice. Some preferred to tend their rural estates, a decision reinforced by the official intolerance shown toward Protestants. Yet even these country landholders served fleeting youthful terms as junior officers and thereby garnered the dignity reserved for those who bore arms. Others in the family, mostly cadets with restricted horizons, fully transferred bureaucratic allegiances and expectations to the army and there continued in the performance of service to the monarch. Now soldiers, they conducted themselves with characteristic ability, vigor, and accomplishment, although here, too, the religious question intruded, restricting ambition and forcing unwelcome, unpleasant choices.

Altogether, fourteen Lacger men took commissions in one or another of the royal regiments from the reign of Louis XIV until the end of the ancien régime. Several had, early on, served briefly in cavalry regiments. Most, however, were infantry officers whose commissions were predominantly in the Regiment of Auvergne. The family contributed ten officers to this particular unit and was among the three or four houses who dominated its officer corps, staff, and command structure. Created already during the early seventeenth century, the Regiment of Auvergne was one of the so-called *petits-vieux*. The *vieux* and *petits-vieux* constituted the dozen oldest, most esteemed, and hence more desirable regiments in the kingdom.[64] Age and honor, however, were not the sole factors to influence the Lacger choice.

Despite the geographic connotation and provincial reference of its name, the Regiment of Auvergne drew from a wide territorial range, including portions of Languedoc. Practically speaking, it was the regional regiment for men of the Castrais who wished to join the army. It also had, by virtue of its recruiting area, a fair number of Protestants or crypto-Protestants within its ranks. The Lacger shared a geographic, cultural, and religious affinity with those whom they commanded or were commanded by. In addition, the family tradition of service to this regiment surely strengthened and supported these bonds. A person trained and fought alongside blood relatives who protected and assisted with an eye toward mutual benefit and advancement. Three close Lacger kin held positions of command in the same battalion for awhile in the early eighteenth century; one was lieutenant colonel; the other two, company captains. For them and others like them, a kindredness of community and family permeated the craft of soldiering.[65]

These associations, on the other hand, neither masked nor muted the reality of the officer's profession. It was bloody and deadly. The Regiment of Auvergne campaigned throughout Bohemia, the Palatine, northern Italy, and Spain in the lengthy series of armed struggles undertaken by Louis XIV and Louis XV. The Lacger fought, were wounded, and died in the Wars of the League of Augsburg, the Spanish Succession, the Austrian Succession, and the Polish Succession. François participated in over two dozen different battles and sieges. He even received a battlefield promotion to lieutenant colonel at Cassano in 1705. His younger brother

Salomon was, in September 1701, among the nearly ninety French officers killed at the disastrous battle of Chiari in northern Italy. Four years later, another Lacger perished at the siege of Verrua, also in the Italian Piedmont. A cousin, Jean-Louis, died of wounds received at Parma in 1734. Jean-Jacques, the chevalier de Lacger, apparently carried a severe facial scar and was wounded repeatedly—at Chiari in 1701, Guastalla in 1734, and Prague in 1742. Louis was also badly wounded, probably in Spain during the last phases of the War of the Spanish Succession. For their efforts during these same years, no less than a half dozen Lacger earned royal decoration, the celebrated Order of Saint Louis.[66]

Valor and honor notwithstanding, military careers did not always flourish. Rather, they could be sluggish and checkered affairs. Lacger men, like many others, typically took commissions while in their late teens. Their average age upon entry into the army was slightly less than nineteen. Most times, however, the family's sons never got beyond the grade of lieutenant or captain. Death cut short the vocation of several: three died in battle and two suffered natural, but nonetheless youthful, demises. At least five others had but brief stints in the royal army before retiring, principally to their estates. In fact, with three notable exceptions, the average length of service among these Lacger officers was about ten years.

François, Louis, and Jean-Jacques differed from their relatives in terms of longevity as well as the grades that they attained. All three were of an age and generation: François and Louis were brothers; Jean-Jacques, a cousin. They received their commissions in the period between 1684 and 1695 and served forty-five, forty, and fifty-one years, respectively. François retired a lieutenant colonel and brevet brigadier; Louis, a battalion commander; and Jean-Jacques, a lieutenant colonel. Still, these three successful officers bore more than a passing resemblance to their less distinguished uncles and nephews, brothers and cousins.

These officers, whether lieutenants or lieutenant colonels, were unmistakably part of a middle stratum of provincial noblemen who lacked sufficient connections at court and who, in any event, were rarely rich. They could not hope to achieve great success in the more exclusive and financially demanding cavalry regiments and consequently gravitated to the infantry. Several Lacger, for instance, were at first cavalry ensigns but soon switched to the infantry. Even there, a man might spend many years in the junior grades, reaching the position of battalion commander or lieutenant colonel only with good fortune and prolonged service. Initial entry into the officer corps did not require purchase. The office of lieutenant, for example, was nonvenal; and after the mid-seventeenth century, it was no longer even necessary to buy the office of captain and with it a company in order to advance. Still, venal captaincies were, as might be expected, much surer avenues for advancement.

Under Louis XIV and his minister of war, Louvois, the growth of the army and a deliberate desire to attract talent opened the higher grades to persons of lesser birth. Length of service along with skill and dedication were increasingly among the factors that governed promotion. After five or six years of service, a lieutenant could reasonably expect to advance to the grade of captain. Noblemen without fortune could rise to even higher positions, mostly administrative, on the basis of merit rather than wealth. They could not hope, however, to match the successes enjoyed by those of highest aristocratic birth and great wealth. These latter privileged men sometimes passed quickly through subalternate grades to become venal captains, proprietary colonels, and in a few instances, generals.[67]

The individual promotion schedules of François, Louis, and Jean-Jacques are models for the meritorious, yet relatively impoverished, provincial nobleman. They collectively and methodically passed through the various grades from lieutenant to captain, and to the nonvenal charges of captain of grenadiers, major, lieutenant colonel, and brigadier. It generally took these Lacger officers about a half dozen years to rise from lieutenant to captain. Unless it was a reformed captaincy—that is to say, when the officer "owned" no company—the advance involved the purchase of a company and probably necessitated some marshaling of family resources. On the other hand, infantry companies were one-half to three-quarters the cost of those in the cavalry or dragoons. The next step, to captain of grenadiers, depended on seniority and required far more time, as many as fifteen, eighteen, or twenty-seven years for these three Lacger officers. Each battalion had a company of grenadiers to complement the usual sixteen infantry companies. Again, a captaincy of grenadiers suited the less wealthy, for grenadiers were recruited without particular expense from the other companies in a regiment.[68]

Longevity and exceptional service could take a soldier even further. The ranking captains became the battalion commanders. For François, who served during the carnage of the War of the Spanish Succession, the dignity came fairly soon, after only twenty years. His brother Louis, on the other hand, languished for nearly thirty years and only received the honor shortly before retirement. Jean-Jacques waited almost thirty years, too, but the pace of his career then quickened when just two years later he was promoted to the nonpurchasable grade of major. As such, he was the regiment's chief administrative officer and functioned as a sort of inspector general. He supervised training, verified the purchase of arms and equipment, and made certain that whether in the field or in garrison, the companies maintained their required strength and that the captains had not defrauded the government by requesting payment for fictitious numbers of troops. The major, along with the lieutenant colonel, was fundamental for the daily and proper functioning of the regiment.

Both François and Jean-Jacques became lieutenant colonels. For François, the rank was bestowed on the field of battle within a year of being appointed battalion commander; he still had twenty-three years' service ahead of him. Jean-Jacques, unable to benefit from rapid wartime promotion, waited until the end of his career, only four years prior to retirement. The lieutenant colonel was second in command of the regiment and frequently better versed in matters than the colonel. In war, he had charge of the regiment's first battalion and if necessary took over for the colonel. Thus, Jean-Jacques assumed command of the Regiment of Auvergne upon the death of his colonel at Prague in 1742. Like the other senior grades held by the Lacger, the lieutenant colonelcy was not venal. Selections were normally made from among the senior battalion commanders or company captains. The lieutenant colonel was often older, without significant financial resources, and from the petty nobility. His chief virtue was long experience with soldiery. He had, moreover, advanced slowly within the regiment. He possessed an intimate, detailed understanding of the organization and the men who belonged to it.[69]

The ultimate achievement for officers with backgrounds and careers similar to those of the Lacger was promotion to brigadier. The crown created this nonvenal brevet grade during the late 1660s. Originally performing the utilitarian function of reorganizing regiments of unequal size into uniform battlefield brigades of four battalions, the position evolved into a reward for outstanding service. Relatively few persons received the honor, and those that did were a roughly even mixture of wealthy privileged officers and individuals from the lesser nobility. Of the 232 brigadiers appointed during the reign of Louis XIV, about one-half arrived via the offices of venal captain and colonel; the other half passed through the nonpurchasable grades of major and lieutenant colonel. For the former, the grade of brigadier often promised admission to the general officer corps, while for the latter, it usually represented the distinguished culmination to a praiseworthy career. François's promotion to brigadier in February 1719 fell into the second category. It was recompense for arduous, loyal, and unfailing performance of duties both on and off the field of battle.[70]

Another, slightly more common distinction was decoration with the Order of Saint Louis. The award, established in 1693, acknowledged merit and recognized achievement among younger officers without having to grant them a promotion. It could also recognize seniority and, accordingly, provided a supplemental pension for valorous retiring officers. François, while decorated as "chevalier de Saint Louis" as early as 1709, received a pension of one thousand livres drawn on the order only upon his retirement in 1728. His brother and cousin were honored with the Order of Saint Louis midway in their careers, too, but it is unclear whether they received much, if anything, by way of a supplemental pension when they retired.[71]

Protestants could not theoretically be admitted as chevaliers of Saint Louis. Members were obliged to "profess the Catholic, Apostolic and Roman Church." In truth, with the Revocation, Huguenots[72] were supposedly unable to serve at all in the officer corps. Though the crown enticed them to convert with promises of money and pensions, the process was slow and not entirely successful. It was not until the late 1690s that Jean-Jacques, for example, publicly converted to Catholicism in exchange for an annual royal pension of three hundred livres. He and the other Lacger admitted to the Order of Saint Louis presumably affirmed their Catholicism at the moment of initiation, too. Recipients knelt and swore an oath of fidelity to Catholicism and the king; they were also required to produce an attestation of Catholicity from their bishop or archbishop.[73] The meaning of these actions for officers of Protestant background can, on the other hand, be ambiguous.

Numerous Huguenots quietly stayed with their regiments after 1685. Some converted as required; others did so but nominally. These latter crypto-Protestants persevered within a climate of limited, practical toleration. They accorded the Catholic Church the respect officially demanded and may, for instance, have attended mass but rarely took Communion. Most, however, balked at the oaths of Catholicity required by the Order of Saint Louis and disdained the pensions offered for public conversion.[74] Not so François, Louis, and Jean-Jacques. Could they have viewed these oaths and attestations as mere formalities, as did some other Protestant officers? Certainly they were careful to follow the requirements of Catholicism. Louis and Jean-Jacques were solemnly wed in Catholic ceremonies; Jean-Jacques received the last rites on his deathbed; François and Louis were buried within the church of la Platé. Louis, heavily influenced by the pious Catholic woman he married only months before dying, even requested a whole series of requiem masses to be celebrated for the repose of his soul.[75]

If these soldiers were willing to satisfy the demands of their Catholic monarch, they likely did so with some regret. François and Jean-Jacques, in particular, were sympathetic to the situation of their confessionally faithful kin. Later, as death approached, they were at pains to insure that these relatives received substantial financial assistance in the form of donations, inheritances, and testamentary legacies. François bequeathed the bulk of his immense estate, including the seigneury of Navès, to a Protestant cousin. Jean-Jacques, despite his public conversion in 1697, spent his final years living in a house owned by a Protestant nephew and then left him a legacy amounting to more than 40 percent of his estate.[76] Such beneficence insured the continuation of the Protestant line; and the donors, after lifelong subservience to a Catholic monarchy, may have been stirred by the conviction that no mortal, not even the king, could touch them beyond the grave.

Economic considerations, naturally enough, had a place in these matters. Officers from circumstances similar to those of the Lacger were unlikely to find great fortunes in the army. Those whose service was brief received a measure of dignity and little else. A lifetime in the regiment might provide a modest, even comfortable retirement. Jean-Jacques, after fifty-one years in the army, had a financial worth of about sixty thousand livres. His cousin Louis, a forty-year veteran, seems to have had fewer assets. Only François, whose career coincided with the War of the League of Augsburg (1688–97) and the War of the Spanish Succession (1702–14) acquired genuine wealth.

François was no doubt blessed with native talent and ambition. Like all military officers, he received a salary. The added pay and accelerated advancement associated with warfare would have given him an extra boost. Supplemental pay and the allowances for subsistence and forage while campaigning augmented a lieutenant colonel's income by 40 percent or more. These allotments for pay and rations naturally increased with higher grade. Here again, the quickened pace of military activities during hostilities favored a career. Seniority came sooner, and there was always a chance of battlefield preferments, such as François's elevation to lieutenant colonel. Another feature of campaign life, one discussed earlier, was irregular income. After the French army's notoriously rapacious behavior in the Palatine during the War of the League of Augsburg, the military administration sought to suppress as far as possible outright looting and robbing. A system of "contributions," taxes levied on enemy and neutral populations, nonetheless continued through the War of the Spanish Succession. Although officially designated for the maintenance of armies, these taxes occasionally enriched the higher officers.[77]

A decorated senior officer with numerous years of combat could also expect pensions and other rewards in retirement. François received a series of royal pensions, or annuities, when he left the regiment in 1728. A regular yearly payment of 466 livres was drawn directly on the royal treasury. A supplement of 200 livres came from the revenues of the Hôtel des Invalides, the famous Parisian institution for old soldiers; and another 1,000 livres per annum, from the endowment attached to the Order of Saint Louis. François by virtue of his conversion derived the far smaller sum of 150 livres from the *économats,* the revenue from vacant ecclesiastical benefices. The crown collected a benefice's income during the period of its vacancy and had, since the mid-1670s, used a substantial portion of this revenue to provide pensions for Protestants who converted. Finally, already some five years prior to François's retirement from the army, the king had appointed him governor for the city of Castres with an annual salary of 1,000 livres.[78] Suitably enriched and influential, he returned to Castres and there spent another thirty years, dying at the age of ninety-seven. His life and career, clearly exceptional, illustrate the possibilities and, by comparison, point up the major disadvantages to service in the army.

Few officers became wealthy and most discovered that the furtherance of their careers came at glacial speed. These drawbacks could be offset somewhat by the prestige and authority traditionally conveyed by the military profession. Yet officers rarely found the immediate opportunity to exercise these qualities within the larger community. They were typically removed from their native towns and regions except in retirement. If men from lesser houses with limited resources occasionally made a life career of the army, it was, one suspects, because they had scant choice. They were younger sons with a meager inheritance; their families possessed no significant landed assets; or there were no opportunities for other offices in the royal bureaucracy. By the late seventeenth century, noble tastes favored a military career. By the same token, provincial noblemen of modest means seldom had stunning success. The Lacger, when possible, seem to have preferred a brief term as lieutenant, perhaps even rising to captain, to be followed by a return to the family estates. The one great exception, however, had a formidable impact upon the family, its fate, and its religious heritage. François de Lacger acquired, at the price of personal conversion, riches in military service to the very king who most persecuted the Huguenots. He then, not without some irony, bestowed this wealth upon the Protestant members of his family, enabling them to persevere steadfastly through the end of the ancien régime to the present.

◌

FOUR

Marriage and Family Life

Marriage held a place of central practical importance in the plans and designs of early modern European elites. It was the institution for the birth and care of children, the crucial next generation who assured the survival and extension of the family, its name, and its power. Marriage was also the focal point and nexus for an array of social, financial, and political arrangements aimed at augmenting the family's influence and prestige, promoting its strength, and protecting its future. Matrimony created and confirmed alliances and exchanges between kin groups. Finally, marital unions offered visible testimony of a family's social assimilation and integration. Marriage was a forum for social synthesis among the power-holding elite. In a society where birth itself conferred privilege and honor, status and wealth, power and position, good matches were essential to good breeding, good blood, and good lineage. As such, marriage was primarily an alliance between families, and their larger requirements took precedence over the affective demands and psychological needs of the individual marriage partners. The personal and emotional bonds between husband and wife were secondary to the greater well-being of the lineage and inevitably subject to its overriding considerations.

Marital unions were, for the Lacger and many other houses, a means of acquiring wealth and power. Through marriage, the Lacger family built and sustained the ties that created and solidified its place in a provincial Protestant judiciary and landed aristocracy. Its men and women, at least until 1685, married within a well-defined, if somewhat regional, pattern typical of families bent on upward social mobility and an expanding network of political alliances and friendships. Thereafter, the arrangements shifted, with marriage partners coming increasingly from an intensely local pool. Whereas the earlier marriages were built on a strategy intended to improve the circumstances of the family, the later unions were designed to preserve it. After 1685, the requirements for the maintenance of confessional identity within the family progressively dominated the criteria for selection of marriage partners.

The half dozen marital alliances struck by Guy de Lacger's sons in the sixteenth century were with women whose family background closely resembled the situation of the Lacger themselves. Their immediate relatives were a mix of aspiring bourgeois, local officeholders in the judicial or financial administration, and newly arrived *parlementaires*. All were well within the Lacger's social group. By the seventeenth century, as the family grew in power and influence, the character of its marital unions changed subtly. Most were still forged within the boundaries of a regional Protestant elite. Yet the family appeared anxious to negotiate strategic matches with houses beyond its traditional economic, social, and geographic range. Aspirations at this juncture may have even disposed the Lacger not to insist too much on the religious question. In early 1613, Jacques de Lacger, *secrétaire du roi* at Paris, briefly considered the possibility of marrying a Catholic woman. His widowed mother, gently but firmly overseeing matters from the family residence at Castres, objected. Happily, he reported to her shortly thereafter that he had found a prospective bride who had been "nurtured and instructed" in the Reformed faith.[1]

The Lacger of Castres arranged fifteen marriages, seven for sons and eight for daughters, in the years between 1600 and 1685. They were uniformly better, more ambitious unions than those of the previous generation. Spouses ideally joined the stature and, if possible, the wealth of their house to the Lacger. In addition, political concerns and an attentiveness to career advancement led to a strong predilection for alliances within judicial and legal circles. Perhaps the two most prestigious matches were those achieved by the parlementary magistrate Jean de Lacger and his eldest daughter, Isabeau, who both married into older, better-established noble houses. Jean, whose mother had been the daughter of the famed Huguenot jurist Jean de Coras, wed Marguerite de Dampmartin, daughter of the *gouverneur* of Montpellier, the chief royal judicial officer within a jurisdiction equivalent to a seneschalsy. Isabeau, the oldest female child of their union, married into the most politically powerful Protestant family of the region, the ancient feudal house of Toulouse-Lautrec. Her husband, Marquis de Toulouse-Lautrec, was seigneur of Saint-Germier and later seneschal of Castres.[2] Female hypergamy of this sort was widespread in France and frequently dominated the marital strategies of the officeholding elite.[3]

Isabeau's two younger sisters fared less brilliantly, but nonetheless well. Their husbands came from families closely tied to the sovereign courts of Languedoc and hence to Lacger interests. Marguerite, presumably with assistance from her mother's relatives, married Guillaume de Clausel, seigneur de Fontfroide, of a distinguished Protestant family of Montpellier. The son of a judge on the *chambre des comptes,* Guillaume himself rose to become a president of the court. He was also an active member of the Reformed Church. Members of the Clausel house continued to serve the *chambre des comptes* as well as the Protestant Church into the early 1680s. The Lacger arranged for the third sister, Louise, to wed François de Rozel, whose father had been a magistrate on the *chambre de l'Edit.* François himself became the tribunal's royal attorney-general, a post to which the couple's son, Pierre, eventually succeeded.[4]

The social and professional integration achieved through the bonds of matrimony was complex and pervasive. In 1600, for example, Jean de Lacger purchased his judicial magistracy on the *chambre de l'Edit* from the Rozel family. It was Jean's daughter, Louise, who subsequently married François de Rozel, attorney-general for the chamber. Such convergence of professional interest and marital alliance spilled into the political sphere as well. During the concluding phase of the Rohan revolt in the late 1620s, François de Rozel, Louise's husband, and the judge Pierre de Lacger, her uncle, diligently cooperated in the futile attempt to maintain Castres in peaceful loyalty to Louis XIII.

The tangle of political, vocational, and familial relationships was even greater in the case of Lacger affiliation with the house of Toulouse-Lautrec. Jacques de Toulouse-Lautrec was seneschal of Castres from 1599 until 1612, when a series of legal complications forced his resignation. The office then passed to Jean de Perrin, a close ally of the Lacger through the marriage of his sister Jeanne and Antoine II de Lacger. The Perrin house had, for example, a role in the guardianship arrangements which Antoine II, immediately prior to his death in 1591, established for his minor children. Jean de Perrin remained seneschal of Castres until 1623, at which time he ceded the office back to the Toulouse-Lautrec. The new incumbent was Marquis, son of the earlier occupant, Jacques de Toulouse-Lautrec. Marquis's wife was Isabeau de Lacger, whose grandmother was, naturally enough, Jeanne de Perrin. These reciprocal, near circular, linkages continued when, for instance, during the 1660s the oldest son of the judge Pierre de Lacger briefly served in a cavalry company commanded by a member of the Toulouse-Lautrec family. Then in 1672 Pierre's second son, Jacques, was betrothed to Marguerite d'Isarn, a granddaughter of Marquis de Toulouse-Lautrec and Isabeau de Lacger. Finally, when both Jacques de Lacger and Marguerite d'Isarn died at an early age, her mother, Louise de Toulouse-Lautrec, became guardian for the deceased couple's two young boys.[5]

Economic motives naturally combined with a family's desire to ally itself with others of similar or superior status. Dowries were always a factor, though as we shall see, they could cut both ways and, among these Huguenot magistrates and lesser nobles, were never lavish affairs. Inheritances from women who married into the family could be more promising. In the early seventeenth century, the enterprising Pierre de Lacger wed a rich young heiress, Roze de Correch, the only child of a deceased magistrate of the *chambre de l'Edit*. Later evidence leaves no doubt that her chief attraction was the valuable landed estates that composed the dowry and her paraphernal property. The latter was the separate property of a married woman and not subject to the *régime dotal*. Thus Roze de Correch's paraphernal assets would never have been made part of the dowry. They remained her own and, unlike the dowry, were free from the control of her husband unless she allowed him their administration. On the other hand, Pierre expected that all would ultimately pass to their children and thereby become part of the Lacger patrimony. A similar case occurred during the mid-1650s when a Lacger son married Magdelaine de Falguerolles. Though in possession of a respectable dowry, her parapherna, which she eventually willed to their children, were worth at least four times as much.[6]

Sometimes the Lacger constructed matches through which the house hoped to expand horizons and establish associations that went beyond the Castrais. Jean de Lacger's betrothal to Marguerite de Dampmartin, from a family of Montpellier, had this effect. More striking was the case of his younger brother Jacques, who, having deployed to Paris, there married the daughter of a magistrate of the Parisian *chambre des comptes*.[7] Though the Lacger neither maintained nor expanded this northern initiative, the marriage represented one of the first steps in an establishment process. On other occasions, bonds of matrimony patched together local affiliations. Marie de Lacger married Jean de Lespinasse, *juge d'appeaux* at Castres and a man with whom her brothers, the judges Jean and Pierre, maintained a regular, if occasionally strident, political relationship. Later, near the close of the eighteenth century, the Lacger renewed this affiliation, arranging a match between Jean-Jacques-Joseph and another Lespinasse daughter.[8]

Marriages with *parlementaire* families and other judicial houses account for about half the Lacger matches during the century prior to the Revocation. The remainder are divided almost evenly between unions with members of the minor landed nobility and those with people involved in the legal professions. These husbands and brides came from families of attorneys, lesser legal officials, and petty seigneurs of the vicinity.[9] Here the design seems less an effort at upward mobility than the perpetuation of a stable regional network of affiliations with households possessing similar financial, social, and political interests.[10]

With the revocation of the Edict of Nantes, the Lacger made a retreat in the marriage market. The requirements for selection of partners changed. Wealth, rank, and prestige—the traditional requirements in matrimonial arrangements[11]—were no longer paramount; confessional compatibility, while always important, now became crucial.[12] The oppressed religious minority banded together for physical security and psychological comfort. In the process, choices were markedly delimited. Ambitious marriage projects with houses at Montpellier and Paris, various *parlementaire* families, or the older feudal aristocracy were no longer discussed. The twelve unions concluded between 1685 and the end of the ancien régime were perceptibly middling, at least in comparison to the confident, aspiring nature of some previous matches. They occurred within the protective confines of the neighboring landed Protestant nobility and, in a few instances, the Protestant bourgeoisie of Castres. When, for instance, Marc-Antoine I married in 1694, the contract unassumingly described his father-in-law as a "bourgeois of Castres." Only the two marriages concluded by a cadet Catholic branch reached outside and beyond, retaining traditional goals of social betterment and economic advantage.[13] The principal lineage of the family remained Protestant, and for these men and women the religious issue reinforced what was a common tendency among early modern elites toward endogamy.[14]

Several of the families to which the Lacger allied themselves through marriage after the Revocation were widely known for their opposition to the royal ban on Protestantism. The Terson, seigneurs of Paleville, were the fiercest. François de Lacger, godson and namesake of the brigadier, wed Julie de Terson de Paleville in 1774. Some twenty-five years earlier, her parents married *au Désert,* that is to say, in one of the illegal and clandestine Protestant gatherings that took place in the countryside or sometimes in a private home. Catholic authorities afterward arrested the couple at the family château near Revel[15] and immediately separated the pair. She was at first confined in a convent at Montpellier, until her pregnancy became obvious. Transferred to an ordinary residence, she nonetheless remained under guard, and at her own expense. Her husband spent two years in prison. His release and return to the family château came only upon agreement, however pro forma, to shun illicit Protestant worship and to baptize their children in the Catholic Church.[16]

While the Lacger selection of spouses was, throughout the sixteenth and seventeenth centuries, influenced by the usual social, professional, and economic considerations, thereafter the concerns of faith and collective solidarity in the face of outside oppression progressively rose to the fore. These affinal kin shared common religious beliefs and values, formed business and social ties, understood one another's political concerns, and together met the external adversary. They eventually formed a solid phalanx of aunts, uncles, cousins, and godparents. Even today the tradition lingers. Relationships initiated by marriage as early as the seventeenth century have been rekindled more than once, and the Lacger still maintain close unifying ties with their "nieces and nephews" and "cousins and godchildren."

Differences among siblings in the choice of marriage partners came, predictably enough, according to order of birth and gender. The eldest son obtained the best match, a preferential treatment in keeping with his position as principal patrimonial heir. The family invested a disproportionally large share of its real property, offices, titles, and other assets in him. A strong marital alliance completed his role as the designated conduit for the continuation of the lineage. The oldest daughter occasionally enjoyed a favored marriage, too, albeit for slightly different reasons. The strategic marriage of a well-dowered daughter offered opportunities for the family to gain social and political advantage through association with families of equivalent or superior position. Yet, in general, the Lacger were fairly evenhanded in securing marriages for their various children, especially when compared to aristocratic houses elsewhere.

The Lacger managed without fail to dower all their marriageable daughters, and a high proportion of their sons married, too. This approach to the marriage of offspring was less stratified, perhaps more egalitarian, than that of nobles at, for example, Toulouse or Aix-en-Provence.[17] Unlike women of the Toulousain nobility during the eighteenth century, younger Lacger daughters were never condemned to spinsterhood. Although female births were likely underreported, particularly for the sixteenth century, twenty-five daughters (including three women of the eighteenth-century cadet Catholic branch) are known to have been born to the Lacger from the sixteenth through the eighteenth centuries. Eight perished in infancy or died as teenagers;[18] three others, born during the 1770s and 1780s, were by the conclusion of our survey not yet old enough to have married. The family dowered and married each of the fourteen women who survived into adulthood.

The marriage pattern among sons conforms a bit more to the traditional historical view. Even so, these young men seem to have had greater opportunity to wed than their counterparts in other areas of southern

France; cadets were not necessarily destined to be bachelors. Thirty-nine male births were recorded among the Lacger between about 1500 and the end of the ancien régime. Thirty-one survived to adulthood. Of these, ten never married; with two exceptions, they were younger sons. Among these bachelors, three entered the church and four the army, both common vocations for cadets.[19] Two of those who pursued church careers did so in the early sixteenth century before the family converted to Protestantism; the third ecclesiastic was from the cadet Catholic line of the eighteenth century. The remaining twenty-one Lacger men married. They represent just slightly over two-thirds of adult males in the family.[20] When women and men are considered together, more than three-quarters of those who survived to adulthood married.

Much of the explanation for the family's consistent ability to marry its children has to do with the nature of the marriage market among the lesser Huguenot nobility of the Castrais. The grouping was relatively small and isolated. None of the families within it were extremely rich or influential, nor did they have much prospect of becoming so. Finally, they shared a common religious culture, one that served to set them apart from a larger outside world. Their fortunes became tightly bound together. They were, by and large, dependent upon one another to furnish marriage partners. Under the circumstances, families rarely demanded or offered extravagant dowries. The Lacger, furthermore, favored an equality in the allotment of marriage portions to their daughters. The combination permitted the affordable marriage of all daughters. The fact that these Huguenots married extensively and repeatedly among themselves also worked against excessive maneuvering for financial gain. The various Protestant houses knew each other well and necessarily returned to one another for future matches. The greater imperative was mutual cooperation for the continuance of their community as well as the maintenance and reinforcement of the cohesive bonds between its members. The smooth intermarriage of daughters and sons was essential to achievement of the larger collective goal.

Because it encompassed so broad a spectrum of financial, social, and political arrangements, marriage was almost never a decision for the two contracting parties alone. Parents exercised extensive authority over their children's marriages, and French royal legislation, beginning with Henry II's edict of 1556, reinforced the notion by requiring parental, principally paternal, permission, written if possible, to the ages of twenty-five for women and thirty for men. The edict further permitted parents to disinherit underage daughters and sons who married without their approval. Yet children rarely married against the parents' wishes. Most families, parents as well as children, agreed on the objectives of marriage.[21] Lacger sons who left Castres, for example, continued to rely upon the counsel of their fathers and mothers in choosing a wife. They wrote asking for advice and seeking approval. Even when parents were dead, they selected spouses whom they sensed their fathers and mothers would have endorsed.

Parents and other family members—grandparents, older siblings, aunts, and uncles—had a compelling voice and played an active role in the choice of spouse and the composition of the dowry. The father usually took the lead in negotiating the marriage contract. If he died before all the children had married, the obligation fell to his heirs and other surviving relatives. Antoine I de Lacger negotiated the marriage of his younger brother with Jean de Coras's daughter in 1559. The arrangements surrounding the marriage of a Lacger daughter to Jean Gaches in 1599 were made by her widowed mother, Jeanne de Perrin, and her maternal grandmother, Astruge de La Roque. Several years later, Jeanne, now assisted by two grown sons, Jean and Pierre, worked out the details in the marriage of another daughter to the seigneur of Saint-Léon.[22]

The terms of these unions were made explicit through the provisions of the marriage contract, a formal legal document written by a notary in conformity with the customary law and juridical practices of the region. Witnesses, generally drawn from the kin, social cohorts, and professional associates of each of the families, publicly attested to and confirmed the agreement.[23] The contract identified the two parties and their parents, explicitly acknowledged the couple's mutual consent to marry, established the reciprocal financial responsibilities embodied in the dowry, and delineated the rights and obligations of the contracting spouses during the marriage and following one or the other's death. Moreover, it usually contained elaborate legal provisions for the division of inheritance among the children born of the matrimonial union. The most pressing elements, however, were the bride's dowry and the mode of its payment.

The dowering of a young woman was a family effort, and the dotal constitution and payment schedule entailed complex financial planning. Parents and grandparents, brothers and sisters, and aunts and uncles inevitably participated. Dowries were typically assembled from several sources and were often paid in installments. Antoine II, upon his death in 1591, bequeathed to each of his daughters a marriage portion of three thousand livres. A few years later, arrangements for the dowry for Isabeau, the first of these daughters to wed, called for two installments—one-half on the day of the celebration of the marriage, the remainder two years afterward. The marriage contract between Jean de Lacger and Marguerite de Dampmartin in 1602 contained similar provisions. Her dowry was seventy-five hundred livres, but only forty-five hundred were advanced immediately. The remainder, contained in a royal bond (*acquit patent*) belonging to the bride's widowed mother, would not be forthcoming until the older woman's passing. About ten years later, terms in the marriage pact of Jacques de Lacger and the Parisian Marguerite de Nets obliged her parents to furnish, upon celebration of the marriage, a dot valued at fourteen thousand livres. The stipulation was for ten thousand livres in cash and the rest in an annuity. The bride's parents further agreed to provide two thousand livres in the form of food and lodging for the young couple over the space of two years. These sorts of elaborate arrangements were common, particularly since sufficient cash was not always readily available. A family was rarely willing to overextend itself. Its resources were often invested in a variety of enterprises, and the members were reluctant to sell portions of their estates or borrow too heavily.[24]

Although the father bore fundamental responsibility for the composition of the dowry, mothers and maternal relatives frequently contributed to the endowment of a child. They augmented and completed the settlement, making it more impressive. Witness the contribution of a royal bond by Marguerite de Dampmartin's mother. The dowry for Jeanne de Lacger's marriage in 1614 included the portion of 3,000 livres that her deceased father had willed her and an equal amount provided by Pierre de Perrin, a maternal cousin. Marie de Lacger's dowry of 1654 totaled 14,000 livres. Her father provided the lion's share, 11,700 livres; her mother contributed another 2,000; a small legacy of 300 livres from a maternal aunt rounded out the sum. The dowry which Marguerite d'Isarn brought to her marriage with Jacques de Lacger in 1672 amounted to 12,000 livres—10,000 from her father, the rest from her mother.

Furthermore, half was paid in cash and jewelry upon solemnization of the marriage, the other half in equal annual installments over the next four years. When their son Marc-Antoine I wed Marie d'Auriol twenty-two years later, her dowry of 12,000 livres included a maternal donation of 900 livres. Toward the end of the eighteenth century, the endowment of Julie de Terson de Paleville for her marriage to François de Lacger consisted of 4,000 livres from her father and 2,000 from her mother.[25]

The dowries that the Lacger granted and received were, with two or three important exceptions, relatively modest. Accurate and explicit information for the period prior to 1600 is extremely limited. Although Jeanne de Carles contributed important property in her 1531 marriage to Guy de Lacger, an estimate of its overall worth was never recorded. Of the unions contracted by her sons, reliable dowry data are only available for the two marriages of Antoine II. Jeanne de Coras, whom he married in 1562, possessed an endowment of seventeen hundred livres;[26] sixteen years later, Jeanne de Perrin provided real property and other assets valued at three thousand livres. Antoine's brother Jean, in the discussion of various marriage proposals, projected dowries between two and three thousand livres; such expectations were seemingly realistic. The wife of a third brother, Adrian, had a dowry in excess of twenty-five hundred livres.[27] Unfortunately, exact dotal figures for these latter marriages are simply unavailable.

During the seventeenth century, there was considerable fluctuation in the size of the dowries of women who married into the Lacger house. In the early years, dowry values increased. The family of Marguerite de Dampmartin provided the relatively handsome sum of seventy-five hundred livres when she and Jean de Lacger wed. Two years afterward, in 1604, Roze de Correch also carried a substantial settlement into her marriage with Jean's brother, Pierre. This dotal allotment consisted entirely of real property whose estimated value, while clearly substantial by local standards, was regrettably never precisely calculated, at least not in the surviving records.[28] After this, the marriage portions that the Lacger expected and received from prospective brides stagnated and, in some instances, declined. Pierre's second marriage, to Marguerite d'Hérail in 1637, produced a mediocre dowry of only six thousand livres. Toward the end of the century, these values again rose, only to falter once more.

Marguerite d'Isarn, in marrying Pierre's son in 1672, had a dowry of twelve thousand livres; yet twenty-two years later, Marie d'Auriol's dot for her marriage to Pierre's grandson was the same amount—twelve thousand livres. By the eighteenth century, the matter only worsened. The matrimonial union of François de Lacger and Julie de Terson de Paleville in 1774 produced a paltry dowry of only six thousand livres.[29] Though this last example may be extreme, it does serve to focus the issue.

Excepting those that had inheritances attached to them, these dowries were, on the whole, relatively meager. They did not compare, for example, with the amounts provided by the older noble houses and *parlementaire* families at Aix-en-Provence. There, financial endowments were immense, involving tens of thousands of livres. Even the averages were striking. Dowries among the *parlementaires* of Aix in the late sixteenth century ranged between nine and twelve thousand livres. These numbers then increased from fifteen to twenty-one thousand livres by the third decade of the next century. As such, they are one and a half to nearly double the size of dowries commanded by the Lacger, who were themselves judicial officials and *parlementaires*. These disparities only increase in a comparison of Lacger dowries with those of Toulousain *parlementaires* at the end of the seventeenth century. The wives of the magistrates at Toulouse had dowries that averaged between twenty and thirty thousand livres and could go as high as fifty thousand. And none of these matched the enormous sums—one hundred thousand livres and more—which were the dowries common to the highest aristocratic circles of France.[30]

Several factors figure in the stagnation and decline of dowry size among the Protestant nobility of the rural Midi. The Protestant *parlementaires* at Castres simply did not possess wealth comparable to their Catholic counterparts at Toulouse, Aix-en-Provence, Bordeaux, Rouen, and elsewhere. Furthermore, the Lacger and their circle were hard-pressed and restricted by the growing offensive against Protestants. After the mid-seventeenth and certainly into the eighteenth century, they no longer possessed the financial and economic opportunities enjoyed by their ancestors. Finally, the pool of eligible marriage partners was narrowly limited to the Reformed nobility and upper bourgeoisie. As previously observed, no one could be too financially demanding under the circumstances; nor would one choose to be. Other corporate considerations took precedence, and among them, confessional cohesiveness was preeminent. The goals in choosing a marriage partner changed, and the community gathered together in the common interest of meeting an external threat.

Information on the size and composition of dowries assembled by the Lacger for the marriage of their own daughters is less readily available. These endowments tended to be roughly equivalent to, or somewhat smaller than, those that the family received. Put more positively, Lacger men generally pursued a strategy of advantageous marriages whereby their wives' dowries exceeded their sisters' portions. During the waning years of the sixteenth century, they set daughters' and sisters' marriage portions at three thousand livres, about what they expected of their own brides. These dowries doubled, on average, by the first decades of the following century, and then doubled again by about 1700.[31] The size of these dowries—which involved little or no conveyance of real property—was about the same as, perhaps even slightly greater than, those of women who married Lacger men; and the pattern of increases generally followed the contours of that for dowries received. In addition, the Lacger consistently avoided dowering sisters and daughters with land or other patrimonial real estate. Almost always, there were sons to inherit the family lands. Women were not to receive or convey land except in the absence of direct male heirs, a position reinforced by customary law.

The Lacger, with the exception of a single incident, never permitted female members to transmit, either through dowries or inheritances, real property to another family. The exception occurred in 1652 when Hercule de Lacger died childless and intestate. His mother and three adult married sisters then divided the sizable inheritance among themselves. Lacger males, for their part, were generally adept and fortunate at the reverse. They sought ideally to marry a rich heiress, the only child of a wealthy family or, failing that, an only or eldest daughter who commanded a lucrative cash dowry and might later receive an additional legacy.

Understandably, brides who stood to inherit substantial real property or whose dowries contained considerable wealth were extremely desirable matches. They offered attractive economic benefits to their husbands and children and, as such, were vital to Lacger prosperity. Although the law barred a husband from disposing of his wife's dowry, he did have usufruct over the interest; and their children inherited the whole. The precise dimensions of these contributions can occasionally be difficult to calculate. The property may have been inventoried, but often no estimate of its value was attached. In several cases, the distinction between dowry and inheritance was blurred. The significance is nevertheless readily appreciated. The dowry and inheritance of Jeanne de Carles, the only child of a prosperous merchant, had lasting value and conferred upon her an importance wholly equivalent to that of her spouse for the future of their progeny. Her assets as listed in the 1531 marriage contract with Guy de Lacger—especially the town house at Castres and the *métairie* of Clot—were, when combined with his judicial office, the starting point for construction of the Lacger patrimony. A century later, the marriage of Pierre de Lacger and Roze de Correch, another only child, held out hope of additional and greater patrimonial enrichment. Roze's many possessions included several houses and nearly a dozen separate farms. But the childless marriage ultimately denied the Lacger her wealth. In the absence of direct heirs, Roze's riches could not stay with the Lacger. Instead, they returned to her family, in this instance to her collateral blood relatives.

The contribution of Marie de Barrau proved more durable. She married Marc-Antoine II de Lacger in the mid-1720s. The sole child and heir of Henry de Barrau, Marie offered a dowry that was set at one-half of her father's possessions as well as one-half of her deceased mother's dowry and paraphernal goods. She eventually inherited the rest and, at her death in 1781, possessed a personal estate, which she bequeathed to her two surviving sons, valued at more than thirty thousand livres. It included over seventeen thousand livres in loans and other financial investments, a house in town whose estimated worth was ten thousand livres, and the remainder in silver plate, jewelry, and other personal property.[32]

The economic attributes of the dotal system unquestionably enhanced the importance of women to the family,[33] while at the same time, the legal arrangements surrounding the dowry offered them safeguards and guaranteed their property rights. Under the customary law of Toulouse, a woman brought the dowry to her husband, yet it was inalienable and, in time, necessarily returned to the wife or her heirs. The husband had free administration of the dot during their marriage and, if he outlived his wife, retained usufruct for his lifetime. Upon his death, the dowry then passed to her heirs, usually their children or, failing progeny, her family.

The marriage contract established a woman's legal rights in the event of her husband's predecease, too.[34] A widow theoretically recovered her dowry and also received an increment (*augment*), a survivor's benefit assigned from the assets of her husband. The *augment* assured a woman a minimum of economic security upon the death of her spouse. The marriage contract normally settled the terms of this widow's supplement, which in the vicinity of Castres was calculated at one-half the value of the dowry. It was legally a "gift" from husband to wife, yet distinct from the jewelry, clothing, and other goods that he might give her at the moment of their marriage.[35] The marriage contract of Antoine II de Lacger and Jeanne de Perrin in 1576 set her dowry at three thousand livres and the corresponding *augment* at fifteen hundred livres. By the terms of the 1637 compact between Marguerite d'Hérail and Pierre de Lacger, her family furnished a dowry of six thousand livres and he agreed to a supplement of three thousand livres. When Marie de Lacger married Marc-Antoine de Noir a few years later, an *augment* of seven thousand livres complemented her relatively handsome dowry of fourteen thousand livres.[36] Local legal customs allowed childless widows to recover the dowry and collect the *augment* as well. In the event of offspring, surviving wives would seldom have had the dowry actually returned. Instead, common practice was to grant her the income from it. The law further restricted a widow with progeny to no more than the usufruct of the *augment*. Again, the terms very much resembled an annuity.[37]

Widowhood was a common experience for Lacger daughters and daughters-in-law, who were frequently much younger than their husbands. Ten or more years sometimes separated them.[38] Jacques de Lacger, who married in 1654, was twenty-five years older than his wife, Magdelaine de Falguerolles. Marc-Antoine II de Lacger, in a more typical case from the early eighteenth century, was eleven years older than Marie de Barrau. François de Lacger, who married Julie de Terson de Paleville in 1774, was more than a dozen years older than his bride.[39] These wives often outlived their husbands. Widows, unless they were young and childless, usually forsook remarriage. They remained at the family residence, acting as guardian for minor children and managing the family's wealth or, in cases where the children were older, living with the family of the eldest son. Nonetheless, marriage contracts routinely established a wife's entitlement upon the predecease of her spouse. Jean de Lacger, in his 1602 betrothal to Marguerite de Dampmartin, agreed to a widow's supplement of three thousand livres. From it she would be able to draw an annual pension, a jointure or *douaire* of five hundred livres "payable by his heirs." Jeanne de Lacger's marriage contract with Guyon de Gavaret in 1614 fixed, in the event of her widowhood, an annual pension of six hundred livres and a choice among several residences belonging to her husband. The family of Magdelaine de Falguerolles, in negotiating her marriage to Jacques de Lacger some forty years later, reached an understanding that she could receive a yearly pension based on the usufruct of her dowry and *augment*. She would also, in typical fashion, be permitted to remain in her husband's house and to retain whatever jewelry, clothing, and household furnishings he had given her.[40]

These matters would naturally be taken up again in the husband's will, and as a matter of practice, the harmonious family—widowed mother and children—would have wished to avoid invoking such stringent legal provisions. They generally preferred less formal, cooperative arrangements built around a pooling of family resources for the mutual advantage of all. Unless the family was rent by disastrous discord, a widow, especially if older, stayed on the patrimonial estates with the principal heir, normally the eldest son. He provided for her comfort in accordance with the accepted standards of filial obligation, and she made no special demands on her dowry or the annuity to which she was legally entitled.

Amid these many legal and financial concerns, the generative focus of marriage ought not to be overlooked. The ideal bride was wealthy, young, and fecund. Of these qualities, the last was indispensable. The economic resources of a prospective wife could be mediocre and she might be slightly older, but she had absolutely to be fertile, for after all, her womb was the instrument for the procreation of the succeeding generation. The stress placed on the maternal aspects of marriage—the bearing and nurturing of children—was formidable, and the occasional failure of a union to produce offspring could be an embittering experience. The lengthy but barren marriage of Pierre de Lacger and Roze de Correch offers eloquent testimony to common expectations and the depth of frustration when they went unfulfilled.[41]

Roze de Correch was born on 7 August 1592; Pierre de Lacger fifteen years earlier in July 1577. As the two families approached the final stages of the negotiations toward their marital union in the autumn 1604, they were twelve and twenty-seven years old respectively. Roze's youth—twelve was the earliest age at which a girl could legally marry—and the couple's difference in ages, while shocking to modern sensibilities, gave less offense in the period. Brides ought to be robust and in their prime; their husbands, more mature and experienced. Popular tradition even praised these unions for their fertility. In the words of a later regional proverb: "A young sheep and old ram have soon made a flock."[42]

Pierre was apparently anxious to wed his prospective bride as quickly as possible. The motivation had much to do with the lure of her fortune. The marriage contracts, for surprisingly there were two in this instance, were signed on 10 and 24 October 1604. Indeed, the existence of two contracts later gave rise to legal confusion and uncertainty. The Reformed pastor blessed and solemnized their marriage six months later.[43]

Roze was, by early modern standards, a great prize. Her father was Paul de Correch, a magistrate of the *chambre de l'Edit*. It was, again, an association that the Lacger had cultivated. As early as 1595, Jean, Pierre's older brother and then judge of Castres, had lent strong support to Correch's request to be appointed to the chamber. By the time of his daughter's marriage, Paul de Correch was dead, but he had bestowed upon this only child the entirety of his estate, which in turn contributed handsomely to the dotal constitution. The paternal legacy included six *métairies* or farms, a manor house, meadows, gardens, and enclosures, along with animals, huts, and furnishings. Most of these lands were situated in the mountainous terrain east of Castres near Vabre and Lacaune. Although no explicit financial worth was assigned them, they were plainly valuable. Roze de Chauvet, the bride's mother, was also well-to-do. The heart of her property was a manor house and five *métairies* toward the west in the vicinity of Puylaurens, Saint-Paul, and Teyssode. While these latter properties would not pass to the daughter until Chauvet's death in 1620 and some outstanding debts relative to her estate had to be settled, it made for an exceptional collection of assets.[44]

The marriage of Roze and Pierre endured thirty-two years, until her death in April 1637 following a prolonged illness, but the prosperous future which Pierre had envisaged slowly soured with Roze's failure to conceive. The absence of offspring spawned acrimony and resentment between them. With her passing in 1637, Pierre, now sixty, was impatient to remarry. He found and was betrothed to a young woman within eight months. The couple celebrated their union in early January 1638, and though she did not immediately become pregnant as Pierre might have hoped, she eventually bore him five children: two boys and three girls.[45] Meanwhile, his first wife was not to be forgotten.

The prolonged and determined hostility between Roze and Pierre became unmistakable in the events that transpired after her death. Following the legal traditions of the region, Pierre fully expected to retain usufruct of his deceased wife's property for his lifetime. It was, he reasoned, her dowry, and normal practice in a fruitless union was to allow a husband use of his predeceased spouse's dowry until his own passing. Yet unbeknownst to Pierre, Roze left a last will and testament. It was a furtive effort, composed in her own hand, and purposely without the publicity a notary might have entailed. Her words, however, had obvious benefit of expert legal advice. She wrote the will in late 1632, nearly five years before she died. At the time, she was living at her estate of la Nourisse near Saint-Paul, a property bestowed by her mother. She likely was, as a practical matter, permanently estranged from her husband by this time. She may have even died in the house at la Nourisse. Jean de Puech, sieur de Fomblanc, her collateral cousin and universal heir under the terms of the will, also had a role in the document, which he dramatically produced on the very day of her death.

The testament opened with the self-confident, unexpectedly assertive, and bitter words by which Roze de Correch wished to be remembered: "The thorn follows the rose and those who are content will not be so for long."[46] What followed, however, was no mere thorn, drawing blood but superficial in its effect. This had more the quality of a well-honed knife aimed deftly, though by no means dispassionately, at the vitals. Roze had prepared a sharp, stunning attack on her husband, and she meant it to be painful. She exploited certain ambiguities and inconsistencies in the contractual arrangements surrounding their marriage in order to take advantage of the distinction between dowry and paraphernal property. It will be remembered that the parapherna were the possessions that a woman held in her own right. They were not made part of the dowry upon marriage, and in contrast to the dowry, she, rather than her husband, had the use and administration of them. A woman was entirely at liberty to control them. She could dispose of them as she wished in her will, and unlike the assets contained in the dot, her surviving spouse would not retain their usufruct.[47]

In naming her cousin Jean de Puech as heir, Roze bequeathed her paraphernal possessions to him. The lengthy court battle that ensued revealed the strategy that she and her cousin had devised. They could not prevent Pierre from usufruct of those assets which Roze had inherited from her father; those lands were beyond any doubt part of the dotal package. On the other hand, there were two marriage contracts, and the second of them, or so the argument went, contained no mention of the properties that had belonged to her mother. Roze only inherited them upon the mother's death in 1620, fifteen years after her marriage to Pierre. Therefore, they were paraphernal rather than dotal resources, and Roze was free to dispose of them as she wished. In fact, at his cousin's death, Jean de Puech took immediate possession of the manor house at la Nourisse and the rich farms associated with it.

Pierre naturally challenged this logic, and the resulting conflict soon went to court. The magistrates who initially examined Roze's will were shocked. Her legal maneuvering impressed them, but they felt obliged to remark upon the expression of her "extreme and brutal passion, and animosity toward the sieur de Lacger." It was, in their opinion, "contrary to accepted standards of good behavior and public decency."[48] Wives simply did not behave in this fashion, even if they were acting within the confines of the law. An expensive legal suit went on for several years, wending its way from the subalternate tribunal at Castres, through the Parlement of Toulouse, to the *chambre de l'Edit* at Castres and the *chambre de l'Edit* attached to the Parlement of Bordeaux. Counter-appeal followed upon appeal. In the end, Pierre successfully pressed his claim to the manor house at la Nourisse and its dependent *métairies,* property that Roze had inherited from her mother and that, he argued, was part of the dowry. He retained use of the entirety of his first wife's possessions for the remainder of his life. Not until Pierre's death in 1655 did they pass to the Puech, sieurs de Fomblanc and collateral blood relatives of Roze de Correch.[49]

While she may not have completely thwarted her much-detested spouse from enjoyment of her familial assets, Roze succeeded in exacting a financial and psychological price. She caused her husband enormous embarrassment. In this heavily masculine world, he may have already been shamed by his inability to impregnate her. To some, it probably appeared that he, rather than she, could not produce children. Her subsequent last will and testament insured even greater humiliation. Roze must have been confident that Pierre would challenge her legal maneuvering. At the same time, she knew that his only recourse was to lay the matter before his judicial colleagues and friends. She would make it painfully obvious to them that Pierre, the honorable royal judge, was unable to control his wife; he failed to command proper obedience and respect. His disgrace, particularly within his sphere of public power and influence, would be assured.

If the biting tragedy of Roze de Correch's marriage stemmed from an inability to fulfill common expectations of maternity, other Lacger wives fared better. The children they bore and cared for satisfied familial, husbandly, and personal needs. The number of offspring, while never great, was adequate and in some ways optimal. A medium-sized family allowed the lineage to continue, even thrive, without the dissipation of resources engendered by too large and unwieldy a brood. Family size among Lacger males who married between the early sixteenth and the late eighteenth centuries was, on average, five children, of whom approximately one-quarter died in youth. The largest single families numbered seven or eight children. Jeanne de Coras, Antoine II's first wife, bore him one child. Jeanne de Perrin, his second spouse, gave birth to another seven; in fact, she was pregnant at his death in 1591 and did not deliver their fourth daughter until several months afterward. Marie d'Auriol and Marc-Antoine I married in 1694 and had seven children over the next eighteen years. She died within months of the birth of their last child. He soon remarried and fathered one more child, but this second marriage only lasted four years before he expired unexpectedly in 1720. Seven years later, his eldest son, Marc-Antoine II, wed Marie de Barrau, and the couple had seven children during the space of a near quarter century.

Women, besides bearing a succession of infants, were expected to care for and educate them for their first six or seven years,[50] as well as oversee the household and sometimes the estate. A wife's maternal and domestic duties extended to the day-to-day supervision of the children's initial moral and religious upbringing, the handling of the household accounts, and the administration of the family's agricultural properties and other business interests, especially during the frequent absences of her husband. She managed the routine details of the home—food, clothing, and furnishings—and supervised the household servants, who in this lesser noble family typically numbered no more than two or three.[51] She also worked with her husband in, for example, securing good marriages for their children. Following the Revocation, the decisive role of wives, mothers, and grandmothers in the education of children at the first stages acquired added significance. A mother's customary charge over the earliest religious training of offspring contributed immensely to the preservation and continuation of the Reformed tradition. These maternal efforts redoubled after 1685 as the forum for the transmission of Protestant religious views and practices shifted from the public to the private sphere.[52]

These were not always easy tasks. Their proper accomplishment required both skill and determination, and other burdens occasionally added to a woman's responsibilities. Jeanne de Perrin, a remarkably able and hardworking person, was obliged to assume direction of the family after the death of her husband, Antoine II, in 1591. It was a complicated and demanding charge, made more difficult by the fact that she was pregnant at the time, yet she acted with tact and diligence. Even before her husband's death, she assumed primary responsibility for her stepson Jean de Lacger's education, arranging for him to join her nephew at Poitiers. It was to her that the boy periodically wrote to request funds for food, lodging, and the like. Before a child left for the Protestant *collège* at Nîmes or Montauban, she would assemble the clothes, shoes, and personal necessities. Furthermore, she as often as her husband arranged for room and board, paid the necessary teachers and servants, and offered moral guidance and emotional encouragement.[53]

Jeanne de Perrin had almost total responsibility for the management of the family's financial and legal affairs after her husband's death. He, through the familiar prescriptive instrument of a deathbed testament, named her tutrix and lawful administratrix for their minor children. Women—the surviving mother or grandmother—customarily acted in this capacity for their children or grandchildren. Marguerite de Nets, widow of the *secrétaire* Jacques de Lacger, became tutrix for their offspring after his demise. When Jacques de Lacger, sieur de Clot and nephew of the above *secrétaire*, died in 1681, his wife, Marguerite d'Isarn, had already predeceased him by three years, most likely in giving birth to their second child. Guardianship of their two infant sons fell consequently to the maternal grandmother, Louise de Toulouse-Lautrec.[54]

Close male relatives—older sons, brothers, and brothers-in-law—assisted and advised the tutrix in her administration of the minor children's property. Antoine II, in naming his wife as guardian, acknowledged the fundamental suitability and essential complementarity of her roles as "mother and tutrix." At the same time, he selected as "honorary tutors" his eldest son, Jean, his brother Jean, and his brother-in-law Louis de Perrin, sieur de La Roque. Jeanne de Perrin was obliged to render an annual account of her management of the patrimonial estates, but beyond this, it is not clear how direct an interest or active a participation these men took or, given the continuing religious strife, were capable of taking in the matter.[55]

Similar arrangements were made for the children of the Parisian *secrétaire* Jacques de Lacger, who died suddenly and probably intestate in late March or early April 1621. His brother Samuel, who also lived at Paris, quickly contacted other family members for their views on settling the matter of a legal guardian or tutor. The choice devolved naturally upon the widow and the children's mother, Marguerite de Nets. Still, her deceased husband's two brothers, Samuel at Paris and Pierre at Castres, worked in unison with her to promote the children's, especially the eldest son's, welfare. Samuel, for instance, acted as their legal representative and safeguarded their rights in the settlement of Jeanne de Perrin's estate after 1628.[56]

Even with a child's emancipation, a mother continued to exercise informal but no less significant power. Jacques de Lacger, despite being in his early thirties, reconsidered when his mother strenuously objected to the prospect of his marriage to a Catholic woman in 1613. He later married the Protestant Marguerite de Nets; together, they had four children before his untimely death in 1621. Marguerite's enduring influence over their eldest son, also christened Jacques, provides another ready example of a woman's authority and direction within the family. The young man studied law, and by 1642 his uncles Samuel and Pierre, seeking to foster his career, arranged for him to practice before the *chambre de l'Edit* at

Castres. The mother, who remained at her Paris residence, subsequently became annoyed with him, commenting that he "only wasted his time at Castres" and was given entirely to the enjoyment of dinner parties and his violin. At her insistence, Jacques, now well over thirty, returned to Paris, where he was received to practice before the parlement there. Yet from her point of view, he was hardly more industrious. He turned to poetry and the circle of the *précieuses,* became entangled in a sordid dueling scandal, then discreetly absented himself from the kingdom for about a year. Finally, in 1653, Jacques's mother and his uncle Pierre arranged for the purchase of a judgeship on the Protestant *chambre* at Castres. Not long afterward, his family also negotiated a favorable match with the relatively wealthy Magdelaine de Falguerolles, and the couple settled at Castres.[57]

The wife and mother had a powerful place in the affairs of the family. She was expected to be the good spouse, the good mother, and the good housewife. Although her contribution tended to be internal to the family's well-being, perhaps more private and less public than that of her husband, it was central. Women bore and cared for the children, managed household matters, and when necessary, administered the patrimonial estates. As principals in a complicated marriage system, they strengthened a family's economic position, adding dowries and inheritances to the existing resources. These marital unions also reinforced familial power, advancing its political position and promoting its social integration by allying it to other, sometimes more prestigious or professionally more prominent, houses. Finally, among the Huguenots of the Castrais, marriage was a means to increase religious solidarity and thereby preserve the values, attitudes, beliefs, and practices shared by the Reformed community. These families formed a relatively small and closely integrated group. Through the mutual exchange of children in marriage, they forged a tight protective network among themselves. Marriage and the accompanying economic, social, and political considerations meant the continuation and, hopefully, the prosperity of the lineage. For Protestants such as the Lacger, these affinities also served to strengthen as well as to preserve kinship bonds and religious traditions.

FIVE

༄

Inheritance Systems and
the Protection of the Patrimony

Death and the accompanying transfer of power and assets was, like the marriage of an offspring, a critical juncture for the early modern family. The demise of kin, especially a father, but also a mother, brother or sister, aunt or uncle, even a cousin, occasioned the reassignment of familial authority and the reallocation of patrimonial resources among the survivors. Every family wished to avoid a ruinous division of power and wealth. Patriarchal prerogatives and patrimonial possessions could not be dissipated among too many heirs, lest the lineage itself be weakened. At the same time, the family needed to insure the rights and privileges of its various members as well as confer upon them some minimum measure of economic security. Again, the welfare of the house took precedence over the individual needs of any one person in an arrangement that aimed, insofar as possible, at the preservation, protection, and continuity of authority and resources. The system strove to provide fundamental stability for the family as generations succeeded one upon another.

The laws and usages governing inheritance varied enormously from one part of the kingdom to another. The western regions, especially Normandy, maintained a strict equality among heirs. Parisian customs were more flexible and offered several options, yet generally favored a rough egalitarianism. In the Midi, on the other hand, an unequal division of the estate prevailed.[1] The practice of the *préciput* (or preferential legacy) and *inter vivos* gifts permitted the father to advantage and "endear" certain of his children or heirs, giving more to one than another. The preferred child was typically the firstborn male. Notions of the preeminence of masculinity and seniority by birth dominated; daughters and younger sons were regularly placed at a disadvantage.[2] In addition, married daughters already in receipt of a dowry tended to be barred from the succession. Yet the exclusion of females and younger males was rarely total. It applied above all to land.[3] Thus the unequal division of the inheritance under paternal auspices and the barring of dowered married females worked to maintain the family property more or less intact and simultaneously enhanced patriarchal authority. While these procedures generally applied to commoners rather than nobles, they were crucial for families such as the Lacger who possessed both noble and nonnoble lands. The somewhat different practices governing noble successions pertained only to seigneurial lands, and the person involved usually had to be noble as well.

The aristocracy had, to be sure, long observed an inequality of inheritance, awarding the eldest son two-thirds or more of the family property. Among nobles, the rule of primogeniture (*droit d'aînesse*) was embedded in the ancient privileges of male succession associated with the feudal legal system, yet it applied solely to seigneurial tenures. The system was designed to maintain the integrity of fiefs and entitled the eldest son to the greatest portion of the patrimony. Originally intended to insure a vassal's military capacity, this effort toward impartibility aimed by the seventeenth and eighteenth centuries at the safeguarding and perpetuation of the patrimonial resources. Primogeniture, along with other legal devices such as the entail, kept the family's landed estates intact. It became the guarantor of the power, splendor, and dignity of every noble house. At the same time, patrilinear, indeed patriarchal, succession reinforced the hierarchical authority of the existing social order.[4]

The last will and testament was the formal civil act that established the details of the inheritance within the confines of customary law and prevailing usage. Drawn up typically by a notary, it was a public document that could be subsequently amended and adjusted through codicils according to the needs and desires of the testator. Final changes could be made on the deathbed. A person often waited until he or she felt death approach before composing these last legal words. The testament was the juridical instrument for obviating the fragmentation of family property and for perpetuating paternal authority.

Southern France, the so-called region of written law (*droit écrit*), was heavily influenced by Roman legal practices, and the testamentary tradition was solidly entrenched. The use of a last will and testament gave the father a powerful means to dominate the family's destiny. The favored descendant was nearly always the eldest male or, failing offspring, the eldest nephew or cousin. Most elite families adopted the strategy of investing a disproportionately large share, one-half to two-thirds and occasionally more, of their resources in the oldest male of the succeeding generation. Those who chose not do so were often regarded with suspicion.[5]

A related and widely observed practice of the Midi reflected an aversion to female heirs and resulted in the near universal exclusion of married and dowered daughters from the inheritance. The marriage portion, it was argued, took the place of the inheritance. The dowry, according to some jurists, was an advance on the inheritance and, once granted, barred these married women from participation in the subsequent succession. While these rules and practices associated with customary law evolved and weakened over the course of the sixteenth and seventeenth centuries, their general effect remained. In any event, shares in the inheritance varied significantly and did so according to both gender and the order of birth. Males had preference over females, the oldest over the younger.[6]

The 1523 testament of Pierre de Lacger, father of Guy and resident of Puylaurens, is the oldest document in the Lacger family archives. It displayed, even at this early date, the essential inheritance strategy that the family pursued over the next several centuries. The elements of masculine predominance and patrimonial impartibility run throughout. Although written in a crude mixture of French, Latin, and Occitan, the text was prepared by a notary and had the requisite seven witnesses, including the notary. It accorded entirely with the legal customs and testamentary practices of the period and region. "Set upon by illness" and knowing full well that "it is ordained for all men to die," Pierre began his farewells with the usual pre-Reformation expressions of religious piety and charitable largesse.[7] He requested masses for the repose of his soul, provided the customary grain and wine for distribution to the poor, and rewarded his two servants with gifts of ten livres each. Pierre named Antoine, his eldest son, as principal heir. The father intended that almost the entirety of the estate should pass to him. Guy, a younger sibling and later founder of the Lacger dynasty at Castres, received a legacy of three thousand livres, payable when he reached the age of twenty-five. Until then, his older brother had the responsibility to provide for him—to "feed and clothe" the younger man, according to the notarial rhetoric. The text did not mention sisters; if there were any, presumably they had been dowered and married off and therefore excluded from the inheritance. We know from other sources that there was also a third brother who was or would soon become a churchman, but the testament made no reference to him. Perhaps he had already been placed in the beneficed clergy and thus provided for.[8]

Nearly three-quarters of a century later, when Pierre's grandson Antoine II de Lacger was "confined to bed by corporal malady," he acted in very much the same manner. Antoine II dictated his intentions to the notary on 4 September 1591, one day prior to death. To be sure, the family was now Protestant and the forms of piety had changed. Elaborate funerals were frowned upon; the Reformers encouraged modest and simple interments. With the Protestant abandonment of belief in purgatory, prayers and masses were no longer deemed useful to lighten the soul's suffering. The highly organized Reformed churches gave greater direction over legacies for the impoverished,[9] and Antoine II was content to leave one hundred livres to "the poor of the hospital of Castres." On the other hand, the character of the partition of the inheritance remained unaltered in its overall contours.

Antoine II married twice. The first wife bore him a single child, a son; the second gave birth to seven children, three boys and four girls, and was expecting the last at the time of his death. The testament made an immediate distinction between male and female children. Each daughter was given three thousand livres, essentially a marriage portion, and was precluded from further participation in the inheritance. Sons, while receiving shares, would find that these varied immensely. The will also made elaborate arrangements for the unborn child. All depended upon its sex. A boy was to have some share in the inheritance: four thousand livres that would be paid by his brothers. A girl—and the child proved to be female—would, like her older sisters, get only a marriage portion of three thousand livres. The strong antifeminine tendencies exhibited in the provisions of Antoine II's will were neither unusual nor unique but conformed entirely with legal practice and the social views to which the laws gave expression.

Among Antoine II's sons, Jean was disproportionately favored. The eldest male and only child of the first marriage, he inherited his father's judicial office and real estate valued at 14,750 livres. The latter farmlands, vineyards, and town house constituted 40 percent of the real property associated with the patrimony. When considered together with the judgeship, Jean received 50 percent or more of the total family resources. His three younger half-brothers had progressively reduced shares of the real property. They received land worth approximately three-fifths, one-half, and three-eighths of that which passed to Jean. On the other hand, the family eventually secured posts in the royal bureaucracy for each of the three. One became *juge ordinaire* at Castres, the other two *secrétaire du roi* and *avocat au conseil privé du roi* at Paris.[10]

When the members of this generation drew up their wills in the mid-seventeenth century, they continued to demonstrate an overwhelming preference for the eldest son in any testamentary distribution of the patrimony. Pierre de Lacger, judge of Castres, left an estate valued at 88,618 livres upon his death in 1655. Under the terms of the will, Pierre's eldest son was named *héritier universel et général*. Except for certain minimum deductions for his brother and two sisters, he was heir to the entirety of the patrimony, inheriting about 62 percent of these assets. His siblings had far more meager shares. An older sister, Marie, had married the previous year, and her dowry of 14,000 livres was subtracted from the patrimony. Moreover, two younger children—a set of twins, boy and girl—each received a *légitime* or minimum share of 10,000 livres.[11] The eldest son and heir was obliged to insure that his older sister's dowry was paid according to the agreed schedule and that the younger siblings received their *légitimes* when they came of age. Aside from these responsibilities

—an imperative embedded in the lineage itself—the patrimonial assets were his.

The *légitime* was that portion of the succession of which a parent could not disinherit a child without legal cause or, from the heir's perspective, that portion of which he or she could not be deprived. The *légitime* guaranteed younger children a minimum share in the estate and was normally paid when a person reached the age of twenty-five, earlier if he or she married. When, for example, Louise de Lacger married in 1726, Marc-Antoine II, her older brother and the reigning family patriarch, paid her the nearly ten thousand livres that constituted the *légitime* from her father and inheritances from her mother and sister. Elder brothers naturally sought to avoid, whenever possible, lump sum settlement of the *légitime,* or other inheritances for that matter. Patrimonial resources were typically tied up in long-term investments, such as real estate or *rentes,* and families were unwilling or unable to divest themselves readily of this property. One solution was to offer younger siblings a pension or annuity. Marc-Antoine I paid his brother Jean-Jacques a yearly pension of four hundred livres, which represented the interest on the younger man's paternal *légitime* and maternal inheritance. The succeeding head of the family, Marc-Antoine II, acted in similar fashion. Rather than immediately advance the five *légitimes* to which his siblings were legally entitled following the demise of their father in 1720, he convinced them to allow him to invest a portion of the assets in a life annuity (*rente viagère*) and accept the yearly interest payments.[12]

By the seventeenth century, marriage contracts increasingly reinforced the practice of preferential legacies by drawing up explicit, detailed provisions that established overall terms for the favored treatment of one or another of the children born to a couple. When Jeanne de Lacger and Guyon de Gavaret wed in 1614, the contract allowed him to nominate one of their male children to receive through an *inter vivos* donation one-half of his "present and future possessions," meaning of course the lineage property (*propres*) of the Gavaret house as well the acquired goods (*acquêts*) that he and his spouse might accumulate over the course of their marriage. If he died before making the choice, his wife could do so; and failing her selection, the preference would automatically fall upon their eldest son. The contractual arrangements surrounding the marriage of

Marie de Lacger and Marc-Antoine de Noir thirty years later contained similar provisions whereby the "first male child" would inherit half of the patrimony. The 1672 marriage contract between Jacques de Lacger and Marguerite d'Isarn endowed the firstborn son with half the family assets. For the other children, they agreed to observe the "order of primogeniture." In later years, the proportion designated in the marriage contract for the eldest son fell from 50 to 33 percent. Marc-Antoine I's marriage contract of 1694 as well as that of his son and namesake, Marc-Antoine II, in 1725 set the inheritance of a son of the husband's choice at one-third. Even then, a father could advantage a child additionally. Marc-Antoine II went beyond the provision of his marriage contract and gave his eldest son a donation *inter vivos* of one-half the Lacger patrimony at the moment of the young man's marriage in 1774.[13]

After the mid-seventeenth century, the Lacger were not nearly so successful as their ancestors in preventing a dissipation of resources and corresponding decline in the family's economic fortunes. Much of the problem had to do with the deteriorating political and economic position of Protestants. Yet there were some internal family difficulties, too. The judge Pierre de Lacger's heir was his eldest son, also named Pierre. This son had a brief military career, never married, and died in 1668 while still in his early twenties. A younger brother, Jacques, then succeeded him as family heir; he was the alternate or substitute beneficiary under the terms of their father's will. These transfers were not, however, without their costs. Their father, the older Pierre, had left an estate valued at more than eighty-eight thousand livres in 1655. After a daughter's dowry and the two *légitimes* were subtracted, Pierre, as oldest son and heir, received an inheritance worth about fifty-five thousand livres. When the estate passed to Jacques, the second son, about a dozen years later, there were further deductions, principally in favor of the youngest sister. Jacques's eventual inheritance was reduced to under forty-nine thousand livres, about 55 percent of the original amount left by his father.[14] Thereafter, with the next generation in the following century, the situation only worsened.

The precise worth of the patrimony upon Jacques de Lacger's death in 1681 is not known, but the family's economic fortunes failed to flourish. The situation remained stable, perhaps more accurately stagnant; it may have even declined. These were, after all, difficult times for French

Protestants. Jacques had followed custom in naming his eldest son, Marc-Antoine I, as heir. Then in 1720, Marc-Antoine I died intestate. It was an unusual and disconcerting development. Only two other Lacger males are known to have passed away without having first composed a will. Hercule de Lacger did so in 1652. His heirs were, by law, his closest blood relatives. Since he died childless, Hercule's property passed to his mother and three sisters. Jean-Louis de Lacger, Marc-Antoine I's younger son, also failed to leave a will when, in 1734, he died of wounds received on the battlefield at Parma. Consequently his assets, a scant five thousand livres, were evenly divided between two surviving siblings, Marc-Antoine II, his older brother, and Louise, a sister.[15]

When Marc-Antoine I died intestate in 1720, the matter was far more complicated, mostly by virtue of the fact that he had married twice and had children from both marriages. Under the circumstances, there was a detailed accounting of the inheritance and its division; and the family could not actively favor the eldest male child but had to abide by the more egalitarian practices set by customary law. Marc-Antoine I's estimated worth at the moment of his demise was a mere 39,100 livres, less than half that of his grandfather sixty-five years earlier. Moreover, some preliminary financial considerations diminished it further. A *légitime* for Marc-Antoine I's younger brother had yet to be paid; his first wife's dowry was set aside to be shared by the four surviving children from that marriage; and there were some outstanding debts to be settled. These items reduced his estate by 23,400 livres, leaving a balance of 15,700 livres. One-third, a bit more than 5,000 livres, immediately went to the eldest son, as stipulated in the 1694 marriage contract between Marc-Antoine I and Marie d'Auriol, his first wife. The remaining two-thirds of the estate was apportioned equally among five persons: the three other children of the first marriage, his second spouse, and their one child. Each share amounted a little less than 2,100 livres. The family, at least this branch of it, was dangerously close to impoverishment.

The four children from Marc-Antoine I's first marriage had a slight advantage. They also received portions of their mother's dowry of 12,000 livres. Marc-Antoine II, the eldest son, got the lion's share, again about one-third, yet he was still left with a paltry inheritance: 5,233 livres from his father and 4,375 from his mother's dowry for a total of 9,598 livres.

His three full siblings—a brother and two sisters—fared considerably worse. When their inheritances from both father and mother are taken into consideration, they received respectively about 5,500, 4,500, and 4,000 livres. A half dozen years later, the youngest sister died and left her share to her sister. Then in the mid-1730s, the younger brother died and his share was divided equally between Marc-Antoine II and his sister, Louise. These two ended up with nearly equal, albeit disastrously meager, inheritances of 12,092 and 10,327 livres.[16]

This calamitous reduction and leveling of inheritance, or at least the tendency to divide it more equally, resulted from several factors. To begin, intestate succession did not "advantage" one child to the extent that a father could through testamentary arrangements; it was considerably more egalitarian in its division of resources. Secondly, Lacger fortunes at Castres had declined with the revocation of the Edict of Nantes in the late seventeenth century. There was simply less wealth to distribute among heirs. This particular branch of the family no longer held royal office of any sort. Its only assets were the *métairies* of Clot and la Planesié and a town house. With less to pass on, the differences in shares were far less pronounced. Finally, the persecution of Protestants probably encouraged the Lacger and other Protestant notables to make allowance for a slightly more egalitarian division of the inheritance in order to insure the minimum welfare of all family members in the intensely hostile environment.

Some commentators have suggested that already in the sixteenth century, the lesser Protestant nobility displayed a noticeable antipathy for primogeniture and the preferential legacy (*préciput*), preferring instead a more even apportionment of the patrimony.[17] Certainly as the pressure on the Huguenot community increased in the following centuries, there was an unmistakable tendency among collateral heirs, siblings in particular, to establish equal portions in the succession or to favor persons who earlier might not have had much if any share. Jacques, sieur de Clot, and his sister Jeanne were coheirs "with equal shares and portions" under the terms of their elder brother's will of 1668. Marie left the entirety of her estate to her older married sister, and not her eldest brother, upon her passing in 1726 at the age of eighteen. When Blanche died a childless widow in 1751, she left her property and possessions to Louis, the youngest and least successful of her brothers.[18]

To be sure, a profound sense of family solidarity permeated the manner whereby members of the Lacger family passed resources to their successors. They never doubted that hereditary property (*propres*) ought to remain in the line whence it came.[19] The notion that assets should be passed to consanguineous relatives—usually direct descendants, but failing them collateral blood kin—tended to apply as well to acquired possessions (*acquêts*), wealth that a person had come by over the duration of her or his life. Already in the sixteenth century, Guy de Lacger's sons had meticulously guarded the inheritance of their siblings who died without issue. Antoine II and Jean, for example, successfully garnered the resources left by their three childless brothers: Antoine I, Adrian, and Sébastien. In later years, Lacger men and women without immediate descendants regularly left their possessions to brothers and sisters, nephews, and occasionally cousins.

Unmarried or otherwise childless Lacger uncles customarily favored their nephews, a common practice throughout ancien régime France.[20] Samuel de Lacger, an attorney and resident of Paris, passed away in May 1652, leaving an estate of some 80,000 livres. It included 27,378 livres in *rentes* and 22,312 livres in cash. In addition, Samuel's heirs sold his two offices, *avocat au conseil* and *secrétaire du roi,* for 24,500 livres. Paul Pellisson Fontanier, the Protestant literary figure whose family figured among the judicial elite of Castres, purchased the office of *secrétaire*—yet another manifestation of the close amicable bonds that united members of the Huguenot provincial magistracy. Finally, Samuel's assets included his personal belongings. Although unmarried, he had rented a fairly extensive and well-furnished apartment on the rue de Seine near Saint-Germain-des-Prés. It doubled as his office and had eight rooms, including a personal study as well as an outer office for his legal clerk and secretary. The personal possessions and household goods contained there sold, after inventory, for 5,542 livres.

The division of the estate followed an established pattern. Samuel bequeathed 1,000 livres to the poor of the Reformed Church of Charenton, where the Huguenots of Paris worshiped under the terms of the Edict of Nantes. Such generosity was exceptional. When his cousin Louise de Lacger died at Castres in the early 1670s, she left no more than 150 livres for the poor, and even then her heirs were reluctant to pay the legacy.[21] Samuel made similar yet smaller gifts of several hundred livres to his secretary and servants. Each of his three surviving sisters received a legacy of 3,000 livres. There were also debts to be settled: back wages for servants, medical and legal bills, and funeral expenses. Once these various items had been deducted, the remaining 67,770 livres were evenly divided between Samuel's two heirs: his elder brother, Pierre, and his oldest nephew, Jacques; each received 33,885 livres.[22]

During the eighteenth century, several unmarried or childless men looked after and occasionally enriched their nephews through testamentary legacies and donations. Jean-Jacques, the chevalier de Lacger, left a modest estate, about sixty thousand livres, when he died in 1746. It will be remembered that he had a long military career during which he converted to Catholicism. His wife predeceased him, and they had no children. The provisions of his will called for several preliminary bequests. He made the traditional gifts: a small amount to the poor of the Hôpital Général at Castres, several hundred livres to each of his two servants, and two thousand livres to a Protestant niece who ministered to him in his final years. He then left twenty-five thousand livres, roughly 40 percent of the estate, to Marc-Antoine II, his eldest Protestant nephew, but "imposed upon him perpetual silence" regarding the legacy. The remainder of the estate, roughly half and valued at thirty thousand livres, went to his heir, the Catholic nephew Jean-Jacques-Joseph de Lacger. There was a distinctly Catholic tone to Jean-Jacques's will.[23] He "implored the intercession of the blessed Virgin Mary and all the saints of Paradise" in addition to requesting burial in the parish cemetery of Notre-Dame de la Platé. Nonetheless, he unmistakably, if not quite openly, sought to impart a measure of economic assistance to his Protestant niece and nephew.[24]

A little more than a decade later, the manner whereby the brigadier François de Lacger distributed the wealth that he had acquired through long and favorable years of military service had an even greater impact upon the Protestant members of the family. The total value of his land and other real estate, financial investments, and personal possessions upon his death in January 1758 was 193,475 livres. His testament, composed just a few months earlier in late October 1757, followed the basic Catholic forms, but just barely. François requested burial within the church of Notre-Dame de la Platé, as was the privilege of the wealthy and prominent, yet he avoided most of the other baroque religious practices associated with Counter-Reformation Catholicism. Furthermore, while he made several pious bequests to various charitable institutions, they were half-hearted, if not niggardly, legacies. The Hôpital Saint-Jacques de Villegoudou, one of two poor houses at Castres, got two hundred livres. The destitute residents of the Hôtel-Dieu in his own parish of Notre-Dame de la Platé received half that amount. Perhaps the most striking aspect of François's testamentary charity was his attitude toward the mendicant orders, a special point in the humanist and Protestant critique of medieval papal Christianity since the early sixteenth century. François, a rich and well-known civic figure, did not forget these monks, but they might have wished he had. In what must have come very close to disparagement, he gave Castres's four mendicant houses—Capuchin, Franciscan, Trinitarian, and Dominican—a pittance of ten livres each.

François provided for a number of relatives. He granted a Catholic cousin, Jean-Jacques-Joseph de Lacger, ten thousand livres and a small meadow. A maternal cousin, Julien de Boisset, received an annuity, 5 percent annual interest on a principal of thirty-four thousand livres. There were also several donations *inter vivos* that François had arranged during August and September 1757, just a few months before making his will. From a legal point of view, these donations were advances upon the inheritance, and all were subsequently confirmed in the testament. His sister-in-law—the widow of his brother, Louis—received six thousand livres. He set aside a similar amount for a distant niece, a woman whom he wished to thank and assist for her "many considerable services." This latter gift was the principal for an annuity that was to take effect upon the donor's death. The niece was to receive an annual pension of three hundred livres, based on a return of 5 percent per annum. Finally, François had established another, dramatically larger donation in late September. By its terms, he irrevocably gave the seigneury of Navès and all his other possessions, excepting the gifts noted above, to his eldest Protestant cousin, Marc-Antoine II. He reserved for himself a lifetime annual pension (*pension annuelle et viagère*) of twenty-five hundred livres, but never drew upon it, as he died within four months.[25]

François and Marc-Antoine II were, biologically speaking, fairly distant cousins. Their common ancestor was Antoine II. He was François's

great-grandfather and Marc-Antoine II's great great-grandfather. Nonetheless, Marc-Antoine II was François's closest and oldest male relative.
He was also Protestant or, more accurately, crypto-Protestant. François
was, in fact, worried that his cousin's questionable religious status might
prevent him from taking possession of the seigneury. He did not wish his
heir, the prospective seigneur, to lose this valuable property "on the pretext" that he stood in violation of the royal edicts regarding the practice of
Catholicism. This anxiety was undoubtedly the reason for François's transfer of the estate by donation *inter vivos* rather than by testamentary succession. Once the gift had been made, François immediately sought royal
confirmation of his act, assuring the monarchy that his cousin had "always
professed Catholicism," much as the young man's father had faithfully
practiced Catholicism "after having renounced the errors of Protestantism." Or so the fiction went. The king confirmed the donation accordingly in early December 1757.[26] The fact that François felt the need to go
to such pains suggests that he knew full well his cousin was Catholic only
insofar as the law required, and that the donation of Navès would dramatically reinvigorate the Protestant lineage.

This contribution by François de Lacger marked an immense water-
shed in the financial position of the Protestant Lacger. During the mid-
seventeenth century, the estimated assets of the richest members of the
family hovered around 80,000 livres. Samuel and Pierre, for example, left
estates in this range upon their deaths in 1652 and 1655. In any event,
their modest economic situation was hopelessly inferior in comparison to
the ten thousand or so French families whose wealth distinguished them
as members of important and relatively powerful aristocratic circles.[27]
Thereafter, Lacger resources actually declined. Marc-Antoine I, Pierre's
grandson, was worth less than 40,000 livres at the moment of his demise
in 1720. Yet his son Marc-Antoine II, well fixed as the chief beneficiary of
the testamentary largesse of François, had a financial worth nearly five
times greater, close to 200,000 livres, when he passed away on the eve of
the Revolution. If the property belonging to his wife, herself an heiress, is
taken into account, the couple bequeathed their children an estate valued
at 375,725 livres.[28] The Protestant Lacger were, after 1758, far more
secure in an economic sense, though still far below the 500,000-livres
threshold that marked significant eighteenth-century noble fortunes.[29]

By the late 1700s, the Lacger adopted a common legal practice whereby the father favored his eldest son with a generous and irrevocable endowment at the moment of his marriage. Marc-Antoine II drew up an *acte de partage* when his son François married in 1774. The act, later confirmed in the father's will, apportioned the patrimonial assets among François, his younger brother Jean-Jacques-Joseph, and their sister Marthe. Marc-Antoine II made the customary provisions. He gave his daughter Marthe a *légitime* that was in fact her marriage portion. It was calculated as a percentage of the estate and eventually set at twelve thousand livres. Jean-Jacques-Joseph received more generous treatment. He acquired the nonnoble ancestral lands of Clot and la Planesié. This second son further enhanced his financial security in later years with his wife's inheritance of property worth some eighty thousand livres.

François, the eldest male and heir, received through the instrument of an *inter vivos* donation the major portion, principally the seigneury of Navès and the *métairies* attached to it. Although the text of this partition indicated that the father gave his son "one-half of his possessions," their actual worth was beyond any doubt in excess of two-thirds of the family's real property. Understandably, Marc-Antoine II and his wife retained usufruct of these possessions for their lifetime. They, along with their son François and his bride, resided at the family château of Navès.[30] This division of the family's real property seems to reflect a sincere desire to provide all children, particularly sons, with some basic means for support, especially since Protestants had so few economic opportunities. In similar fashion, when Marie de Barrau, Marc-Antoine II's wife, died in 1781, she was careful to provide for both her sons, even though the older received a greater share. She also established *légitimes* for her two granddaughters, the children and heirs of her daughter Marthe, who was by that time deceased.[31]

The terms of Marc-Antoine II's act of *partage* were fully implemented upon his death in 1785. His testament, written four years earlier, had a slightly more seigneurial ring than those of his ancestors. He, for example, left twelve *setiers* of wheat for distribution among the "poor" tenants on his lands at Navès and Clot. The will also confirmed the *légitime* of his daughter Marthe. Although she had died several years previously, there were the two young girls born of her marriage, and they were entitled to their mother's share. The bulk of the document, however, was given over to the details of the bequest of Navès to François, the older son, and Clot and la Planesié to Jean-Jacques-Joseph, the younger one.[32]

Although this donation detached the *métairies* of Clot and la Planesié from the seigneurial estate of Navès, the tendency to reassemble the dismembered patrimonial property eventually reasserted itself. This time it came through marriage rather than inheritance. In 1832, Auguste de Lacger, grandson of François, rejoined Navès to Clot and la Planesié when he and Marie de Lacger, granddaughter of Jean-Jacques-Joseph and heiress to the latter *métairies,* wed.[33] These lands remained united until Fernand de Lacger, grandson of Auguste and Marie, sold Clot and la Planesié at the end of the century.

Given the limited horizons and relative stagnancy of the economy, inheritances and the dowries that were sometimes tied to them assumed primal importance. The disputes over them were consequently some of the hardest fought of the ancien régime, and the Lacger family provides more than a few examples. Antoine II filed suit against his brothers Jean and Adrian in order to establish his claim as the "universal heir" of their brother Sébastien. Seven years later, following the death of Adrian, Antoine II and Jean engaged Adrian's widow in court battle to insure their proper share in his estate. Earlier, in 1576, Antoine II, acting for his son, had been peripherally involved in a tangled legal squabble among the heirs of Jean de Coras. Coras's daughter had been Antoine II's first wife, and their son had certain claims, through his deceased mother's dowry, on the estate. In the late 1630s Pierre and the collateral relatives of his deceased wife, Roze de Correch, engaged in a protracted series of suits over her dowry and inheritance.[34] Wealth was never easily attained, and those families who possessed it, even in lesser amounts, jealously guarded their resources.

At the same time, inheritance and the family arrangements related to it were far from being purely a business transaction.[35] The economic aspect, though important, was always understood by families such as the Lacger in tight conjunction with considerations of kinship and ideology. A sense of what was best for the family's future governed the whole. The solidarity of the family and the lineage demanded, insofar as possible, the indivisibility of the patrimony. The favoring of the eldest son with shares of one-third or, more commonly, one-half to two-thirds of the family's assets kept much of the estate intact. It acted, though not always successfully, as a counterbalance to prevent fragmentation and morseling. The practice assisted undeniably in the long-term perpetuation of the family. Any suggestion of an equality of inheritance among noble sons was looked upon as foolish, if not dangerous. On the other hand, the tendency toward impartibility of the patrimony came at the expense of younger sons and the female line.

Another element that acted favorably for family survival was the tendency to reassemble family property and goods. The wealth of collateral relatives contributed frequently and significantly to the support of the principal line. This particular kind of familial assistance had additional meaning for the Protestant Lacger. Newly converted Catholics within the family, especially several military officers during the first half of the eighteenth century, made sizable donations to their economically weaker crypto-Protestant nephews and cousins. They thereby assured the survival not merely of the family, but the Protestant line of the family. Taken together, the preferential legacy for the eldest male as well as the system of primogeniture for seigneurial fiefs, the strong antifeminine bias, the reassembly of inheritances, and the support of the Protestant line after 1685 formed the basis for the preservation of the patrimony and, thus, the economic foundations for the continuance of the Lacger.

෮

Educational Structures and
Intellectual Traditions

Education among the nobility in general and the Protestant elite in particular served a number of critical, interrelated functions. Formal instruction at the level of the municipal *collège* and the university law faculty provided vital training for future civic leaders and satisfied the professional needs of aspiring noble officeholders in the royal judicial hierarchy. Schooling also served purposes that went beyond the specific political requirements of the community or occupational prerequisites of the nobility of the robe. By the time of the Renaissance and for several centuries thereafter, aristocratic circles viewed education, whether at home with a tutor or in the classroom of the college, as an important component for the proper formation of the gentleman.[1] It provided the sophistication and manners that supplemented and completed traditional aristocratic virtues such as physical prowess and skill at arms.[2] Coupled to this was the important humanist notion that moral education engendered noble virtue.[3] Finally, the learned tradition had a special place within the French Reformed community.

The Huguenot nobles, as members of a religious minority, recognized the utility and benefit offered by education. Schooling opened vocational opportunities and helped balance the disadvantage of being Protestant in a Catholic realm. Education simultaneously provided the safeguard and protection that came from being informed and knowledgeable. The Reformed tradition, moreover, had been from the outset deeply imbued with an educational and scholarly orientation.[4] The intense focus upon Scripture fostered, among other things, the growth of literacy and an interest in the study of language. In time, this approach became more secular and popular among Protestant families like the Lacger, but the essential emphasis remained. In the half century or so prior to the revocation of the Edict of Nantes, for example, Huguenots throughout France actively engaged in literary and scientific pursuits, contributing to an unmistakable and energetic cultural flowering among the elite of Protestant society.

As previously observed, a number of Lacger sons, especially in the early seventeenth century, attended the Protestant colleges in towns such as Nîmes and Montauban. Pierre and Jacques studied at Nîmes in the 1590s; their younger brother, Samuel, was a student at the college of Montauban during the next decade; and Pierre's eldest son was at Nîmes for a time in the early 1660s. Castres itself had a municipal college by the 1570s. Antoine II, as a member of the municipal elite, had a deciding role in its establishment.[5] And while it appears likely that the Lacger sent their sons there for at least the early portion of their schooling, the boys later transferred to Nîmes and Montauban for completion of their studies. Pierre and Jacques left Castres for Nîmes in the autumn 1590 in order to continue their education. At the time, they were about thirteen and eleven years old, respectively. The pair remained at Nîmes under the tutelage of the famed master Anne Rulman for four years,[6] then left for Toulouse, where Pierre enrolled in the law school. Jacques remained with his older sibling for several years, perhaps attending a college at Toulouse or even the university. He afterward went to the University of Montpellier, again in legal studies. Samuel, after spending a half dozen or so years at the college of Montauban, also went on to take a university degree in law, although it is not clear where.[7]

Several of these Protestant schools, most prominently the one at Nîmes, predated the foundation of a Reformed church and were very much Renaissance in inspiration. They were, in fact, municipal efforts, which the Protestants subsequently embraced and remolded. The Nîmes consulate, for example, once convinced of the Reformation, proceeded to hire only Protestant masters for the college. The local consistory, meanwhile, succeeded in pressing the consulate to add a school of theology. One of the town's pastors, scholarly men such as Pierre Viret, served as the principal theology professor. The national synod of the Reformed Churches of France, for its part, encouraged the local churches to establish grammar schools for the instruction of young boys. Furthermore, each ecclesiastical province ought, in the opinion of the national church, to set up a college for more advanced studies. Beyond these, there were several Protestant academies to train pastors.[8]

Education of this sort was exclusive to males; women seldom received much, if any, formal academic instruction. They did not attend the college or university; instead, their schooling took place privately, usually within the confines of the home. Members of the family or private tutors taught young girls reading and writing in the vernacular. The emphasis was upon sensible and useful skills. Education for girls aimed at the fundamentals and rarely sought to achieve broadly based knowledge. The more intellectual formation associated with training in Latin was by and large disregarded. Lacger daughters and women who married into the family appear to have been able to read and write French, and a few may even have benefited from exceptional training. Jeanne de Coras, who married Antoine II in 1561, appears to have been knowledgeable and well read.[9] Protestant women were generally more literate than their Catholic counterparts. On the other hand, what little formal education these women received seldom went beyond the rudiments. They frequently married at a young age, and their mothers and other women of the household emphasized the practical domestic and managerial skills associated with the art of housewifery. The emphasis was very much upon domesticity. Women were expected to bear and raise children, to be thrifty, and to exercise good sense. Their elders, male and female, instilled in them the perceived feminine virtues of chastity and modesty, patience and gentleness, piety and reverence, submissiveness and obedience. A woman's education was intended to assist in fulfilling her role as virtuous wife and mother.[10]

Boys, in contrast, learned to read and write both Latin and the vernacular tongue at an early age. At about seven, their formal academic training began. As it progressed, they passed through the various forms, typically from the seventh to the first.[11] Students began with the rudiments of grammar, oratory, and rhetoric. They studied Latin closely, declining nouns and conjugating verbs. As their knowledge and sophistication increased, they embarked upon Latin literature, reading a range of standard classical authors, including moralists—here Cicero was the favorite—as well as Caesar's *Commentaries* and poets such as Virgil and Ovid. There was also some attention to historians and philosophers. Language preparation invariably predominated. By the fourth form, occasionally later, students began to learn Greek in addition to Latin. In some cases, Hebrew was available during the final two years.

These Protestant schools also offered religious studies, taught, in this instance, in the vernacular. Instruction went beyond the usual prayers or attendance at religious services. Pupils studied the catechism diligently and read regularly from a French New Testament. The provincial Reformed synod, meeting at Réalmont about the time of the founding of the Castres college in the mid-1570s, saw as one of the goals of these institutions to "faithfully instruct children in the true religion." In all, the course of studies was the standard, classically based Renaissance curriculum. It emphasized rhetorical skills and upheld the ancients as the best standard for literary judgment. Within the Protestant community, there was the important addition of scripturally based religious education in the French language.[12]

Matriculation at the university and the study of law subsequent to the years spent at the local college had a practical objective for the Lacger and families like them. They were part of the robe nobility, a group that sought to secure and perpetuate ennoblement through service as royal officials, predominantly in the judicial but also in the financial bureaucracy. Though these families might eventually abandon their offices, purchase seigneuries, and achieve an integration with the older nobility of the sword, most depended heavily upon judgeships and similar posts during the initial phases of the process. These positions, in turn, demanded a certain amount of training. Several generations of Lacger took law degrees at Toulouse and Montpellier before undertaking careers as lawyers, judges, and royal bureaucrats at Castres or, to a lesser extent, Paris. The matter was doubly important for Protestant robe families, who faced confessional barriers in addition to the usual competition among those seeking to improve their status. Jean de Lacger, eldest son of Antoine II, expressed an honest concern in the early 1590s when he wondered aloud whether his younger brothers would be excluded from the university because of their religion.[13] Shortly thereafter, the Edict of Nantes helped allay some of these fears, and Protestants continued to have access to the educational and vocational training that they desired, at least until the last decades of the seventeenth century. After that, Lacger interests shifted to military commissions and landed seigneuries, neither of which depended directly upon extensive formal schooling. At the same time, the Revocation reduced the ready availability of university education to French Protestants.

A second element of the learned tradition that helps us understand its place among Protestant notables centers on preferences in reading. Individual and family libraries tended to reflect the educational, professional, and religious background of the owners. Altogether, the disposition toward legal, classical, historical, and religious volumes was emphatic.[14] Three surviving Lacger book lists, one clearly a probate inventory, allow a ready, informative appreciation of this leaning.[15] The first listing, from 1588, enumerated the small library of fifteen books which Antoine II had assembled during his fifty or sixty years at Castres. It had an assessed value of only 30 livres, 5 sous. The second library belonged to Antoine II's youngest son, Samuel. The listing, drawn up as part of the settlement of his estate in 1652, was considerably larger at 143 volumes. They sold, after his death, for a total of 169 livres, 8 sous. Having spent the last forty years of his life at Paris, Samuel plainly had greater access to printed books. Unfortunately, the inventory specified no more than twenty-four, a mere 17 percent, of the titles. The third collection was owned by Jacques, sieur de Clot and son of Pierre. Jacques was Antoine II's grandson and Samuel's nephew. The list of nineteen titles that composed his library was compiled sometime before his death in 1681.[16]

These meager collections were no match for the hundreds, occasionally thousands, of volumes that members of the upper aristocracy—the ducal and similarly high placed feudal families—amassed for their libraries, yet they shared some common interests. Works of classical and contemporary literature as well as books on history and theology figured prominently on the shelves of the great and the less-than-great noble houses. The most striking difference, on the other hand, was in the realm of professional tomes. The older sword nobles saw themselves as distinguished military leaders and the proud possessors of important fiefs. They were rarely jurists and accordingly had fewer law books and jurisprudential studies, the very texts upon which parlementary magistrates and other lesser members of the robe nobility depended heavily.[17]

The libraries of Antoine II and his son Samuel corresponded to the reading tastes of Protestant noble officeholders—Huguenot members of the nobility of the robe. Both men were judicial officials, the elder a royal judge at Castres, the younger an *avocat au conseil privé du roi* and later a *secrétaire du roi* at Paris. As a result, they owned a number of standard legal texts, treatises, and commentaries. Antoine II, for example, had a copy of Justinian's *Institutes*.[18] His son, sixty years later, possessed far more legal texts. They included commentaries as well as collections of royal ordinances and parlementary decisions by jurisconsults, such as the celebrated Georges Louët and Pierre Guénois as well as the Protestants Jean de Coras and Samuel d'Escorbiac.[19] He owned an edition of the *Code Henri III*, actually a private compilation put together by the jurist Barnabé Brisson at the request of the Estates of Blois in the late sixteenth century.[20] There were other handy reference manuals, such as the obscure but undoubtedly useful book entitled *Les successions testamentaires*. Samuel was, after all, a Parisian attorney with a successful and demanding practice; these were working volumes.

All three libraries had a strong concentration of classical texts. Here were works first encountered while a schoolboy and then reread over a lifetime. The ancients, both Latin and Greek, and their Renaissance commentators were extremely popular during the sixteenth and seventeenth centuries.[21] Antoine II owned copies of the Augustan poet Grattius "Faliscus" and the naturalist Pliny the Elder, editions of Cicero's letters and the moral maxims of Epicurus, as well as a collection of Catullus, Tibullus, and Propertius. Several of these editions contained commentaries by Renaissance humanists such as Joseph Justus Scaliger and Marc-Antoine de Muret.[22] Along similar lines, Antoine II's library included the published correspondence of the sixteenth-century stoic Justus Lipsius.[23] There were also a Greek-Latin edition of Homer and a copy of Aldo Manuzio's widely circulated grammar.[24]

Samuel was equally interested in language and classical literature. His library contained Ambrosius Calepinus's standard polyglot dictionary and a translation of Plato's Timaeus by the Greek scholar Louis Le Roy,[25] in addition to the cherished works of the poet Horace, the celebrated tragedian Seneca, and the classical historians Herodotus and Dio Cassius. A Greek-Latin copy of Dio Cassius's Roman history found its way onto the library shelves of Jacques, too. He also owned a Greek-Latin edition of Demosthenes' Orations and a Latin edition of Plutarch's Lives.

This appreciation for the classics and classical histories was part of an immense general curiosity about history, especially noticeable in the seventeenth century, when, for example, the Paris printers published a great many historical studies.[26] Samuel's library contained several well-known histories of France: the Italian Davila's ultramontane narrative of the Wars of Religion, Etienne Pasquier's Gallican account of the kingdom, and the royal historiographer Du Hallain's very popular history of the French monarchs.[27] Samuel had also purchased a number of other historical works for which the inventory mentioned no author. He had yet another history of France; perhaps it was the widely read one by Scipion Dupleix. There was a genealogical history of the great houses of Auvergne, a region that was often broadly defined to encompass the Lacger's native Castrais. Finally, Samuel owned a history of England, most likely by André Duchesne, another popular and prolific historical writer.

Samuel's nephew Jacques shared this taste for histories. Like his uncle, he had a copy of the genealogical history of Auvergne, though Jacques had clearly not inherited it from his uncle. Moreover, there were multivolume accounts of the Holy Roman Empire and the Crusades by Louis Maimbourg,[28] a seven-volume work by Gilbert Saulnier, sieur du Verdier,[29] and a two-volume history of the Moorish conquest of Spain. Along more religious lines, Jacques's library had a four-volume French translation of Flavius Josephus's history of the Jews[30] and one or another edition of Johann Sleidan's Protestant history of the early German Reformation during the reign of Emperor Charles V. Altogether, this propensity for legal, classical, and historical texts was typical of the world of lesser nobles, royal bureaucrats, and men of law.[31]

Religious books, by far the most popular genre of the age, were not missing from the libraries of the three Lacger men. Counter-Reformation French Catholicism, for instance, took full advantage of printing to make available a wide range of scriptural texts and commentaries, ecclesiastical histories, and devotional tracts.[32] Protestants, who had pioneered the publication of religious works, were no less anxious to print and distribute their own materials. The Lacger libraries contained the standard works of Scripture. Antoine II owned a large Bible in quarto and counted it as the most expensive book in his library. He also possessed two New Testaments. Samuel had the familiar Bible and a folio Latin edition of John Calvin's *Institutes of the Christian Religion*. Jacques, too, had copies of some of Calvin's writings: his commentary on the Pentateuch and his lessons on the prophet Daniel.[33] Somewhat more unusual were Jacques's several volumes from the works of Saint John Chrysostom, patriarch of Constantinople and church father.

The trio naturally had an interest in contemporary French Protestant authors. Antoine II's library included Philippe du Plessis Mornay's *Traité de la verité de la religion chrestienne;* his son Samuel's, a copy of Michel Le Faucheur's *Traitté de la Cène du Seigneur.*[34] The first book appeared initially in 1581 and, as the title suggests, made a reasoned argument for Christianity. Mornay, assuming the existence of a natural religion, proceeded deductively to establish such doctrines as the creation of the universe and the immortality of the soul. It was among the better-known tracts written by this most eloquent of sixteenth-century Huguenot political propagandists and religious apologists. Even more famous was the *Vindiciae contra tyrannos,* a leading treatise in the history of Huguenot resistance theory and commonly attributed to Mornay.[35] Frequently labeled the "pope of the Huguenots," he was a friend of Admiral Coligny and an advisor to Henry IV, a trenchant writer, and a principal in the founding the famous Protestant academy at Saumur. Mornay's celebrated dispute over the Eucharist with Jacques Davy du Perron, bishop of Evreux, at the conference of Fontainebleau in 1600 even served as the origin for Le Faucheur's treatise. Du Perron is generally thought to have been the victor at the conference, and Le Faucheur offered a subsequent comprehensive and extremely detailed response to the bishop's arguments.

Jacques also possessed several volumes in this controversialist tradition. There was, for example, a copy of Edme Aubertine's *L'Eucharistie de l'ancienne église,*[36] a book that flowed from the debate between Le Faucheur and Du Perron. Aubertine, a Reformed pastor, attempted to establish, over and against Du Perron, Robert Bellarmine, and other Catholic authors, the essential harmony of the Reformed doctrine of the Eucharist with that proposed by Augustine. Jacques's library contained one more title along these same lines. It was a two-volume work published in the 1660s by Jean Daillé, yet another Protestant pastor and savant.[37] Daillé, like so many before him, was responding to Catholic challenges regarding both religious doctrine and pious practices.

The most conspicuous absence in these several libraries was any mention of scientific studies or treatises. Could it be that the popularity of science, particularity in the sixteenth and early seventeenth centuries, had not yet made its full impact upon Huguenot robe families like the Lacger, preoccupied as they were with professional legal interests and political-religious concerns? Might their classical humanist training and subsequent instruction in the law have also contributed to a relative indifference toward scientific discoveries? Certainly other Protestants of the bourgeoisie and petty provincial nobility demonstrated an interest in the developments surrounding science, and the cultural tastes of the Lacger possessed remarkable breadth in other ways.

By the mid-seventeenth century, these literary and intellectual interests moved considerably beyond the special concerns engendered by professional, educational, and religious background. The Reformed community of Castres became a center for literary activities, especially poetry. The literary salons of Paris welcomed several poets and writers from the Protestant families of the Castrais. The most distinguished were Samuel d'Isarn and Paul Pellisson Fontanier. At Castres itself an academy devoted to literary, moral, and scientific pursuits flourished. The poet and jurist Jacques de Lacger, cousin to the Jacques whose library we have examined, participated energetically in both endeavors. He was, for a time, a regular in the *cercle précieux* of the comtesse de La Suze at Paris. Later, after settling at Castres, he routinely contributed to the academy there.

This Jacques de Lacger was in many ways the *enfant terrible*. The eldest child of the *secrétaire* Jacques de Lacger and Marguerite de Nets, he could be rash and undisciplined, indolent and self-serving. He was born at Paris and raised there principally by his mother; the father was dead before

Jacques's eighth birthday. His paternal uncle, Samuel, also lived at Paris, and he, along with a second uncle, the judge Pierre at Castres, offered her help and counsel during the long years devoted to raising and educating Jacques and the three other surviving children. The youth received, much as his father, uncles, grandfather, and great-grandfather before him, training in the law. His schooling complete, Jacques departed Paris for the family seat at Castres, where his mother and uncles hoped he would find a successful legal practice, pleading before the *chambre de l'Edit*. Yet he proved indifferent to the barrister's life and preferred the whirl of social, literary, and musical gatherings. His mother felt that he was simply squandering time and money on parties and violin lessons. After a few years, she insisted that he return to Paris where, presumably, she could keep a closer eye on him. Whatever her intentions, the effort was soon frustrated. Jacques returned to Paris in 1646, but rather than devote his energies to the law or some other sensible enterprise, he joined a group of young poets, many of them Protestant and several from the Midi.[38]

The *précieuse* poetess Henriette de Coligny, comtesse de La Suze, and her literary salon became the young man's passion. The eldest daughter of the maréchal de Châtillon, she descended from a prominent Huguenot family. Her first husband, whom she married in 1643 at the age of twenty-four, was the Scot Thomas Hamilton, earl of Haddington. When he died a year afterward, she returned from Scotland and soon married Gaspard de Champagne, comte de La Suze. One malicious observer described the new husband as "one-eyed, drunken and indebted"—that is to say, physically, morally, and financially disreputable. The marriage, in any event, quickly faltered. She displayed absolutely no affection for her husband and turned entirely to poetry, in particular the delicate and often sentimental verses associated with the *précieuses*. The comtesse wrote a number of elegies and, with Paul Pellisson Fontanier and several others, authored a *Recueil de pièces galantes*.[39] She is probably better remembered for the salon that she began about the time Jacques de Lacger returned to Paris in 1646. Frequented by Saint-Amant, Boisrobert, Lignières, and the abbé Cotin, it was an annex to the more famous salon at the Hôtel de Rambouillet and, as such, formed part of the *cercle de la préciosité*.[40]

Cast by the scandalmonger Gédéon Tallemant des Réaux in his anecdotal *Historiettes* as a "rascal" who was "fat and round, completely lacking in manners,"[41] Jacques de Lacger was nonetheless a favorite of La Suze. For his part, he became completely enamored, and dedicated to her the lau-datory *Vers pour Iris,* a series of sixty well-constructed, if undistinguished, sonnets, madrigals, stanzas, and elegies. In these gallant poems, Lacger openly proclaimed his admiration. Sonnets began with "Allez, jeune beauté, merveille de nostre age," madrigals confessed that "Iris n'a rien d'une mortelle," while elegies declared that "Je ne sçaurois souffrir de vous voir si contente."[42]

Whatever the measure of his poetic spirit, discretion and caution were not qualities that governed Lacger's personal life. He bragged of his rela-tionship with the comtesse de La Suze, shamelessly embellishing the matter and, naturally enough, causing her embarrassment.[43] A far more serious incident occurred in 1650–51 when he became entangled in a senseless quarrel with Henri, marquis de Sévigné. Lacger by late 1650 had fixed his amorous attentions on Ninon de Lenclos, whom he met through his friend Pierre de Rambouillet, oldest son of the rich Prot-estant financier Nicolas de Rambouillet. Ninon was, at the time, the younger Rambouillet's lover, yet had only just ended an affair with Henri de Sévigné. When she rebuffed Lacger, he lashed out in confused and mis-directed, albeit fatal fashion. Perhaps he put the blame for his amorous failure with Ninon on de Sévigné. In any event, he invented and spread a malicious tale concerning Henri de Sévigné's current lover, Madame de Gondran. The elaborate fabrication cast de Gondran as little more than a harlot, and de Sévigné felt obliged to defend her. He publicly announced his intention to avenge the insult to Madame de Gondran and administer the insolent Lacger a sound caning. Lacger, answering in kind, challenged de Sévigné to a duel. Resort to arms was the classic fashion whereby knights, since Carolingian days, had settled a point of honor. Under the circumstances, the duel must have held special appeal for a romantically inclined and socially insecure provincial such as Jacques de Lacger. The two men met on 3 February 1651 near the convent of Picpus in northeast Paris. De Sévigné was mortally wounded when Lacger's sword opened a deep diagonal cut across his body. The bleeding could not be stanched, and he died the following day. Several months later, Lacger abandoned Paris in apparent disgrace over his behavior.[44]

In mid-August 1651, Samuel de Lacger reported to his brother Pierre at Castres that their nephew had departed the capital, going first to Calais and then by sea to Holland and, ultimately, to Sweden. He arrived at Stockholm in early autumn. Christina, the young Swedish queen, was a lavish patron of the arts and had a particular interest in French culture.[45] A number of French intellectuals, in disfavor after the Fronde, established residence at her court around 1649. She also maintained an active correspondence with literary figures throughout France, including the essayist and stylist Jean Guez de Balzac, the dramatist Boisrobert, the Huguenot Valentin Conrart (who was perpetual secretary of the Académie française), and the comtesse de La Suze.

Whether through the good offices of the abbé Bourdelot, a French writer and physician who was at the time personally attending the queen, or by virtue of letters of recommendation that he may have carried from one or another member of the Parisian salons, Christina offered Lacger a position as royal secretary. Once installed as *conseiller et secrétaire des commandements de la reine de Suède,* he had charge of her Latin letters and a portion of the correspondence with the French literary world. He was in communication with literary personages such as Balzac, Conrart, and Chapelain. The queen employed Lacger's poetic talents, too. He composed a long ode in her honor and penned several shorter verses for specific occasions. Among the latter was a piece on "the flight of Armide before Renaud," the theme of a royal tapestry. Armide was the dangerous enchantress and Renaud the chivalrous crusader introduced by Torquato Tasso, an Italian Renaissance poet, in his *Jerusalem Delivered (Gerusalemme liberata).* Artistic and literary productions of seventeenth-century France popularized the subject;[46] the fashion evidently extended to Sweden. Lacger also wrote a farcical *"combat de barrière"* for the celebration of the queen's birthday; and he played in a number of light dramatic sketches performed at the Swedish royal court. Then in May 1652, Christina sent him to Italy on a book-buying expedition. By August he was in Venice. Yet Jacques de Lacger never returned to Sweden.[47]

Samuel de Lacger died at Paris in May 1652 and named his nephew as coheir. The legacy—not quite thirty-five thousand livres—made it possible for Jacques to return to France and buy a post in the royal judiciary. Coincidentally, about a month after Samuel's death, a cousin, Hercule de Lacger, passed away. Hercule had been a judge on the *chambre de l'Edit.* He was childless, and the heirs, his mother and three sisters, were unable to succeed to the judicial office. They were therefore anxious to sell it. Pierre, Jacques's uncle at Castres, immediately initiated negotiations to acquire the position for his vagabond and profligate nephew. By mid-September the bargain was struck. Jacques's inheritance from his uncle Samuel, a substantial loan from his uncle Pierre, and funds from his mother and deceased father enabled Jacques to meet the purchase price of eighty thousand livres. He returned to France in late 1652 or very early 1653. On 6 January, the royal chancellery approved his appointment to the chamber at Castres, and the tribunal seated him by early March.[48]

The move to Castres marked a turning point for Jacques, who was by this time close to forty. The following year he married the comparatively young Magdelaine de Falguerolles—she was only fifteen when they wed. Over the next decade and a half, he and his wife, along with their six children, carried on the rather uneventful existence of a provincial *parlementaire* family.[49] Whatever calm may have settled over Jacques's life dissolved in 1670, however, when the monarchy transferred the *chambre de l'Edit* to Castelnaudary. The Protestant judges had little choice but to pack their belonging and follow to this newly selected Catholic seat. They moved again nine years later when Louis XIV abolished the chamber altogether. This time the magistrates were integrated into the Parlement of Toulouse. The final act occurred in 1685 with the Revocation. Jacques, like so many other Reformed judges, converted to Catholicism, at least in part, that he might save his office. Ironically, when he died three years later, this convert of convenience was buried in the Cathedral of St-Etienne, unquestionably one of the sacred grounds of conservative Catholicism at Toulouse.

The fifteen or more years which Jacques de Lacger spent in relative quiet at Castres after 1653 by no means marked the end of his literary and intellectual career. Rather, soon after his arrival he joined the Academy of Castres and over time established himself as one of its leading members. The Academy had been founded in November 1648 during roughly the same period that several others were created at such diverse provincial centers as Toulouse, Soissons, Caen, Nîmes, and Arles. It endured twenty-two years, until the *chambre de l'Edit* departed Castres for Castelnaudary; the final session took place in August 1670. The enterprise, as such, approximated a kind of golden cultural and intellectual age for literary and scholarly activity among the Huguenots. The Academy's demise marked, at the very least, the beginning of the end for the open and thriving Protestant community at Castres and other towns throughout the Midi.

The notion of an academy for Castres originated with the Protestant magistrates and lawyers of the *chambre*. During the enterprise's twenty-two years, a dozen judges and nineteen attorneys belonged. They were the mainstay of the creation, and the departure of the *chambre* in 1670 signaled the Academy's finish. There were, as might be expected, other participants. They included at least one physician, the town's Reformed pastors—seven over the life of the Academy—and nine members of the local gentry and bourgeoisie. The Academy made a sustained effort to welcome Catholics as well. This aspect of the undertaking reflected in large measure the influence of the Protestant judges of the *chambre de l'Edit,* men who were themselves engaged in a bipartisan attempt to administer justice. Some few Catholics responded positively to the invitation. Four became permanent members; several others were occasional guests. Among the latter were jurists of the *chambre,* various priests, and even a Jesuit father and Franciscan friar. Toward the end, the Academy's meetings took place in the home of the sieur de Donneville, the Catholic *président* of the *chambre de l'Edit.* Moreover, the Protestant members, though the overwhelming majority, were hardly fanatics on the religious question. Several of them—notably Isarn, Pellisson Fontanier, Lacger, and Ranchin—adopted Catholicism near the end of their lives. In all, the Academy of Castres was part of the wider attempt, however belated and ill-fated, to bridge the gap between Protestant and Catholic. The membership sought, within the context of the sessions, a forum for toleration and a ground of common culture, where followers of both faiths could conduct an ameliorating dialogue.[50]

The members of the Academy were originally twenty "persons of erudition." Their numbers progressively rose to forty and included several respected writers and poets. Those already belonging to the Academy proposed candidates for membership, who were then subject to election by the secret ballot of the members. Jacques de Lacger, for instance, was elected in January 1553 to replace a recently deceased participant. The group was organized in egalitarian fashion by seventeenth-century standards. There was no president; rather, a moderator presided over the weekly meetings, initially Thursday and later Tuesday at noon. Members served as moderator according to an ordered alphabetic rotation. A permanent secretary, for many years Jacques d'Espérandieu, the older of the two poetically inclined brothers, kept an abbreviated record of the sessions, noting the name of the moderator, the other members present, and the subject of their discussion. Finally, two treasurers regularly accounted for each member's annual dues of five livres. The money went mostly for renting, lighting, heating, and cleaning their meeting place. The sessions originally took place at the *hôtel* of the Protestant *parlementaire* Jacques de Ranchin. The tragic poisoning of Ranchin's mother by a servant in December 1650 obliged the group to rent meeting quarters elsewhere, and it continued to do so for another seventeen years. Only toward the end of its existence did the Academy return to Ranchin's residence. Yet once again, misfortune struck when, in June 1669, fire destroyed much of the house. Thus the Academy met during its final months at the home of the Catholic judge de Donneville.[51]

Most of the "academicians" were from Protestant families associated in one way or another with the *chambre de l'Edit*. Jacques and Jean d'Espérandieu were attorneys, empowered to practice before the tribunal, in addition to being classicists and poets of local repute. The Pellisson brothers were sons of a *parlementaire* and themselves trained in the law. Jacques de Ranchin and Jacques de Lacger were associate judges on the chamber; Pierre de Rozel, its royal attorney-general; Benoît d'Isarn, Samuel's brother, the chief clerk of the court.[52] The *chambre de l'Edit* of Castres offered the highest positions to which Huguenot officeholders of the Midi could aspire, and around it they fashioned an extensive cultural edifice. These persons maintained close professional and social relationships: they worked together, they worshiped together, their families intermarried, and they found mutual support and entertainment in promoting their own erudition and literary talent.

Jacques de Ranchin, whose inclinations were at once legal and literary, offers a fine example of the membership of the Academy of Castres. Born around 1616 and trained in the law, Jacques was the third generation of Ranchin to sit on the *chambre de l'Edit* when, in 1643, he succeeded to the office of associate magistrate held by his father and his father's uncle before him. The family, originally from Uzès, subsequently established itself at Montpellier, where its members were prominent jurists at the university and in the *chambre des comptes.* The Ranchin then went on to Castres and service with the Protestant court there. Jacques de Ranchin joined the Academy of Castres at the moment of its founding. Indeed, his home was the first site of its meetings.

He seemed to have thoroughly enjoyed the sort of cultural entertainment that the Academy represented. Occasionally, he even stepped beyond the bounds of the puritanical moral code laid down by the French Reformed Churches. In 1650, for example, the Protestant consistory at Castres chastised him for attending the theater. The transgression, for which he offered profuse repentance, was in direct contravention of the accepted standards of Protestant behavior.[53]

This jurist and literary devotee spent time at Paris in 1654 and there frequented the salon of Madeleine de Scudéry. A novelist originally from Provence, she wrote several long romances. Her house served as the gathering place, for nearly ten years beginning in 1653, of a literary society known as the *samedis* after its habit of meeting each Saturday. The group was less aristocratic than some other salons and more open to lesser nobles and provincial Protestants such as Ranchin. He wrote some sonnets and epigrams as well as paraphrases of various psalms, canticles, and hymns. His best-known work was probably the *Stances à Philis.* Generally considered a minor figure among the *poètes galants,* he also composed and read to the Academy a poem entitled "The Meadow of Love" (*Le pré de l'amour*). As with so many within this circle of Protestant judges and poets, Jacques de Ranchin converted to Catholicism as pressure mounted toward the end of the century. The conversion—which occurred in 1680, about a dozen years before his death—was something of a showpiece and even merited announcement in the prominent Parisian weekly, the *Mercure Galant.*[54]

Samuel d'Isarn, thought by Tallemant des Réaux to have been a handsome youth capable of highly entertaining verses, was another, more talented poet whose family roots were also among the Protestant legal professionals of Castres. His brother, also a member of the Academy, was clerk of the *chambre de l'Edit;* a niece married into the Lacger house. Samuel d'Isarn himself left Castres for Paris in the mid-1650s. There he continued his poetic efforts in the company of the *précieuses* and the salon of Mademoiselle de Scudéry. Isarn eventually became a protégé of

Jean-Baptiste Colbert, writing a *Life of Colbert* and serving as governor for the education of the great minister's son. Again, like so many in this circle, toward the end of his life, in the mid-1660s, he turned to Catholicism.[55]

Paul Pellisson Fontanier was undeniably the most famous member of the Academy of Castres. He and an older brother, Georges, were friends of Jacques de Ranchin, with whom they shared a similarity of age and background. Born in 1624, he was, like Ranchin, the son of a Protestant magistrate on the *chambre de l'Edit*. Although too young at the time of his father's death in 1631 to succeed him as judge, Paul Pellisson Fontanier eventually studied law at Toulouse. Afterward, he went to Paris but returned to Castres by 1648 and was one of the leading figures in the establishment of the Academy. For two years, he attended nearly all its gatherings, often reading his own poetry or other works, such as his translation of Homer's *Odyssey*. Then, he once again departed for Paris, this time definitively. There he secured a position as *secrétaire du roi*, purchasing it from the Lacger family in 1652. Jacques de Lacger had first acquired this office in the early seventeenth century. Following Jacques's death, it passed to a younger brother, Samuel; and when Samuel died, the family sold it to Pellisson Fontanier for twenty thousand livres.[56]

The following year, Pellisson Fontanier met Madeleine de Scudéry. They became fast friends, and he was soon dubbed the Apollo of the *samedis*.[57] By 1657, Pellisson Fontanier had become the principal secretary to Nicolas Fouquet, Louis XIV's able but overly ambitious *surintendant des finances* who was disgraced in the 1660s. He published an eloquent and spirited defense of his patron,[58] but in the end was himself tainted by the affair and spent several years in the Bastille. Louis XIV afterward rehabilitated Pellisson Fontanier, and when he abjured Protestantism in 1670 amid the religious turmoil of the period, the king rewarded him handsomely with several remunerative royal posts.[59] In return, Pellisson Fontanier aided the royal cause for some two decades preceding his death in 1693 by penning anti-Protestant tracts and persuading other Huguenots, some of them influential persons like his friend Jacques de Ranchin,[60] to convert. For a time, he even had administrative charge over a "conversion fund" from which he could reward these converts, notable or otherwise, with royal pensions large and small.[61]

As a literary figure, Pellisson Fontanier is better known for his prose than his poetry. His *Histoire de l'Académie française* first appeared in 1653. It is perhaps the most acclaimed of his works and won him a place on the Academy itself. Besides this early history of the *Académie française,* Pellisson Fontanier's letters and a critical preface to a collection of Jean-François Sarasin's poetry are thought to be his best literary accomplishments. Of course, he and the comtesse de La Suze published their popular collection of verses, the *Recueil des pièces galantes* of 1664. And as previously noted, toward the end of his life he acted as an advocate and propagandist for Versailles, writing and publishing several pious apologies in which he urged Protestants to follow the example of his religious conversion.[62]

Georges Pellisson, while never possessed of the talent and energy of his younger brother, may have been the most assiduous member of the Castres Academy. Of the 207 sessions that took place between 1650 and 1654, he failed to attend only seventeen. He, too, wrote both poetry and prose; and at various times, he presented his sonnets, burlesque verses, various translations, and scientific treatises to the other members of the Academy. Georges Pellisson made frequent visits to Paris, where his brother introduced him to salon society and, in particular, the literary coterie of Mademoiselle de Scudéry. Finally, by late 1655 or early 1656, he, too, moved permanently to Paris, thereafter returning only briefly and occasionally to his native Castres.[63]

Pierre Borel was the best-known participant of scientific inclination. Upon completion of medical studies at Montpellier, he returned to his native Castres and there practiced medicine from 1641 until 1653. Then he spent several years in Paris as *conseiller et médecin ordinaire du roi.* He returned to Castres in 1657 and assumed teaching duties in the college. Borel wrote a diverse number of works on medicine and natural history, chemistry and physics, language and poetry, philosophy and history. He also published the first biography of René Descartes, the *Vitae Renati Cartesii* of 1656. These wide-ranging interests were surely as exemplary of the Academy's endeavors as the polished verses and published prose of Samuel d'Isarn or Paul Pellisson Fontanier.[64]

Most members of the Castres Academy did not, understandably enough, frequent the highest literary circles, nor were they especially well known. They were content to read and discuss one another's more amateurish literary efforts at their weekly meetings or engage in what they took to be salutary debates over lively and topical issues. Unfortunately, the secretary's abbreviated accounts give no more than the titles of the discussions and debates. The subject matter fell into several related categories: political, moral, and religious questions; historical issues; scientific matters; and, above all, poetry and literature, classical as well as contemporary, French and foreign.

It comes as little surprise that the members discussed such political issues as the proper behavior of the prince or his power with respect to the church. Royal authority was one of the most hotly debated topics of the age, whether by absolutist theoreticians in the employ of Cardinal Richelieu or Huguenot *parlementaires* and attorneys at Castres. An especially favored author was the Academy's own Christophe Balthazar, a convert from Catholicism who spent much of his adult life at Castres. In several different treatises, he defended the claims of the French crown against the Spanish in Burgundy, Flanders, Luxembourg, and Italy.[65] Following his election to the Academy in early 1658, Balthazar and the scientifically inclined Pierre Borel tended to dominate its proceedings.

The moral questions were a mixed lot. Some had a prophetic ring, as when the pastor Gaches, moderating in a 1651 session, asked "Whether persons banished from their country by their prince could legitimately take up arms against him?" A few years later, not long after the 1654 abdication of his former patron the queen of Sweden, Jacques de Lacger posed the question "Whether a sovereign deserves glory or blame in abandoning his crown?" Other subjects of moral debate were altogether more predictable and pedestrian: "If one ought to praise one's friends in their presence?" "Whether virtue alone will make people happy?" "Which is better, to love or be loved?"

Occasionally the savant spirit ran to excess, as when, in March 1649, the Academy treated the proposition "Whether persons who administer love philtres ought to be punished as poisoners?" About ten years later, Lacger was moderator for a session in which he introduced a similarly sophistic debate: "Who are to be criticized more, the Spanish for never changing the style of their dress, or the French for changing it too often?" More to the point in seventeenth-century France was a topic that he proposed several months afterward: "Whether there is greater glory for a prince in encouraging the development of his state through peace or extending its frontiers through war?" Members of the bar could hardly resist treating juridical matters. The Academy periodically posed such queries as "Whether it is proper that punishment be left to the will of the judge?" Or the perpetual dilemma of "Whether a judge must declare a mistrial over a simple technicality?" And a society with so fundamental a respect for family and parents inevitably asked the question "What is the true gravity of parricide and what ought its punishment to be?"[66]

The Academy debated religious issues far less frequently than moral questions. Moreover, the specific subjects and the nature of their treatment were very much in keeping with the moderate religious position of many of its members—prominent, often noble men of the law who were tied to the royal judiciary. They had little fondness for religious quarrels and avoided heated controversies over Holy Writ or Christian doctrine, preferring instead to busy themselves with translations of the Epistles or paraphrases of the Psalms. Jacques de Lacger, in a wholly representative exercise, wrote a paraphrase of Psalm 130, the well-known *De profundis.*[67] Members probed the meaning of Easter, composed sonnets directed against atheists, and even pondered the miraculous. They devoted an entire session to the eclipse that was said to have occurred at the moment of Jesus' death and whether it was "universal and miraculous or particular and natural."

Among other favorite topics were various historical issues. Members exchanged views on the historical accuracy of the deeds and actions attributed to Joan of Arc and investigated the origins of hereditary fiefs, particularly the duchies and counties of the medieval French kingdom. The physician Pierre Borel even wrote a long antiquarian treatise on the ancient Gauls.[68]

The scientific enquiries undertaken by the Academy covered a broad range of natural phenomena. Its adherents examined the process of rain, the nature of dew, and the causes of thunder and lightning. They discussed geological questions focusing on mineral formations, both precious and base. The ebb and flow of the tide as well as the salinity of the sea made their way onto the agenda. The Academy even engaged in the occasional scientific test, as when in late 1649 it purchased some mercury in order to perform the "experiment of the void," thereby re-creating Pascal's celebrated experiment of the previous year. Both tests were based on the breakthrough of Evangelista Torricelli, the Italian physicist who, in creating a sustained vacuum, had discovered the principle of the barometer. The Academy appeared to have been keenly aware of Torricelli's work.

One of its members, Pierre Saporta, translated his short tract on hydraulics into French, publishing it together with two other pieces on the same subject, one a translation of a work by Benedotto Castelli, the other an essay by Saporta himself.[69]

Besides these popular yet scholarly exercises, the Academy carried on a lively series of literary readings and accompanying critiques. Nearly all members took a hand at composing poems, in both Latin and French. This sort of literary creation—writing poems, sonnets, epigrams, stanzas, elegies, and the like—was extremely fashionable among the elite, particularly the judicial elite, of the seventeenth century. It spoke to creative talent, good breeding, intellectual spirit, and eloquent sensibilities. Some among them—Pellisson Fontanier, Isarn, Lacger, and Ranchin—were clever, and more. Lacger, at various times, offered the poems that he had written while a young man at Paris and later in the employ of the Swedish queen.

Sometimes the members discussed the ancients, authors whom they had all pored over and memorized as schoolchildren. Again, Lacger read scene 2, act 4 of Terence's *Eunuchus* in a 1655 session and then opened discussion on the meaning of the final words, *"Certe extrema linea amare haud nihil est."* Many of the participants also prepared and read French translations of the ancient Greeks and Romans as well as contemporary Italian and Spanish authors, such as Giovanni Battista Manzini and Lorenço Gratian. Paul Pellisson Fontanier translated Homer's *Odyssey;* his older brother, Cicero's well-known speech *Pro Murena.* Others rendered selections from Livy, Seneca, and Ovid into French, and expounded on grammatical challenges and obscure passages in Thucydides, Xenophon, and Cicero. Readings from contemporary authors, Jean Chapelain's *La Pucelle* or Corneille's *Oedipe* and *La Toison d'or,* had a place in the weekly meetings, too. Members relished the work of their own Pellisson Fontanier, particularly his *Histoire de l'Académie française.* They kept abreast of recent developments throughout France and Europe in the weekly *Journal des Savants,* an early literary and scientific periodical founded in 1665 by an erudite Parisian jurist.[70]

The lively intellectual discourse sponsored by the Academy suggests in many ways the condition of French Protestants by mid-seventeenth century. Deprived of traditional political and military power after the defeat of Rohan and the Peace of Alès in 1629, they concentrated their considerable energies on intellectual endeavors. They set about once more to prove their worth and make their contribution. The Huguenots drew upon the solid scholarly foundation that was intimately bound to the Reformation. The Reformed Churches of France had long encouraged the establishment of schools and the spread of literacy. Lacger sons attended the Protestant colleges. In later life, Bibles and other books intimately connected to Huguenot religious interests were readily available on their library shelves. The Protestant nobility of the robe, moreover, had sound professional reasons to support these activities. They depended upon the legal tomes associated with their judicial functions. Somewhat more fundamentally, education was critical to advancement in the royal bureaucracy. Furthermore, the display of rhetorical refinement and literary appreciation was thought essential for the complete gentleman. Huguenot notables, to be sure, generally shared the educational background and literary tastes of the social elite throughout France. They, too, studied the classics and devoured popular histories.[71] Finally, the achievements of the poetic salons of Paris or the literary and scientific discussions within the Academy of Castres testified to the strength and quality of Protestant values and character. These poets and jurists strove for, even if they did not always achieve, sensitive, elegant expression. They debated contemporary moral issues and apprised one another of the latest advances in human knowledge. Such enterprises, in their own special way, compensated for the loss of power and influence suffered in the political, military, and even economic spheres.

SEVEN

~

Family Allegiances and
Kinship Ties

Family as structure, practice, and ideology is fundamental to any study
of elites. Taken in the broad sense of persons connected by blood and
marriage, it was the essential framework for possession and disposition of
power as well as mediation and reconciliation of disputes. In an earlier
world, one where the bureaucratic state intruded far less, the family was
an invaluable instrument for social control. It was, in addition, a vital
institution for the allocation of rights and privileges. Indeed, the family's
access to and control of power within society contributed to its very
shape. Finally, the family stood as a powerful symbol commanding authority in firm and deliberate fashion. Nobles, above all, had a keen appreciation of family and lineage—their ancestors and descendants, cognates
and affines, living, dead, and yet unborn. Here was the solidifying foundation for the honor, privilege, and power of the house.[1]

The structure of the early modern European family was patriarchal and
authoritarian, emphasizing stability and continuity.[2] It was, in this respect,

deeply rooted in the existing social structure, economic conditions, legal order, and political organization.[3] The husband and father "naturally" exercised extensive, unified hierarchical control over his wife and their offspring as well as other members of the household—blood relations, in-laws, and servants. In this divinely ordained order, the head of the family was expected to govern all with a stern but fair and benevolent hand. The elements of deference, respect, obligation, and obedience were meant to permeate the relationship.

A husband, as previously noted, had considerable power over his wife, notably in the public sphere. He stood close watch over her and was, in many ways, responsible for her actions. Husbands deemed incapable of controlling their wives were publicly mocked and ridiculed. A man had the "right," and was often expected, to discipline physically a disobedient or unfaithful spouse. For her part, a married woman understood that she might be beaten, despite limited legal and moral restrictions on this sort of abusive treatment.[4] In financial affairs, a husband legally enjoyed complete management of the patrimonial property. He also conducted the routine administration of goods associated with the dowry, even though he could not dispose of them, or any portion therein, without his wife's agreement. As a practical matter, a wife frequently invested him with the stewardship of her paraphernal property, as well. Altogether, the husband administered without restraint the bulk of the family's economic assets, the wife intervening only in certain specified circumstances. Other practices were no less restrictive of wives. According to the customary law of Toulouse, for instance, a woman could enter into a contract in her own right. Nonetheless, the requirement for her husband's concurrence became the norm. A wife, moreover, was ordinarily barred from bringing legal suit unless authorized by her husband. These legal limitations and the seemingly ubiquitous requirement for a husband's authorization left women in a position of extreme juridical dependency.[5]

A wife's subordination was unmistakable and severe, though certainly not absolute. Nevertheless, a woman's lack of legal independence did not always correspond accurately to her power and capacity within the family. The traditional feminine domain was the domestic, which in lesser noble houses such as the Lacger house meant, among other things, supervision of routine matters related to the provisioning and care of food and clothing, governance of the household servants, and tutelage of the small children.

A wife's place in the childrearing process accorded her a voice in decisions affecting these offspring. She played an important role in their schooling, participated in the arrangements surrounding their marriages, and usually acted as the guardian for minor children following her spouse's death. A married woman, in addition, controlled her paraphernal possessions, unless she had delegated administration to her husband; and she could always freely dictate her last will and testament, thereby disposing of her parapherna. Other circumstances further attenuated her juridical incapacity. The short-term absence of a husband sometimes improved a woman's situation and enhanced her power, if only temporarily. While he was away, she managed the household and estate in his stead. Later, as widows, women found some measure of emancipation in escaping the legal domination of their husbands. Many widows, for example, were left to execute family decisions in whose making they had but limited participation.

Children were, as a matter of course, subject to rigorous parental control. Here, too, the father predominated, though the mother had a complementary role. Symbolic of this paternal rule is the fact that both sons and daughters, even after marriage, used the patronymic surname. The father, normally with the assistance of his wife, was expected to be attentive to the overall plans for a child's education, first in the home and later, in the case of boys, at school. Parents oversaw their children's moral, religious, and professional training. Discipline was strict and generally included physical correction. Career choices for sons were, like schooling, settled by the parents. They also arranged their daughter's or son's marriage, dominating the selection of a spouse and negotiating the details of the dowry. In France, young persons who married without parental permission could be legally disinherited. The period of a child's minority was, for the purposes of marriage, extremely long. The law required that males to the age of thirty and females to twenty-five seek parental approval to wed. Inheritance was one more area that came under patriarchal direction. The father enjoyed a pivotal role in assigning shares in the patrimonial succession. He actively favored the eldest male through a preferential legacy or *inter vivos* donation, while other siblings received minimal shares or, in the case of most daughters, marriage portions.[6]

Protestantism reinforced the patriarchal structure of the family. The weight of Holy Scripture seemed clear. The Apostle Paul urged, "Wives, be subject to your husbands, as to the Lord" and "Children, obey your parents in the Lord." The Decalogue commanded to "Honor thy father and thy mother."[7] Calvin and his followers, fully cognizant of these biblical injunctions, likened the household to a small individual church where the pious father, as the head and master of his family, supervises and instructs the members in accordance with the talents and capabilities that he has received from God. The father, the ancient and sacred *paterfamilias,* once again assumed a sacerdotal role at the very heart of the family. Much as he directed other aspects of family life, the father became its spiritual and moral guide. Ideally, he conducted himself with a firm benevolence. Among the literate bourgeoisie and nobility, in particular, he officiated over the household—wife, children, and servants—reading each evening from Scripture and leading prayers as well as joint singing of psalms.[8] Women, to be sure, participated with their husbands in these activities. Their place within the family as conduit for religious traditions and practices, the more so after 1685, ought not to be overlooked.[9] Still, the Protestant tendency to place much of the burden of piety on the home strengthened the concentration of power in the hands of the father. In the end, his patriarchal position and undivided authority within the family are critical to understanding kinship and the relationships that flowed from it.

The bonds of blood and marriage created a dense network of kinfolk. A ready departure point for examining this fine mesh of human connections is the pattern of forenames, the so-called Christian names that parents bestowed upon their children at baptism. An infant's forename incorporated her or him into the family and the community, while simultaneously reinforcing kin attachments and affiliations.[10] Unlike modern Western culture, where a person's name is oftentimes an expression of individuality and distinctiveness, Lacger parents, along with numerous others, regularly chose to name their offspring for someone in the family. The name possessed an integrative function, serving to unite and join persons rather than set them apart. Children frequently shared names with cognate and affine kin—parents and grandparents, aunts and uncles. Names cemented bonds of spiritual kinship, too; many newborns were called after their godfather or godmother.

By early modern times, names tended to be selected from a relatively restricted inventory centering on biblical figures as well as a variety of later Christian saints and martyrs. Local saints' names, for example, became very popular during the Middle Ages. In earlier times, prior to the eleventh or twelfth centuries, the custom was to name children after grandparents; the subsequent tendency was to choose saintly Christian names from the names of godparents. There was a shift of emphasis from blood kin to spiritual kin, although ideally the two would be combined. Grandparents or other close blood relatives were usually looked upon as the best choice for godparents. This development in naming patterns maintained family continuity while simultaneously emphasizing the godparent's role as spiritual protector. The shared name symbolized the family's biological endurance. Children, in body and name, perpetuated what their ancestors had begun. The memory and the reality endured. The system also established a link through the godparent to the child's distant yet more powerful heavenly protector, her or his name-saint.[11] While the theological beliefs and notions of piety surrounding these usages changed among Protestants, the time-honored customs often remained intact.

The Protestant Reformers were, as might be expected, very fond of biblical names. Yet the ordinary faithful often clung to traditional ways. The result in some instances was a tension between the Reformed Churches' formal notions of correct and appropriate names and people's attachment to customary family names. The first generation of Lacger after the family's conversion christened most of its children with older medieval favorites such as Anne, Isabeau, Jacques, Jean, Marie, and Pierre. These were New Testament names, and the fact that several had a faintly Catholic ring seemed not to matter. More importantly, they fell within an established and ongoing family naming pattern. The naming of Jeanne for her mother was emphatically so. Only one child, Samuel, received a distinctive Old Testament name, and even it was not especially popular among Protestants.[12]

Subsequently, in the seventeenth and eighteenth centuries, naming practices among the nobility and bourgeois began to underscore the individuality of their children. These families wished as well to distinguish themselves from the *menu peuple*. It became fashionable to give children multiple names and to borrow names from classical antiquity. Again, the Lacger offer numerous examples. Infant boys were christened Jean-Jacques, Jean-Louis, and Jean-Jacques-Joseph; girls, Marie-Marguerite,

Catherine-Antoinette, and Antoinette-Louise-Rosalie. For the classically inclined, there were Hercule and his two cousins, father and son, each Marc-Antoine. Yet the focus of names for the Lacger, as with most parents, remained on those appellations shared by others in the family.

Family names passed from one generation to the next, vividly expressing the child's membership in the lineage. This process occurred even when children were named for godparents rather than a father or grandfather, mother or grandmother, since godparents were usually family members, either paternal or maternal. The reader is, by this point, keenly aware of the constant repetition of names among the Lacger. Initial favorites for males were Antoine, Jacques, Jean, and Pierre. Pierre, the early resident of Puylaurens and historic founder of the house, had a grandson, a great-grandson, and a great-great-grandson who bore his name. Jean, baptized in 1567, was called after his maternal grandfather and godfather, the *parlementaire* Jean de Coras. He also had a paternal uncle Jean. Later, a nephew would bear the name Jean.[13] There were equally as many Jacques. The first, born in the 1570s, had a son and a nephew named for him. There was a cousin Jacques in the Castelnaudary branch of the family, too.[14]

The two brothers named Antoine, sons of Guy de Lacger, appear to have been namesakes of a late-fifteenth-century ancestor, perhaps Guy's grandfather.[15] This sort of double-naming of siblings is further evidence of the desire to see a cherished family name persist. During the Middle Ages and the sixteenth century, families commonly gave a newborn child the same first name as an elder sibling, especially if it was the traditional name for the head of the family. The hope was that at least one of the children would survive the demographic ravages of the age. The name, and with it a tangible thread joining generations, would live on.

Sons were, naturally enough, named for maternal kin, too. The practice seems to have been less common in the sixteenth than in subsequent centuries. On the other hand, there is the example of Jean, given the name of his maternal grandfather, Jean de Coras. Louis and Marc-Antoine were, in the seventeenth century, named for maternal uncles. Later, Henri, Honoré-Joseph, and Gabriel bore the names of their maternal grandfathers. In most of these cases, the relative for whom an infant was named was also the godfather.[16]

Girls, no less than boys, were named for relatives on both their father's and mother's side. Whereas males were occasionally called after a distant and deceased, but direct, paternal ascendant, females were almost invariably named for living kin—grandmothers, mothers, and aunts. The most common names among Lacger women were Isabeau, Jeanne, Louise, and Marie. A succession of women bore the name Jeanne. The tradition began when Jeanne de Perrin married Antoine II de Lacger in the mid-1570s. She had several namesakes, including a daughter and a granddaughter. Likewise, several series of aunts and nieces were christened Isabeau and Marie, one after the other.

A major difficulty in tracing female names is created because families generally neglected to keep some written trace of the children of married daughters. There are very few glimpses of the tortured path by which a female name could attach and reattach itself to the family as daughters moved by marriage among the Protestant houses of the Castrais. The name Louise in the Lacger lineage offers a rare and complex example. The first recorded Louise de Lacger, born in the early seventeenth century, was a daughter of Jean de Lacger and Marguerite de Dampmartin. Louise's older sister married Marquis de Toulouse-Lautrec and the couple named one of their daughters Louise, presumably in honor of her aunt. This niece, Louise de Toulouse-Lautrec, in turn, had several children by her husband, Jean d'Isarn. Among them was a daughter who eventually married a Lacger son, and one of their granddaughters would be called Louise after her great-grandmother, Louise de Toulouse-Lautrec.[17] The name passed from aunt to niece, mother to daughter, and from great-grandmother to great-granddaughter, while simultaneously wending its way through two other families before returning to the Lacger. Altogether, the process lasted nearly one and a half centuries.

Intertwined in this arrangement was the practice of naming a child for the godparent. Here examples abound. Blanche was named for her maternal aunt and godmother, Blanche de Falguerolles; Jean-Jacques, for his godfather and paternal uncle of the same name; François, for his godfather, the brigadier François, who also happened to be his father's cousin and benefactor. Occasionally, the process reached beyond consanguineous and affinal kin to friends, professional associates, and patrons of the family. Salomon, born in 1670, was named for his godfather, Salomon de

Faure. This latter person was, like the infant's father, a judge on the *chambre de l'Edit;* he was also the husband of the baby's maternal aunt. An eighteenth-century Pierre, to take another example, was so called perhaps less for his ancestors of the same name than for his godfather, Pierre de Julien, a retired army officer and minor benefactor of the child's father.[18]

Godparents in these elaborate family interconnections had a place that went beyond the occasional bestowal of a name. Although Protestants no longer regarded godparentage as creating a fundamental and sacral relationship that, for example, acted as an impediment to marriage, sponsors at baptism retained great significance. Baptism created a special attachment between godfather and godson or godmother and goddaughter. A godparent promised to look after a child's religious welfare, often conferred his or her name upon the infant, and occasionally favored this spiritual charge with a testamentary bequest, though in truth such gifts were often more symbolic than real.[19] The system also furthered the connections between the godparents and the natural parents. It strengthened friendships, solidified kinship ties, and, in addition, cemented social and economic relationships between the sponsors and the parents of the child. Families chose godparents from among their patrons, clients, friend, and associates or, more commonly, from among consanguine and affinal relatives. Evidence from seventeenth-century Bordeaux, for example, indicates that more than one-half of all godparents there were kin. Baptism and the web of godparentage created a "kinship-group partly natural and partly artificial." Among the Lacger, baptism served to intensify family bonds. For them, the ties of godparentage occupied a central position in revitalizing blood relationships and fortifying those that had been created through marriage.[20]

The Reformed Churches' *Discipline,* a basic official statement of ecclesiastical polity, established the obligations of the godparents and, more particularly in this patriarchal society, the godfather. By the seventeenth century, each infant usually had at baptism both a godfather and godmother. The godparents presented the baby for the ceremony at the temple and answered in her or his stead the rudimentary questions for induction into the Christian community. A basic spiritual responsibility obliged these sponsors to watch over the godchild's proper religious instruction. There was also a social responsibility, for godparents were expected to contribute to the material welfare of their godchildren in the event that they were orphaned. Consequently, sponsors had to be of suitable age and circumstances. They could not to be too young to assume responsibility. Nor would the Reformed Churches permit women alone to present the child for baptism. Presumably, they were deemed incapable of fulfilling the godparents' duties on their own.[21]

The birth of a child offered, then, a preeminent opportunity to reinforce existing affiliations and to create fictive or artificial kin relationships through the selection of godparents. The common pattern was for a father and mother to turn to grandparents, siblings, and other relatives or to people who could be associated with a system of patronage. Information regarding godparents is available for thirty-five Lacger children baptized between the mid-sixteenth and late-eighteenth centuries. In all, sixty-nine godparents—thirty-four women and thirty-five men—can be identified. Eight, some 12 percent, were grandparents: four grandfathers and four grandmothers. The most popular choices, however, were the parents' own siblings. Maternal and paternal aunts and uncles account for well over one-third (36 percent) of all Lacger godparents. In these instances, there was a tendency to favor the father's brothers and mother's sisters: two out of three choices among these parental siblings followed a gender inclination for paternal brothers and maternal sisters. Along related lines, the spouses of the parental siblings constituted fully 7 percent of the godparents. Selection of children's brothers and sisters occurred with about the same frequency (6 percent) as the choice of slightly more distant relatives, such as cousins (7 percent).[22]

GODPARENTS TO LACGER CHILDREN

Relationship	Number	Percentage
Grandparents	8	12
Aunts and uncles	25	36
Aunts and uncles by marriage	5	7
Brothers and sisters	4	6
Cousins	5	7
Family patrons	3	5
Agricultural tenants	12	17
Relationship unknown	7	10
TOTAL	69	100

The Lacger rarely chose godparents from among patrons, a reflection perhaps of the family's status as minor provincial and Protestant nobility. They simply did not possess the wide range of client-patron relationships that characterized larger and more important houses bent upon and capable of regional and national prominence.[23] Furthermore, as Protestants they tended to be somewhat inward looking, seeking the security of a well-defined and proximate kindred—persons to whom they were related and with whom they safely shared a religious culture. The singular exception occurred in the early seventeenth century, when Antoine II's son Jacques moved to Paris and purchased a position as *secrétaire du roi*. There he married Marguerite de Nets, the daughter of a magistrate in the Parisian *chambre des comptes,* a sovereign court with responsibility for fiscal cases. One of their several sons had, as his godparents, Gilles de Maupeou, the prominent Huguenot financial intendant, and Charlotte de Nassau, duchesse de La Trémoille. The La Trémoille, one of the leading families of the Protestant aristocracy of the sword, were the Lacger's most influential patrons during the troubled first three decades of the seventeenth century.[24]

Another unusual aspect of godparentage within the Lacger house was a consequence of their religious position. During the half century following the revocation of the Edict of Nantes, the crypto-Protestant Lacger frequently resorted to having their agricultural tenants acts as godparents. Four offspring of Marc-Antoine I and Marie d'Auriol and two infants of Marc-Antoine II and Marie de Barrau had as godparents gardeners (*jardiniers*), peasant farmers (*travailleurs de terre*), and their wives. It would appear to have been a short-term political maneuver. Protestants found it distasteful to have their children baptized by the Catholic curé. After 1685, it was necessary to have this done for their own protection and to safeguard the child's legal status; yet, who among their family and friends would have been inclined to swear, as the ceremony required, that the newborn would be nurtured in the Catholic faith? Instead, they called upon tenants, some of whom may have been Catholic. These tenants could honestly declare their best intention to have a child raised Catholic, knowing full well that they had no control over the process. This saved Protestant nobles from lying to the parish priest. Tenants, by the same token, endeared themselves to their landlord or, in some cases, may not have been able to refuse the request to serve as godparents.[25]

The consequences of these kinship solidarities were sometimes quite tangible. The members of the kindred group—individuals fused by blood, marriage, and spiritual obligation—provided for one another. They extended help, protection, and advancement in a widely practiced and universally acknowledged system that historians have designated kin patronage. Family affection, lineage loyalty, a sense of duty, and the compulsion to maintain the house's honor prompted members of the kindred to assist one another. Such support was not simply a matter of parents aiding their children. Obligations and responsibilities extended broadly within the lineage to brothers and sisters, aunts and uncles, nieces and nephews, occasionally to distant cousins.[26] However, paternal patronage was likely the most common form of assistance. Fathers helped their offspring by means of the purchase of judicial and administrative offices, offers of financial loans, gifts of landed estates and town houses, and arrangements for favorable marriages and advantageous inheritances. Another sort of widespread kinship patronage link was the uncle/nephew pairing. A predictable association was between father's brother/brother's son, though that of mother's brother/sister's son appears to have been commonplace, too.[27] The Lacger were no exception in the development of these beneficial and constructive kinship connections.

A number of maternal and paternal uncles aided one or another nephew in different ways and at various times. Pierre and Samuel fostered the career of their brother's oldest son in the 1650s. Samuel made this nephew, Jacques, his coheir in his last will and testament of 1652. Pierre subsequently arranged for the young man's purchase of a prestigious judicial office and loaned him the generous sum of eighteen thousand livres on extremely favorable terms, less than 2 percent per annum. Later, this nephew was permitted use of the family town house at Castres in exchange for certain "repairs and improvements" to it.[28]

Other nephews fared equally well. Jean-Jacques-Joseph, in the eighteenth century, received important legacies from both maternal and paternal uncles. His original prospects had not been bright. He was the youngest of Marc-Antoine I's eight children and, to compound the disadvantage, born of his father's second marriage. He inherited very little of the comparatively sparse paternal resources, and his mother, the daughter of a minor judicial officer, had even fewer assets. Three separate male relatives, however, came to his assistance. The brigadier François, his distant cousin, initially boosted the young man's career by helping him secure an appointment in the Regiment of Auvergne. In addition, this military benefactor, at his death in 1758, bequeathed Jean-Jacques-Joseph land and cash with a combined value of fifteen thousand livres. Even before this beneficence, two uncles advantaged Jean-Jacques-Joseph. His mother's brother left him three small *métairies;* and Jean-Jacques, a paternal uncle and godfather for whom he was at least partially named, made him his chief heir in 1746. The latter inheritance amounted to thirty thousand livres and some household furnishings.[29] These gifts and legacies rescued Jean-Jacques-Joseph from what surely would have otherwise been a long and stable, but financially unrewarding, career in the army. He quit his regiment in 1747, a year after receiving the handsome legacy of thirty thousand livres from his father's brother. He publicly converted to Catholicism, took a wealthy Catholic bride, and with the assistance of his wife and her family, soon established an extremely prosperous cadet line.[30]

Uncles generally promoted their nephews' careers in the church and the army. In the years prior to the Reformation, the canon Jean de Lacger took a strong interest in his nephew Sébastien's ecclesiastical career. The younger man followed directly in his uncle's path, becoming a canon and thereafter dean of the collegial church at Burlats. Several centuries later, François de Lacger, a leading officer of the Regiment of Auvergne, assiduously fostered the careers of his brothers, nephews, and cousins. He became lieutenant colonel, second in command of the regiment, at an early age and subsequently used this power and rank to help members of his family. Both of his younger brothers served in this same regiment. Though one died in combat at an early age, the other appears to have benefited in terms of promotions and preferments from his older sibling's position as a senior officer in the unit. François may also have assisted the career of a younger cousin, Jean-Jacques, the chevalier de Lacger, who later rose to become lieutenant colonel for the Regiment of Auvergne.

François and Jean-Jacques, the chevalier de Lacger, unquestionably watched over the military careers of Marc-Antoine I's three sons. Marc-Antoine I was François's second cousin and Jean-Jacques's brother. The pair, uncle and distant cousin to the three young men, helped secure each of them their initial commissions in the Regiment of Auvergne. Marc-Antoine II served seven years, until his father died and he inherited the family estates. Jean-Louis, a younger sibling, probably would have made the army a lifelong career had he not died of battlefield wounds at Parma in 1734. The youngest brother, Jean-Jacques-Joseph, was the obvious pro-tégé of his military uncle and godfather, for whom he was named. He remained with the regiment for more than a dozen years and won several promising promotions. Only the previously mentioned inheritances and an opportune marriage convinced him to retire. Finally, François fur-thered the military career of Julien de Boisset, a cousin on his mother's side. Boisset eventually became a company captain in the regiment and later received a generous testamentary bequest from his cousin François.[31]

The assistance that a family typically extended to women was by com-parison modest, but it did exist. The Lacger took pains to insure that their daughters and nieces had suitable marriages. Here the most important element was the provision of a dowry. Both fathers and mothers partici-pated in the process. A mother's contribution to a daughter's dowry in the Lacger house was often about 15 percent of the total. Aunts and uncles occasionally donated to the dowries of their nieces, too. Pierre de Perrin gave three thousand livres to the dowry of his sister's daughter, Jeanne de Lacger, in 1614. Toward mid-century, Marie d'Hérail provided a small gift of three hundred livres for the dowry of her sister's daughter. The young bride, Marie de Lacger, was likely the aunt's namesake and god-daughter as well. Sisters supported one another, too. Yet another Marie de Lacger, when she passed away in the early eighteenth century, made her sister Louise her sole heir. Parents and siblings also provided other material assistance, things such as housing. Marthe and her husband lived in the family's town house during the middle decades of the eighteenth century, while her father, mother, and two brothers resided at the châ-teaux of Navès and Clot. Finally, there were the usual legacies and gifts *inter vivos*. Samuel left testamentary bequests to his three sisters; Jean-Jacques similarly remembered a niece; François provided for his elderly sister-in-law and a niece.[32]

Another way in which kinship and clientage combined occurred in the professional and social sphere. For the Lacger these were usually occupa-tional and business ties rather than the complex reciprocal relationships of dependency and service associated with a political patron. The recurring association of blood relatives and affines was particularly pronounced within the judicial ranks of the *chambre de l'Edit*. Offices almost always passed from father to son or between brothers, occasionally cousins. Jean de Lacger's post, in typical fashion, went to his son, Hercule, and from him to a cousin, Jacques. Even when a family relinquished an office, it did so within a professional network defined largely by kinship and marriage. Jean purchased his judgeship on the *chambre de l'Edit* from the Rozel house in 1600 or, perhaps more accurately, the family bought it for him. A few years later, Jean's daughter married a Rozel son. The young man's father had occupied the judicial post now held by his father-in-law; and he was himself the court's royal attorney-general.

These *parlementaire* families intermarried extensively and repeatedly. Antoine I, magistrate on the Parlement of Toulouse in the mid-sixteenth century, married the widow of a high court judge. Her first husband, in fact, had been the previous possessor of Antoine's office. The *parlementaire* Jean's son-in-law was attorney-general for the *chambre de l'Edit*. Jacques, *parlementaire* from 1653 until his death in 1688, was married to Magdelaine de Falguerolles, whose sister was married to another of the tribunal's judges. There were, in addition, numerous matrimonial links with families on other sovereign courts, such as the *chambre des comptes* and various subalternate courts associated with the seneschalsy. Roze de Correch, first wife of the subalternate judge Pierre, was the daughter of a magistrate on the *chambre de l'Edit*.[33] In these instances, marriage nurtured and solidified professional connections, assisted in career advancement, and secured vital patronage.

Matrilineal kinship played as important a role as patrilineal associations in acquiring and retaining a powerful patron. The Lacger's successful, if fleeting, client-patron relationship with the La Trémoille during the early seventeenth century flowed from the family of Marguerite de Nets, wife of Jacques de Lacger. Her father had originally secured an appointment in the La Trémoille household. He subsequently aided his son-in-law and his son-in-law's house in becoming La Trémoille clients. At about this same time, the Lacger established a valuable connection to the house of Toulouse-Lautrec. The association began with the 1617 marriage between Isabeau de Lacger and Marquis de Toulouse-Lautrec. There was, at this point, a professional connection: Isabeau's maternal uncle Jean de Perrin was seneschal of Castres. The office had previously been held by her father-in-law, Jacques de Toulouse-Lautrec, and in 1623, returned to the

Toulouse-Lautrec when Isabeau's husband became the seneschal of Castres. Later, her nephew Pierre obtained a commission in a cavalry company commanded by a member of the Toulouse-Lautrec, while another nephew, Jacques, sieur de Clot, married her granddaughter. Finally, when both Jacques and his wife died at a young age, it was the maternal grandmother, Dame Louise de Toulouse-Lautrec, who became the children's legal guardian and saw to their upbringing. Her role fell within another established matrilineal linkage by which families traditionally called upon mothers and maternal grandmothers to be guardians for fatherless minors. Uncles, whether paternal or maternal, usually acted in an advisory capacity. In the end, the Lacger did not have many prominent patrons. Their allegiances and alliances arose mostly within the local, lesser Protestant elite and centered on the nearby court system. Their two most powerful patrons were the La Trémoille at the national level and the Toulouse-Lautrec locally. Both connections were established through marriage and had strong matrilineal associations. Neither relationship proved long-lasting, however. The Lacger's thin ties to patrons of national importance faded rapidly with the decline of Huguenot political fortunes following the failure of Rohan's revolt in the late 1620s. Regional client-patron networks endured longer, but inevitably contracted after 1685.

How might sibling relationships within the Lacger house be accurately characterized? Were they, to take the two obvious extremes, marked by rivalry or cooperation? To begin, it would appear that the gulf between eldest son (and heir) and younger brothers was less than in higher aristocratic circles.[34] This is not to deny Lacger investment of a disproportionate share of the house's social prestige, political power, and economic assets in the oldest son. A sense of interdependency and cohesion, nonetheless, permeated this Huguenot family, and the feeling only intensified after 1685. Marc-Antoine II, for example, carefully divided the patrimony upon the marriage of his older son in 1774. Though the tradition of favoring the eldest male remained in place, the younger brother received a substantial settlement. He was made heir to the *métairies* of Clot and la Planesié, long the cornerstones of Lacger fortunes. There are other cases, particularly among siblings, of mutual assistance and kin cohesiveness. François, after retiring from the military, invited his younger, less affluent brother to share his house with him. If unmarried or childless, siblings made one another their heirs, or failing brothers and sisters, they endowed nieces, nephews, and cousins. Nieces and nephews, for their part, cared for childless, unmarried, or widowed aunts and uncles as they grew old. Such behavior and the sentiments upon which it was founded stood in apparent contrast to feelings among the elite elsewhere. Within the Catholic aristocracy of nearby Toulouse, for instance, at least one historian has suggested that "the eldest son felt little obligation toward his younger brothers once their portions had been paid."[35]

Cooperation among siblings was an important strategic device for the advancement, if not the very durability, of this particular Protestant house. Divisive quarrels exacted an enormous price. The religious wars of the sixteenth and early seventeenth centuries as well as the aftermath of the Revocation possessed the capacity to disrupt families severely.[36] The Lacger successfully managed to avoid such disasters. Differences in confessional adherence occasionally developed, but they rarely affected kin relationships. Religious divisions were simply not permitted to shatter family solidarity. Reconsider for a moment the exchange of godparents and names in the eighteenth century. In several cases, godparentage and naming bridged religious differences within the family. Jean-Jacques publicly abjured Protestantism in the interests of his flourishing military career. The act did not, however, dissuade his crypto-Protestant elder brother from asking him to be godparent to his youngest son in 1718. Twenty-five years later, Marc-Antoine II, a staunch Protestant, did not hesitate to have his Catholic half brother as godparent for a son. He even named the child for his sibling. The same Catholic half brother would later reciprocate and have Marc-Antoine II as godfather for one of his daughters.[37] The bonds of family affection overcame confessional rifts.

Did this developed sense of family also act as a deterrent in keeping the Protestant Lacger from emigrating after 1685? Not a single family member left the kingdom, and vigorous kinship solidarity seems to have been at least partially responsible. Family members helped see one another through the difficulties. Along similar lines, did these crises revive and expand lineage loyalties and kin networks?[38] Of this there can be no doubt. Not only did immediate relations—parents and siblings, aunts and uncles —come to one another's aid, but more distant relatives, such as second cousins, took special care to enrich their less prosperous Protestant kin.

How far did these kinship solidarities extend? Or, put somewhat differently, what was the genealogical proximity of family ties? The Lacger at Castelnaudary in the Lauragais, for example, diverged from the rest of the family by the end of the sixteenth century. This cadet branch quickly became detached and distinct, having few if any dealings with the older lineage at Castres after 1600. The development resulted from geographic distance, the branch's adoption of Catholicism, and the historical moment of the separation. None of these factors alone would appear to have been sufficient for a permanent separation. By comparison, the Lacger sons who migrated to a more distant Paris remained close to their relations at Castres, and the children of the next generation continued in this vein.

The nature and timing of the Lauragais branch's conversion to Catholicism also differed from subsequent abjurations. During the late sixteenth and early seventeenth centuries, conversion conveyed a sense of political and cultural division. It had connotations of abandonment and disloyalty toward the cause, of opting for economic, social, and political gain through the adoption of Catholicism. The Edict of Fontainebleau and the proscription of Protestantism in 1685 dramatically altered the context of conversion. Those in the family who abjured the Reformed faith in the late-seventeenth and eighteenth centuries acted typically from constraint. It was not a matter of choosing voluntarily to embrace Catholicism. Their Protestant brothers, sisters, nephews, and nieces understood these complicated pressures and remained on relatively good terms with them. Protestant and Catholics family members depended upon one another, assisting financially or offering support in old age. The ties among consanguineous Lacger kin at Castres extended broadly, as far as second cousins and occasionally beyond. Certainly, this developed sense of the kin group was not unusual among families of the petty French nobility.[39]

The strength of these bonds also meant that the family maintained tight control over economic assets. Legal customs and practices aided considerably in this regard. The law demanded that patrimonial property remain within the line whence it came. The wealth of unmarried or childless family members passed to their closest blood relatives—parents, siblings, nephews and nieces, or cousins. Antoine II and Jean laid claim to most of their three childless brothers' inheritances in the sixteenth century. In the following century, the unmarried Samuel left his estate to a brother and nephew. Jean-Jacques and François, when they died in the mid-1700s, also without issue, bequeathed their possessions to nephews and cousins.

Attention to the impartibility of the patrimony and a strong desire to reassemble it whenever fragmentation occurred also took place outside the direct influence of the law. Marc-Antoine II, for instance, split the property of Navès from that of Clot and la Planesié in the later eighteenth century. The oldest son received Navès; the younger, Clot and la Planesié. Then, in the early 1830s, the grandchildren of these two brothers rejoined the lands through marriage. The Lacger, like most petty Protestant nobles of the Castrais, had since the Revocation become accustomed to selecting marriage partners from a small regional and confessional pool. The marital union of these Lacger second cousins in 1832 seems an especially strong confirmation of the practice. Matrimony knitted the family ever closer and, in the process, reunited its resources.

The family preserved and promoted its own collective memory in several other ways. Genealogy and portraiture became popular, particularly in the eighteenth century.[40] The five volumes of transcribed documents, which a younger Lacger son assembled over the space of half a decade in the early 1770s and which are the basis for the present study, stand as learned testimony to this interest. No sooner had this amateur historian and genealogist completed his honorable task than the family published a brief but elegant *Généalogie historique de la maison de Lacger*. The genealogical impulse then continued into the nineteenth century. Gabriel de Lacger, born in 1833, put together a series of thick dossiers in which he arranged, for each of his principal male ancestors as far back as 1523, the many original documents still in the family's possession.

Portraits of the more illustrious Lacger also graced the châteaux at Navès and Clot. The oldest to survive is that of the seventeenth-century poet and judge Jacques, clad in the crimson robes of his office.[41] There are also two highly idealized portraits of military officers from the eighteenth century. The one is François, adorned with the Order of Saint Louis; the other, Jean-Jacques, the chevalier de Lacger, dressed in the handsome black armor befitting a lieutenant colonel. At least one additional eighteenth-century portrait, that of an unidentified woman, has survived. All appear to have been painted by professional artists contemporary to the subjects. Finally, there are several early nineteenth-century miniatures, including one of Jean-Jacques-Joseph, the ardent copyist and genealogist. It is a slightly amateurish effort undertaken by a nephew in ten one-hour sittings in 1804. Taken together, these portraits bespeak the esteem in which houses held their ancestors, not to mention the subjects' pride in their own achievements.

The Lacger cherished close blood kin. They were, in this respect, hardly different from other houses in early modern France. If anything, their religious position—a minority repeatedly subject to violence and persecution—reaffirmed sentiments of interdependency and cooperation, the need to remain united and harmonious. They shared as well other traits common to families of the early modern French elite. A series of patriarchal fathers, for example, long dominated the Lacger line. Given the strategy for survival that most clans adopted during this time, it was essential that familial authority remain undivided. Patriarchy provides a key to understanding early modern European kinship relationships.[42]

Some simple biological realities reaffirmed this patriarchal structure within the Lacger lineage. Many of the male heads of family had exceptionally long lives. Pierre, the judge at Castres during the turbulent decades of the early seventeenth century, was seventy-eight years old at his death in 1655. His nephew, the *parlementaire* Jacques, lived into his mid-seventies. François was ninety-seven when he passed away in January 1758. His cousin Marc-Antoine II, the man to whom he bequeathed the seigneury of Navès, lived to the age of eighty-seven.[43]

The Lacger, furthermore, never wanted for male heirs, although there were rarely so many sons as to create conflict. In the sixteenth century, Guy had five sons; yet only two produced children and continued the line. Pierre, Guy's grandson, had but two male children and only one of them married. Pierre's son fathered two sons and again only one married. The latter, Marc-Antoine I, had five sons, of whom two survived to adulthood and had children. The next generation saw two sons as well.[44] The Lacger possessed the basic assurance of biological perpetuation without an expensive and dangerous dispersal of resources. Stable, well-defined continuity and a dense network of relatives gave force to lineal solidarity. Agnatic succession—a strong sense of patrilinearity—clearly dominated.

The importance of women in the kin group is equally apparent. Marriage contracts and baptismal records, for example, suggest a close association of both patrilineal and matrilineal kin. Traditional family names for women wound their way from mother to daughter or granddaughter, from one generation to the next, in and out of the Lacger house as daughters married into neighboring families and their offspring later returned in marital union. Women in the Lacger house, perhaps more than men, served to bind kinship to clientage, professional ties, and personal friendship. Witness the Lacger–Nets–La Trémoille affiliation or the Lacger–Toulouse-Lautrec connection, both in the early seventeenth century, at the height of Lacger aspirations. Each was secured through Lacger daughters or women who married into the family.

The family structure and kinship relationships of the Lacger from the early sixteenth through the late eighteenth centuries are familiar to those who have studied these issues for other French houses of the period. Certain characteristics are, nonetheless, closely related to the Lacger situation as petty Protestant nobility from the provincial world of southern France. The family's religious posture unmistakably reinforced traditional ties of mutual support and solidarity. Kin depended upon and drew strength from one another. Secondly, southern French legal customs and cultural practices added to the power of patriarchal authority. Protestantism may have contributed here too, enhancing the role of the father. Finally, Lacger status as Huguenot stock of mainly regional importance likely stunted the growth and development of client-patron relationships, at least when compared to the elaborate networks surrounding the highest aristocratic houses of the kingdom. The Lacger focused on nurturing and maintaining carefully delimited associations with houses of similar political and professional status within close geographic proximity. These particular families also shared fundamental religious views and, for this reason, protected one another. Throughout, the Lacger drew upon themselves in repeated and profound demonstration of their understanding of family loyalty and reciprocal obligation.

༽

EIGHT

Confessional Identity and the Crucible of the Revocation

An elaborate array of competing, often conflicting requirements relentlessly molded and defined the religious identity of Huguenot families such as the Lacger. Whatever the balance between personal conviction and the broader social forces that prompted members of the Lacger house to adopt Reformed Christianity during the 1560s, the perpetuation of the decision by later descendants proved an arduous, unremitting task. Although the Lacger had a sophisticated understanding of their faith, they did not have a close interest in either the internal bureaucracy of the local Reformed church or matters that were essentially theological and disciplinary. They preferred, instead, to channel their efforts into the arena of Huguenot political affairs, within the specific context of local municipal governance and regional consultative assemblies. This role better suited their position as judges at Castres and in the province of Languedoc. The Lacger were part of a regional Protestant political elite whose stature determined, at least partially, the family's position in the religious sphere. The Lacger also belonged to an aspiring robe nobility that depended upon royal officeholding. The crown, which the Lacger and other Protestant magistrates served, was Catholic and as such, it ultimately insisted upon religious as well as political loyalty. The balance of these various demands was always difficult and, after 1685, impossible.

Piety among the Lacger was in keeping with their social status, religious-political interests, and educational formation. They owned and read the Bible, composed paraphrases of the psalms, studied Calvin's *Institutes* and scriptural commentaries, and even pored over the church fathers. Politically active members of the family followed various national controversies through the writings of Du Plessis Mornay, Le Faucheur, and Aubertine. Fathers presided over daily family prayer, and mothers took charge of the religious training of the very young. They worshiped with the congregation each Wednesday and Sunday, married and baptized their offspring in the temple, left pious bequests to the poor, and were laid to rest by the pastor. Altogether, their religious practices and the literate, lay, and often personal traditions surrounding them were the shared attributes of the Protestant provincial notables.

Lacger involvement in the administrative affairs of the local Reformed church, however, was infrequent. Only one member of the family participated directly in the workings of the inner ecclesiastical circles. Jacques, second son of the judge Pierre de Lacger, was selected as one of the twenty-one elders for the Reformed church at Castres for a two-year term beginning in January 1674. The pastors had, some thirty years earlier, attempted to persuade Pierre himself to serve in a similar capacity, but he evidently declined.[1]

Jacques de Lacger's tenure as elder proved disastrous. His attendance at the various meetings of the consistory during these two years was abysmally poor. Of 163 sessions, he was present at not more than 57—only slightly better than one-third of the time. Moreover, on two different occasions, the very consistory on which he sat disciplined him. In February 1674, barely a month after his selection, the consistory asked Jacques to explain the scandalous rumors that he and his wife had attended a "ball and dance." The new elder responded lamely that he had not himself attended. Rather, his wife had gone in the company of her parents. About a year and a half later, in July 1675, the Castres consistory again chided Lacger, this time for a public legal squabble with his brother-in-law and fellow elder, Raymond Dumas. Once more, Lacger excused himself by claiming that his father-in-law was behind the matter.[2] Aside from the issue of his personal character, his repeated neglect of duty and overall fecklessness suggest little, if any, commitment to or interest in his position and function within the church. Not surprisingly, he was never again asked to assume the post of elder.

Pierre de Lacger's reluctance to serve as elder and his son's apparent disinterest was doubtless unusual for Protestants of their social and economic condition. The position reinforced noble power and allowed these men to pose as protectors of the Christian community. Other notables of Castres—especially men of legal training associated with the *chambre de l'Edit*—seemed more than willing to be church elders. Many of them were from families whose social and professional situation mirrored the Lacger; some were, in fact, allied to the Lacger through marriage. They included several members of the Escorbiac and Ranchin families, attorneys and sons of magistrates on the *chambre de l'Edit*. The Espérandieu, men of the law and faithful members of the Academy of Castres, assumed the duties of elder, too. Another participant in the Academy, the lawyer Benoît d'Isarn, served as elder for a time; and Raymond Dumas, attorney and husband of Jeanne de Lacger, fulfilled a term as elder during the mid-1670s. On the other hand, judges, whether seated on the *chambre* or in the local subalternate courts, rarely took on such positions within the church.[3] It seemed incompatible with their political standing and dignity. Pierre was no exception in this regard. Nonetheless, these magistrates could and did wield great power within the church.

The Huguenot judges possessed considerable influence in the ecclesiastical realm by reason of their political prominence. Pierre, in his capacity as royal judge for the city and county of Castres, occupied the preeminent position at the regular meetings of the so-called *corps d'Eglise* at Castres. The notion, even the existence, of a *corps d'Eglise* varied from one Reformed church to another. This particular forum was not a recognized ecclesiastical institution with widespread status and uniform character, as was, for instance, the consistory.[4] Within the Reformed community of Castres, the term designated a gathering that was distinct from the local consistory. Whereas the consistory directed the overall religious life of the church—watching over the moral behavior of the faithful, providing assistance for the impoverished, and attending to the many details of daily ecclesiastical administration—the *corps d'Eglise* resolved sensitive administrative matters within the church and guided its delicate relationship with other churches, superior ecclesiastical bodies such as the colloquy, and, most conspicuously by the seventeenth century, outside political powers. The *corps* at Castres had much the flavor of a general assembly of the most distinguished men of the congregation. The membership included the royal judge, the two Protestant municipal consuls,[5] three Reformed pastors, and the church's elders, as well as a substantial number of other influential persons from the Protestant community.

Pierre attended most all the meetings of the *corps d'Eglise* from the mid-1640s, when the surviving records begin, until his death in 1655. He was clearly the foremost participant, was always mentioned first in the litany of attendees, and presumably presided over the sessions. The group does not appear to have had a fixed schedule for gathering. More likely, it assembled according to the particular need. The body sometimes acted to settle thorny internal matters, such as disputes over pastors' salaries or the hiring of a new pastor. The members of the *corps* occasionally handled the church's affairs with other Reformed churches, as when in 1647 the Church of Montpellier requested the loan of the pastor Gaches for six months. The consistory of Castres refused, but it took the power and influence of the *corps d'Eglise* to make the refusal stick. On other occasions, relations among the various churches were more amicable, as when the *corps d'Eglise* at Castres decided that it would join the churches of Montauban and Montpellier in organizing a delegation to remind the king of his promise to safeguard the legal position of his Huguenot subjects.[6]

The *corps*'s discussions repeatedly focused on issues of potential political and religious discord, matters which threatened to disrupt its uneasy relationship with the Catholic state. Throughout 1646 and 1647, for example, it guided the negotiations with royal officials in seeking permission to construct another temple at Castres. A few years later, the same body worked out the details for building a new bell tower. It was the *corps* that, in 1654, inquired about what appeared to be irregularities in the conduct of the municipal *collège*. The faculty of the *collège* had been divided along confessional lines, with equal numbers of Catholic and Protestant instructors since the early 1630s. Predictably, the arrangement was a source of constant friction. As previously noted, the *corps* also regularly named those persons dispatched to protest the increasingly frequent violations of Huguenot privileges under the terms of the Edict of Nantes.[7] In all of this, Pierre seems to have been something of a guiding force. After his death in 1655, the *corps d'Eglise* met less regularly, and the place of honor went to a series of Protestant magistrates from the *chambre de l'Edit,* according to what appears to have been an ordered rotation. In any event, none had the strong, abiding interest so evident in Pierre de Lacger.

Pierre had long appreciated the conjuncture of political and religious influence afforded by his position as a Huguenot leader and royal magistrate at Castres. He attended a number of local and national Huguenot political assemblies, beginning in the early 1610s. Perhaps the most famous was the national meeting held at Grenoble in 1615. By the 1620s, Pierre had also become a familiar figure at the regional Protestant synods. On these latter occasions, he served as the royal commissioner whose essential job was to report the proceedings along with his observations to the crown.[8] This role seems to have suited Pierre, who cast himself as an intermediary, if not mediator and negotiator, in the conflict between the national Catholic monarchy and local Protestant community. Acting in the capacity of peacemaker and power broker, occasionally even protector, was hardly unusual for Huguenot robe nobles such as the Lacger, who sought to be at once Protestant and firmly loyal to the crown. The Escorbiac family occupied a similar niche at Montauban. Naturally, the actions of these men were not always appreciated by fellow Protestants, especially during the troubles of the 1620s. In the longer term, however, these endeavors afforded the Lacger and similar houses a pivotal and powerful position within the Huguenot towns of southern France.

Others in the family were similarly involved in this nexus of political and ecclesiastical affairs, though usually to a lesser extent. Pierre's father, Antoine II, had been a principal in the *politique* group that attempted to achieve civic and religious stability at Castres beginning in the mid-1570s. Again, his position as royal *juge ordinaire* lent the necessary prestige and authority. Later his several sons—chiefly Jean and Pierre, who, each in turn, succeeded him as judge at Castres—continued in the same vein.

Jean, the eldest, became judge upon his father's death in 1591. He immediately found himself in the midst of a divisive and emotionally charged religious controversy.

Gaspard d'Olaxe, an eloquent Protestant pastor of Spanish origins, threatened to split and weaken the Reformed church at Castres in the mid-1590s. He appears to have secured a post at Castres only after abandoning improperly his ministry at Sorèze, a town about twenty-five kilometers to the southwest. There was, in addition, the vague accusation that he had spread heresy among the faithful of the region. The quarrel quickly mingled with other local issues, and the Protestants of Castres divided into two hotly opposed camps on the subject of Olaxe. The local Colloquy of Albigeois debated the matter, yet amid the turmoil reached no decision. It referred the matter to the neighboring Colloquy of Lauragais, which promptly condemned Olaxe for preaching doctrinal error and deserting the church at Sorèze. The colloquy then excommunicated Olaxe and dismissed him from the ministry. The provincial synod and, ultimately, the national synod, both meeting at Montauban, confirmed the decision. Olaxe, for his part, eventually converted to Catholicism, returned to Spain, and there entered a Franciscan monastery.

Jean de Lacger, by virtue of his civic and judicial standing, could not avoid entanglement in these intricate and emotionally charged developments. He and the municipal consuls met with the pastors and elders of the Reformed Church of Castres following Olaxe's condemnation by the Colloquy of Lauragais. The group appointed him, with two others, to accompany Olaxe to the meeting of the provincial synod at Montauban. There, following its reaffirmation of Olaxe's condemnation, the synod charged Jean to reconcile the principal feuding parties at Castres. Several acrimonious lawsuits had been initiated, and the synod wanted a swift conclusion to the fracas. The affair and Jean's part in it again suggest the power that civic and judicial officers such as the Lacger occupied within the Reformed Churches and the pacifying or mediating role that they frequently played.[9]

Whether these Lacger men and women conformed to traditional historical notions of a strict Calvinist morality is more difficult to gauge. With one or two notable exceptions, they seem to have acted with an unobtrusive correctness. Though perhaps not exemplary models of virtue, neither were they thought to be wayward or morally delinquent. Their plainly ordinary behavior is perhaps more typical of most French Protestants than the unbending and stern "Puritanism" that is often associated with followers of the Calvinist Reformation. While the modern observer might find the ambitious, often overbearing, conduct of a person such as Pierre de Lacger distasteful and disturbing, the faults recorded by the Castres consistory against his son Jacques, sieur de Clot—dancing, quarreling, and the disregard of ecclesiastical duties—are wholly typical of the minor infractions that Reformed churches throughout France sought to eradicate.[10] More serious transgressions, as judged by the standards of the age, were fewer or perhaps better concealed. The only recorded illegitimate children, for example, were those fathered in the seventeenth century by men of the cadet Catholic line at Castelnaudary in the Lauragais.[11] The great exception to these behavioral patterns is the seventeenth-century poet and jurist Jacques. His unsettled life, replete with self-indulgence and profligacy as well as a deadly duel and hints of sexual dalliance, differed sharply from the sober and dignified lives of his kinfolk.

The Lacger, and others like them, found that their calming influence within Huguenot circles and the attempted balance between confessional fidelity and obedience to the Catholic sovereign could not prevent the worsening of Protestant fortunes and the complete suppression of the Reformed Churches by the final quarter of the seventeenth century. Under the circumstances, most in the family withdrew from public life and discreetly but firmly held on to their Protestant heritage. A few others, mostly magistrates and army officers, abjured the Reformed faith and became Catholic. These conversions naturally occurred within a far larger context and ought to be examined accordingly. The *parlementaire* Jacques was the earliest of the family to convert, and his actions offer a ready, instructive set-piece for introducing the broader questions surrounding conversion and constancy among the Lacger and other Huguenot houses of southern France.

As the French monarchy moved deliberately and firmly during the early 1680s toward the revocation of the Edict of Nantes, a Protestant *président à mortier* and eight Reformed *conseillers* still sat, with their more numerous Catholic counterparts, on the Parlement of Toulouse, the sovereign court for the province of Languedoc. These Protestant judges, however, were not part of a traditional urban magistracy. They came from the small-town hinterland of southern French Calvinism and had previously been associated with the *chambre de l'Edit,* the Protestant-Catholic tribunal established at Castres during the last phases of the sixteenth-century religious warfare. Although these Reformed magistrates retained their parlementary offices upon the chamber's dissolution in 1679, they were obliged to move to Toulouse and to integrate into the various other chambers of the parlement.

Immediately upon arrival at ultra-Catholic Toulouse, the Protestant judges faced intense pressure to convert. Such constraint was part of a general attempt directed at Huguenot pastors, nobles, and wealthy bourgeois. The reaction of these *parlementaires* demonstrates that they were not as well equipped as other Protestants, even other members of the petty provincial nobility, to withstand royal pressure. Lacking substantial landed wealth, these magistrates were heavily dependent upon royal favor for their livelihood and therefore open to considerable leverage. A few buckled quickly. The *président* Charles de Vignolles surrendered first, sometime in the winter of 1679–80. The next spring, Jacques de Ranchin, judge and occasional poet, abjured and received in exchange a handsome annual pension of three thousand livres. The slippage stopped at this point, at least until late June 1685, when the crown presented the Protestant judges with a far more difficult choice: it gave them three months in which to convert or resign from the court. It came as no particular shock that the remaining Reformed *parlementaires* chose Catholicism and thereby protected their considerable financial investment and social achievement.[12] To what extent these men were, in the language of the day, *mal convertis,* remains a subject of some debate. Simply put, were the conversions sincere or just a matter of convenience? Part of the response can be found in the fact that the decision to abjure frequently engendered religious fissures, authentic or otherwise, within these families. It is to the nature, intention, and effect of these splits that we therefore must turn.

The most common sort of religious division within Huguenot families at the time of the Revocation was that between parents and children, or among siblings. The *parlementaires* proved no exception. A brother and sister of the *président* Vignolles sought asylum, probably in the Swiss cantons. His other siblings, however, remained in France. Vignolles's children stayed at Toulouse, where the family continued a tradition of service to the parlement. Among the sons of Thomas d'Escorbiac, one stayed in France and eventually succeeded to his father's office on the high court. Three others chose to emigrate: one joined the Dutch army and two found employ in the service of the king of Denmark. The *parlementaire* Claude de Juge converted, but his brother, a Reformed pastor at Castres, left for Holland.[13]

A more revealing type of split was that between husband and wife. To return to a previous example, Thomas d'Escorbiac, shamelessly declaring in 1685 that not a single Huguenot could be found "at Montpellier, Nîmes or elsewhere," traveled to Versailles, where he abjured in the presence of the Sun King himself. In return, Escorbiac retained his judicial office and, a few years later, was able to pass it to his equally *nouveau converti* son. The elder Escorbiac had, in addition, wrangled an annual royal pension of three thousand livres. His wife, however, was far more reluctant and much slower to convert, though she eventually capitulated.[14]

Jacques de Lacger, himself a Protestant *parlementaire* seeking to retain his office, adopted Catholicism in a less dramatic and more ordinary fashion. Nonetheless, a similar sort of division occurred between him and his wife, Magdelaine de Falguerolles. He abjured in September 1685, near the end of the three-month grace period that the royal administration granted Protestant magistrates. Magdelaine de Falguerolles, however, refused to declare for Catholicism, most likely by explicit agreement with her husband. Presumably, she intended to remain, quietly and privately, the family conduit for Reformed beliefs and practices. Such a strategy appears consonant with the fundamental role assigned to women, both mothers and grandmothers, in the religious upbringing of children.[15] Moreover, royal pressure to convert may have initially been stronger for men, especially prominent public figures, than for women. Jacques and his fellow jurist Claude de Juge successfully petitioned the crown to "forgive" their wives' refusal to convert. Such female defiance could have easily jeopardized a husband's judicial post, yet the royal bureaucracy chose to overlook it in these instances.[16]

This well-planned but short-term stratagem floundered, however, when Jacques died in 1688. Royal officials subjected his widow to unrelenting coercion. They even threatened Magdelaine de Falguerolles and her sister

Blanche, the wife of another "new Catholic" *parlementaire,* with exile to Burgundy in 1698. Magdelaine seems to have been briefly interned at Albi in the autumn 1699. Yet her personal religious constancy was not in doubt. The greater difficulty arose with regard to her children or, more precisely, her sons, the only children about whom we are reasonably well informed. They showed little of their mother's defiant resolve, but instead followed the paternal example. The sons' conversions, such as they were, tended to be a matter of acquiescence and submission to the monarchy. They were not anxious to declare actively and openly for Catholicism, yet like many Huguenots, they were susceptible to pressure. Protestants whose families depended upon royal officeholding would have found open resistance to the king's will distressing, even on so fundamental an issue as religion. Opposition would, at the very least, have endangered their offices and called into question their monarchical loyalties. They preferred to remain silent, but if absolutely necessary, assented to the sovereign's wishes.

For the sons of Jacques de Lacger and Magdelaine de Falguerolles, part of the incentive for what we might call passive or, better yet, tacit conversion was the desire to retain the legal rights to their deceased father's parlementary office. Although the family sold the post at a loss in 1692, the thirty-nine thousand livres that it fetched was still a large sum by provincial standards. Another financial consideration centered on the annual royal pensions that each of the sons received as *gratification* or reward following their father's death. François, already a captain in the Regiment of Auvergne, received eight hundred livres; each of his brothers, three hundred livres. Typically, payment of such a pension was contingent upon presentation of a "certificate of Catholicity," signed by the pensioner's curé and attesting to proper religious behavior. Finally, these sons needed to be mindful of their future careers.[17] They, like their father, held royal posts, even though the focus had shifted from the judiciary to the army. Their continued service inevitably entailed compliance in the religious domain. Jacques's eldest son and legal heir, though trained in the law, chose not to succeed to his father's judicial post.[18] An unwillingness to make a public profession of Catholicism probably had much to do with his decision. He, of course, fell back upon the preferential legacy which he received as eldest male. However meager, this inheritance was more than his brothers could anticipate. They opted for service in the royal army and the inevitable yielding to Catholicism.[19]

Other couples attempted this same delicate tactic of having the husband convert to save his office, while the wife and hopefully the children remained Protestant. Jacques's sister-in-law, Blanche de Falguerolles, and her husband, the parlementary magistrate Salomon de Faure, pursued a similar course: he abjured; she remained adamantly Reformed. The strength of commitment among these women is unmistakable. As late as 1700, the Parlement of Toulouse condemned in absentia Dame Daubiais, wife of the formerly Protestant magistrate Claude de Juge. Her particular attempt to remain Protestant must have been especially arduous, as she had already fled the realm.[20]

Barbara Diefendorf, in a study of "religious schism" among Protestant families of northern France during the sixteenth century, offers some much earlier but equally compelling instances of husband-wife splits. By comparing the rolls of Protestants who abjured at Coutances in Normandy during the late 1580s with lists of persons who fled rather than convert, Diefendorf found what appears to be "a very high proportion of women who remained Protestants, even though their husbands returned to the Catholic Church." While fully endorsing Diefendorf's conclusion that the evidence demonstrates considerable courage and independence among these women, I should like to draw attention to the fact that religious division among married couples occasionally resulted from a deliberate and mutual decision.[21]

As an immediate response to the revocation of the Edict of Nantes, artificially constructed religious schism within the family possessed a certain logic. Men were typically in greater legal and personal peril if they failed to convert. Women, moreover, had traditionally attended to the rudimentary religious training of children. Finally, the device must be understood as the short-term stopgap that it could only have been meant to be. After all, who within the Huguenot community was willing to predict that the Revocation would be so lasting? Only as the years wore on did it become painfully obvious that this temporary remedy had failed these Protestant magistrates, their wives, and their children.

This not uncommon response to religious persecution points up the dilemma of Huguenots who held offices from the state. How are we to account, on the one hand, for the seemingly effortless conversion of

Protestant *parlementaires* and, on the other, for the intricate plans to retain the Protestant faith among at least some members of the family? The explanation for this apparent ambiguity lies in the peculiar position that Protestant royal officeholders had occupied since the beginnings of the religious conflict in the mid-sixteenth century.

Families such as the Lacger of Castres, the Escorbiac of Montauban, or the Ranchin and Vignolles of Montpellier retained traditional ambitions within the civic and judicial elite, while exploring new roles that opened to them as the result of their Protestantism. They were active in the many Huguenot political assemblies that met throughout France from the earliest years of the Reformation. Another prospect, one again connected to Protestantism, was patronage by important Huguenot military and political figures such as the prince of Condé or Henry of Navarre. Yet it was access to the highest levels of the provincial magistracy which these families ultimately sought. The opportunity came with the creation of the *chambre de l'Edit*, the special Protestant chamber of the Parlement of Toulouse, at Castres during the late sixteenth century. The Reformed magistrates were entitled to nine seats on the *chambre:* one presiding magistracy (*président*) and eight associate judgeships (*conseillers*).

The aspiring Huguenot houses immediately set about securing these royal positions for themselves and their heirs. As might be expected, once acquired, the offices were rarely relinquished. Fulcrand de Vignolles, a Huguenot jurist from Montpellier, became a *conseiller* when the chamber was first established in 1579. Upon his death in 1595, the office passed to a son, Jacques. When Jacques died some thirty years later, the position passed to a third generation in the person of Gaspard de Vignolles. And in 1660, the parlement received Charles de Vignolles as *conseiller* in the *chambre de l'Edit,* even though he had not yet attained the required age of twenty-five. The last three of these successive magistrates were, in addition, *présidents* of the chamber.[22]

If the Vignolles example seems a bit too predictable, it might nonetheless be viewed as the model after which others patterned themselves. Three generations of the Ranchin and Juge families methodically passed coveted offices from one generation to the next. The Escorbiac, to cite another case, first achieved the rank of *conseiller en la chambre* in 1579, at the very beginnings of the bipartisan venture. Guichard d'Escorbiac, his son, Samuel, and his grandson, Thomas, served on the court until its last days, and beyond. Jean de Lacger's family purchased the office of *conseiller* for him in 1600. It passed first to a son, Hercule, in 1624 and then to a nephew, Jacques, in mid-century.[23]

Historians have never seriously doubted that the minor Protestant nobility, dependent as it was on royal judicial offices, could not easily afford to relinquish its principal source of political power, social prestige, and economic sustenance. The Lacger and other Protestant families within the royal magistracy were, at best, treading a very tight path. This segment of the Protestant community was prepared to defend its status with dogged determination. Accordingly, family divisions at the time of the Revocation and the manner whereby they were mutually defined and determined become understandable. Even before the Edict of Fontainebleau, the formal act of revocation promulgated in October 1685, tension between political loyalties and religious adherence was an ever-present fact of life for the French Reformed community and nowhere more acute than among the judicial order. Afterward, the pull in different directions only worsened.

Conversion was not always a matter of coercion or constraint, at least not in any crude or overt fashion. The reasons could nonetheless be convincing. Jean Bruniquel, a pious and unassuming Huguenot from the rural uplands northeast of Castres, reflected upon the relatively early religious fracture within his own family. Writing in 1630 after the failure of the rebellion directed against Louis XIII and Richelieu, Bruniquel presumed that those of his kin who had abandoned the Reformed faith and "adopted the Roman religion" had done so in order to guard, keep, and protect their children.[24] The requirements of family integrity and a sense of parental obligation sanctioned, in Bruniquel's view, the decision to shift from Protestantism to Catholicism.

Within elite circles, conversion was frequently linked to the realization of professional and financial ambitions.[25] Religious conformity became a necessity for royal officials after the Revocation, and it could make a significant difference in the fortunes of others. Take, for example, the effect of conversion upon the careers of military officers or upon the wealth and position of those who abjured and then married Catholic heiresses; Jean-Jacques-Joseph de Lacger fits both these patterns.

A dozen Lacger men, many of them crypto-Protestants, served in the royal army during the century following the revocation of the Edict of

Nantes. Though Huguenots were theoretically barred from service in the officer corps, few encountered serious obstacles to admission. Whole units were reputed to be unofficially Protestant. The Regiment of Auvergne, the favorite among the Lacger, sought its officers and soldiers in the villages and towns of southern France, the very heartland of the Huguenots. Inevitably, they figured among the recruits, and as a result, the regiment acquired a certain notoriety for being Protestant.

Most "new Catholic" officers could get by with a minimum of formal compliance with the official requirements of Catholicism. In most cases, the obligations would have been no more severe than the demands made by their village curé or parish priest. Attendance at mass, for example, might be required,[26] but no one would insist too heavily upon taking the Sacrament. Younger men with commissions as lieutenants accommodated themselves to these relatively lenient circumstances. Marc-Antoine I de Lacger and several of his sons and grandsons enjoyed limited careers as junior officers. Yet promotion to the higher ranks, coveted decorations, and remunerative pensions required more substantive attestations of Catholicity.

François, Louis, and Jean-Jacques de Lacger became battalion commanders and lieutenant colonels; they were awarded the Order of Saint Louis and favored with royal pensions. The price of these considerable favors was public abjuration of the Reformed faith, oaths of fidelity to Roman Catholicism, and a life in conformity with the precepts of the king's religion. These men married according to the Catholic liturgy, sought the sacrament of extreme unction when dying, and were entombed in Counter-Reformation churches. One of them even requested the celebration of requiem masses for his eternal benefit.[27] Although such conduct suggests men who were more accommodating and docile than many other "new Catholics,"[28] their actions were, nonetheless, suffused with guilt, perhaps even shame. As they approached death, François and Jean-Jacques, for example, carefully supported, often handsomely, their Protestant relatives, making them financial legacies and substantial donations of land.[29] Moreover, François, after his retirement from the army in 1728, became a powerful civic figure at Castres for the next thirty years. His position surely enabled him to watch over the safety of his Protestant kin. Though these officers had not been able to remain Protestant themselves, they could improve the situation of, and in some ways protect, those in the family and the larger community who remained faithful to the Reformed tradition.[30]

Less rueful of his abjuration was Jean-Jacques-Joseph de Lacger. Although the motivation may have been similar—social and financial security—the circumstances of conversion were different from those of his military kin. Jean-Jacques-Joseph was born in 1718, well after the Revocation. Though the only child of Marc-Antoine I's second marriage, he had seven older half brothers and half sisters. Compounding the difficulty was the fact that, when his father died in 1720, only two years after this youngest brother's birth, family financial fortunes were at their lowest point since the early sixteenth century. Jean-Jacques-Joseph had but a paltry inheritance and few prospects. His Protestant background was a further hindrance. He initially joined the army, where moderately influential family members boosted his career in limited fashion. Bereft of substantial inheritance or professional opportunity, Jean-Jacques-Joseph opted for betterment through marriage. His choice settled upon the daughter of a newly arrived yet very rich Catholic family. It meant, of necessity, his public disavowal of Protestantism and full commitment to Catholicism. His wife, Marguerite de Roux, was a devout Catholic who, at the moment of her passing in 1762, was said to have died in the "aura of sanctity" (en odeur de sainteté). Their descendants, among whom figured several ordained priests, continued in this dedicated observation of Roman Catholic forms of piety.[31] This branch of the family remains firmly Catholic down to the present.

Yet even in this latter case, confessional fissures never alienated and did not even separate members of the family. Marc-Antoine II, a clandestine yet resolute Protestant, named a son for his Catholic half brother Jean-Jacques-Joseph. This half brother was the infant's godfather as well. Later, Jean-Jacques-Joseph had Marc-Antoine act as godfather for one of his daughters. The various Lacger officers who converted to Catholicism were also namesakes and godparents for the children of their crypto-Protestant relations.[32]

In a religious sense, the Revocation and its aftermath split the Lacger: some remained quietly Protestant, while others embraced Catholicism in varying degree and fashion. However, confessional differences born of the Revocation failed to shatter family solidarity: relatives supported and shielded one another financially and politically, and they continued to reinforce time-honored kinship relationships through the exchange of names or godparents. Family bonds transcended religious differences.

For those who struggled to resist the political and religious pressure after 1685, the course was treacherous. Active resistance was hardly a realistic possibility for the Lacger. The family's understanding of royal power and the obligation to dutiful obedience militated against it. None chose to emigrate, and they were not sympathetic with the heroic Protestant uprisings that occurred throughout the Midi in the early eighteenth century.[33] There is no evidence that the Lacger even participated in the secret religious assemblies that abounded in the Castrais beginning in the mid-1740s.[34]

There was a kind of quiet opposition, but it too was tempered by the Lacger's economic and social position as well as the legal necessity to be at least officially Catholic. Recent converts—*nouveaux catholiques* or *nouveaux convertis,* as they were frequently called—were hard-pressed in this regard. Many within the ranks of the notables played a sort of double game, performing obligatory gestures such as marriage or the baptism of children in the Catholic church, but little else. They frequently tried to avoid mass and confession unless royal commissioners and their accompanying soldiers forced them.[35] These crypto-Protestants continued to read the Bible and sing from the Psalter privately each evening. At the moment of death, some attempted to evade confession and extreme unction, the deathbed presence of a priest, and burial according to the Catholic rite.[36]

The great danger for Protestants who refused Catholic baptism, marriage, and burial was the potential loss of civil status. Since the close of the Wars of Religion in the late sixteenth century, the clergy, both Catholic and Protestant, became responsible for the legal registry of births, marriages, and deaths.[37] The development moved the community one step closer to the modern practice of a standardized *état-civil* and recorded vital statistics—births, marriages, and deaths—while permitting the churches to retain their traditional role in presiding over these fundamental rites of passage. Once the royal government expelled Protestant pastors from the kingdom in the 1680s, persons wishing to insure the legality of their marriages, the legitimacy of children born of these marriages, and the unchallenged transfer of economic assets from one generation to the next necessarily turned to the Catholic church, whose parish registers established their legal and civil status.

The baptism of infants according to the Catholic rite encountered less opposition from the Reformed community than marriage or those rituals associated with death and burial. Protestants regarded baptism at the hands of a Catholic priest as valid[38] and, in any case, did not share the strong Catholic insistence upon the absolute necessity of baptism for salvation. They might, nonetheless, be tempted to drag their feet and delay their appearance at the parish church for the ceremony, even though they generally wished the child's birth recorded in the parish register. Parents or midwives now and again privately administered a provisional or emergency baptism on the pretext that the newborn was sickly. The measure, they could always tell the authorities, had been essential to insure the salvation of an ailing infant. The practice also concealed an illicit Protestant baptism.[39]

Lacger conduct points to one especially vexing aspect of being forced to baptize children in the Catholic church—namely, the selection of a godfather and godmother. A godparent could not be a heretic, schismatic, or declared excommunicate. He or she had to be a reputable member of the church. Godparents were, after all, meant to be the spokespersons, literally the sponsors, for the infant. They promised as well to look after the child's religious upbringing. Such pledges of belief and assumptions of responsibility placed crypto-Protestants in an extremely awkward, if not precarious, position. One solution, invoked by noble and bourgeois families at Castres and Montauban,[40] for instance, was to turn to servants and agricultural tenants. Marc-Antoine I and his son Marc-Antoine II had members of the local peasantry serve repeatedly as godparents for their daughters and sons. The baptismal records describe these persons as gardeners and sharecroppers, midwives, and the wives, widows, and daughters of peasant farmers. Simon Gras, the Lacger's tenant at the *métairie* of Clot, was godfather for no less than four of Marc-Antoine I's children.[41] Some of these persons were probably Catholics; others may have been crypto-Protestants. In any event, they could, if pressed, always claim they had agreed to be godparents out of constraint. Nearly all must have been honored by the request to assist their betters. This sort of development also hints at the remarkable fashion by which the Reformed community united across socioeconomic barriers in order to contend with adversity. Oppression fostered an extraordinary cohesiveness among these Reformed coreligionists.

An altogether more irritating point of friction for crypto-Protestants attempting to endure the state-imposed Catholic religion was marriage. French Protestants, especially those with economic assets, were deeply concerned with the legality of their marriages.[42] After 1685, "new Catholics" of the nobility were, for legal and pragmatic reasons, obliged to marry before a Catholic priest. Once again, with the Revocation, the Catholic church maintained the only official registry of marriages. Yet the requirement for Catholic marriage was not as unpalatable as it might first appear. Protestants agreed that the marriage contract drawn up before the notary formed the basis for their union. Marriage was in many ways a civil matter and, in their view, certainly not a sacrament. The celebration in the church, despite the mass and other "popish" trappings, was merely a public ceremony attesting to the couple's union and assuring its proper registration.[43]

Nonetheless, marriage in the Catholic church was not always an easy matter for "new converts," particularly those in the heavily Protestant southern provinces. Many ecclesiastical officials were suspicious of their sincerity and demanded proof of Catholicity before celebrating a marriage. Young persons sometimes sought out curés who had acquired reputations for being less exacting.[44] More often, they faced long delays until they agreed to some precise renunciation of Protestant beliefs and practices, or a firmer demonstration of Catholic deportment. Marc-Antoine II de Lacger and Marie de Barrau, for instance, concluded their marriage contract in December 1725, but did not celebrate the union in the church of Notre-Dame de la Platé until February 1727, fourteen months later.[45] The reason for the delay is not wholly clear, but it likely related to the couple's uncertain religious posture. Still, families with even minimal wealth were generally careful to follow the proper forms, however onerous and distasteful, if for no other reason than to assure the legal registry and hence the validity of their marriages. Marc-Antoine II's parents had done so in 1694, his sister Louise in 1726, and other members of the family in the years that followed.[46]

By the second quarter of the eighteenth century, many Huguenots adopted the practice of marrying au Désert (in the wilds), a term recalling the scriptural language of which they were fond.[47] They celebrated their marriages before their pastors in the countryside or in private residences. French law refused to recognize the validity of these Protestant marriages and, as a result, the contracting parties left themselves open to disputes over the legitimacy of progeny and the devolution of property. A Protestant couple who married *au Désert* constantly feared that the law would declare their union concubinary. As such, it would render their children bastards, depriving them of their name and their inheritance. Protestant noble and bourgeois families, the Lacger among them, tended as a result to shun these sorts of arrangements.[48]

After 1750, increasing numbers of French writers and enlightened critics, Catholic and non-Catholic alike, argued that the law's refusal to recognize "Protestant" marriages—those contracted *au Désert*—was unduly harsh and detrimental to the entire society. Jurists and others sought a way to legalize marriages and births among these determined Calvinists without offending the Catholic clergy. The eventual but belated result was the Edict of Toleration of November 1787. Though incomplete and contradictory, it publicly acknowledged the failure of the Revocation and guaranteed Protestants the civil status that the crown had so long denied them. The Edict of 1787 offered Reformed couples several different ways to conclude valid marriages and insure the legitimacy of their children. Henceforth, Protestant marriages would be properly registered and the children born of them indisputably legitimate.[49]

Protestants resented, above all, Catholic practices surrounding death. They found the sacrament of extreme unction and the deathbed presence of the curé repugnant. The anointing with oils seemed unscriptural and superstitious. An informal comforting of the dying by the pastor was the only parallel in Reformed practice. Thus crypto-Protestants occasionally suffered an unexpected or "sudden" death.[50] Through this device their families sometimes managed to avoid summoning the Catholic clergy to the deathbed, yet they could still bury the deceased properly in the local cemetery and obtain the curé's requisite registration of the death, thereby fulfilling civil status requirements and safeguarding inheritance rights.

Other families were more wary. When Marc-Antoine I lay dying in November 1720, he and his family took the precaution of summoning the parish priest to administer the "sacraments of penance and extreme unction." A half dozen years earlier, Marc-Antoine I had acted similarly at the time of his eighteen-year-old son's death, and this despite the fact that both men were secretly Protestant.[51] The Lacger, in these instances, carefully conformed to the legal requirements in order to protect the testamentary succession and, with it, the family's continuity as well as its financial welfare. In other, less vital areas, they were defiant of Catholic practices. In 1709, for example, Marc-Antoine I refused to contribute to a Catholic charitable organization. Although the group's directors complained to the authorities, there was not much anyone could do, and his refusal did not create serious complications for him or his kin.[52] Behind this careful and frequently evasive behavior was the firm recognition of the practical necessity of being officially and legally Catholic, while meticulously protecting confessional identity and occasionally offering guarded glimpses of a firm inner spirit.

The administration of extreme unction and the Catholic burial of clandestine Protestants was an area where, by the second quarter of the eighteenth century, Catholic and royal authorities first relented in their ill-fated attempt to eradicate the Reformed tradition. By the 1730s, parish curés refused to provide the last rites and burial to persons who were Catholic in name only. Finally, a royal declaration of April 1736 permitted the civil interment of persons who had been denied "ecclesiastical burial." Persons benefiting from the royal proclamation were usually buried privately and certainly not in the local Catholic cemetery.[53]

Marc-Antoine I and at least one of his children had requested and received the last rites as well as burial in the parish cemetery when they passed away in the first several decades of the eighteenth century. Other members of the family probably did likewise at this juncture. Sixty years later, in the early 1780s, when Marc-Antoine II and his wife, Marie de Barrau, died, the family again went through the formality of asking the local priest for Catholic burial. This time, the Catholic church's response was wholly different. In both cases, the local curé refused to bury them, adding formulaically that Marc-Antoine II and Marie de Barrau were "the issue of parents who professed the *Religion Prétendue Réformée*" and that they followed it themselves. The lieutenant general of the police at Castres then authorized interment according to the provisions of the declaration of 1736. The city had for some time maintained a separate civil register for Protestant deaths.[54] Although not yet permitted an openly Protestant funeral, at least the Lacger and others were no longer obligated to follow the Catholic forms and defer to the priest.

This pattern of patient obedience, followed by gradual reemergence and resurgence, is far from exceptional. It is by no means unusual to find Huguenot lineages wherein persons baptized in the Protestant temple prior to 1685 married as "new converts" in the Catholic Church during the first decades of the eighteenth century. Their children were baptized, married, and perhaps even buried by the parish priest. Their grand-children, however, behaved differently. They celebrated their marriages before the Protestant pastor by the 1770s and had infants born of these unions christened in the Reformed church. Protestant fears concerning the legality of their civil status dissolved more than a full decade before the Edict of Toleration (1787). Beginning in 1775, for instance, François de Lacger and Julie de Terson de Paleville took each of their four infants to the Reformed pastor for baptism. She came from a staunchly deter-mined and defiant Protestant family and may well have influenced her husband; equally likely, the couple shared resolute Protestant views. Evidence of the latter comes from the fact that François's younger brother and his brother's wife had the Protestant pastor baptize their children, too. When their aunt Marthe de Lacger died in 1777, she was buried in Protestant fashion.[55] Though these actions were still not completely legal, they were by this point relatively safe. The crown and its agents showed little further interest in contesting them. Accordingly, the Huguenots of the Castrais cast off the last vestiges of concealment and subterfuge.

Reaction to the Revocation was, in the end, complex. That it could vary considerably within a single house is made clear by the Lacger expe-rience. Women often remained strongly Protestant, sometimes to the point of imprisonment. The response among men was diverse. Royal officeholders tended to convert halfheartedly, almost regretfully. A younger son sometimes submitted to Catholicism for reasons of personal advancement, and these conversions could be more definitive. Their effect was certainly more lasting. Most men and women, however, especially those of the family who could take refuge on their estates or who had other independent economic assets, quietly persevered. Among these lat-ter persons, resistance to the intense political and religious pressure required deeply rooted personal convictions, family reinforcement grounded in such matters as the private daily exercise of a Reformed piety, and above all, the continuing protection and support of a cohesive kin network.[56]

The Lacger were neither excessive nor extreme in their commitment to Protestantism. Instead, they are typical of what might be taken to have been a more ordinary approach within Protestant circles to the unceasing challenges and difficulties encountered throughout the ancien régime. These men and women vigorously maintained Protestant beliefs and practices. Mothers and fathers, particularly during the eighteenth century, took care to preserve and nurture religious traditions. Some family members, by virtue of their social and professional position, assumed leadership roles in the political dealings of the Protestant church and community. Yet they tended not to become involved in what were, strictly speaking, the church's administrative and disciplinary concerns. There were, naturally enough, some confessional defections after the Revocation. Such conversions, however, were few in number and often ambiguous in character. In any event, the differences were not permitted to divide the family. Not until the twentieth century and the emergence of a highly mobile pluralistic society did the Protestant and cadet Catholic branches drift decisively apart. From the sixteenth through the eighteenth centuries, the Lacger generally sustained, in close mutual relationship with the stable union of kin, their commitment to the Reformed tradition.

NINE

☙

Conclusion

This portrait of a provincial Huguenot family does not end with the collapse of the ancien régime. Much as they had persevered in earlier centuries, so the Lacger weathered the Revolution and the upheavals that followed. Like many Protestants, they welcomed the events of 1789 and thereafter, for the changes served to lift an oppressive royal Catholicism. The only member of the Lacger house known to have emigrated was a military officer of the cadet Catholic branch. During the nineteenth century, the family prospered on a moderate scale, building a textile mill and later establishing a private bank. Even today, while nowhere near so active as their ancestors in the political, economic, social, and religious spheres, the Lacger continue. This fundamental endurance returns us finally to our original set of questions.

How did the early modern European family undertake and adapt to change? What was the impact of larger structural shifts—the Reformation and Wars of Religion, the profound social and economic transformations that began in the sixteenth century, the development of the absolutist state, and the later proscription of Protestantism—upon its domain? Many families planned for, initiated, and, when they deemed necessary, resisted change. Their actions were hardly a succession of blind or passive responses. How, in particular, did the Lacger family interact with the processes of change? In what ways did it take advantage of opportunities and adjust to constraints? What does the process tell us about other families?

Although this has been the story of the internal dynamics of one family, the events are representative of those experienced throughout the ancien régime by numerous Protestants who belonged to the lesser provincial nobility. In addition, the Lacger struggle reveals something of the wider history of the higher social groupings in preindustrial France, and in western Europe generally. The evolution of Lacger family status was, in its broadest contours, characteristic of the development of many houses. Originally participants in an intensely local notability, they soon aspired to a regional judicial and political elite. Such accomplishment peaked, however, by the second half of the seventeenth century. Thereafter, fortunes stagnated, and the Lacger settled into the rural Protestant gentry, even adopting a faintly seigneurial style. Historians acknowledge that even within noble circles, few families met with resounding success in the endeavor to advance their situation. Many were of decidedly unexceptional stature, content in the enjoyment of the modicum of prosperity and influence that they were able to attain. Moreover, maintaining even this meager achievement could, over the long haul, be extremely difficult. Only a relative handful of families had the seeming capacity and good fortune to do so. More likely, most houses partook of a minimum level of accomplishment—they survived. Here the Lacger example serves us well.

In the attempt to describe and explain this durability, the present study has concentrated on the dense complex of family functions among the so-called notables of early modern France. A variety of elements—economic, political, social, reproductive, cultural, protective, and religious—have weighed heavily in the argument. Understandably, all were densely woven together. The family was the fundamental economic unit of early modern society, in addition to providing the basis for the political and social order. It also served as the focal point for the rearing and training of children as well as for the creation of a tenacious mesh of sheltering and supportive kinship relationships. Finally, in preindustrial Europe, the family was an important framework for bestowing and sustaining traditions of religious belief and practice.

In economic terms, the Lacger house was moderately prosperous. Its members were energetic and frugal. With one or two exceptions, they carefully husbanded their resources, passing as much as possible to the succeeding generations. Altogether, the family was neither extremely wealthy nor heavily indebted. This modest situation was far removed from that of the comfortable and leisured court nobility. Those who have studied the highest levels of the aristocracy have logically underscored the immense visible wealth associated with the great houses. William Weary, in his examination of the prominent and powerful house of La Trémoille, for instance, emphasizes the economic and political in accounting for long-term resilience and adaptability to change.[1] The Lacger were obviously not among the most important aristocratic houses, and the practices that molded their existence were not always similar to those of the more important lineages, despite certain resemblances and echoes. The Lacger pursued an unadorned lifestyle in keeping with the modest economic and social circumstances of most provincial nobles and the announced standards of Protestant comportment.

Economic and political factors were not, of course, wholly ignored by lesser families such as the Lacger. Rural estates and urban residences, rentes, judicial offices, and military commissions formed the accumulated array of assets acquired and preserved over the years and, to the extent possible, transferred to successive generations. Curiously, the pattern of inheritance and distribution of property within the Lacger family appears to be more egalitarian than in other noble houses studied by other historians. This situation may, in part, be a function of their petty noble status and rural focus. It also relates to their position as Protestants living in a hostile environment. The family took care to insure the maintenance and support of each of its members. Parents, siblings, cousins, and the like engaged in a deliberate process of collective support. Historians generally consider persistence and continuation among early modern families as dependent upon an impartibility of resources and, whenever possible, the reassembly or reconsolidation of collateral resources. Such mechanisms were no doubt critical, but no more so than mutual concern and consideration among kin.

The established patrimonial possessions, especially land and offices, also had strong linkages to the political sphere. The Lacger wielded substantial political power at Castres and in the adjoining region from roughly the mid-sixteenth through the mid-seventeenth centuries. This period corresponded to the tenure of several of its sons as judges in the municipality and county. The family's political clout waned with the abandonment of local judicial office after 1655 and then definitively evaporated following the Revocation of 1685. Meanwhile, they bore the distinctive hallmarks of the developing royal bureaucracy. There was staunch loyalty to the crown, perhaps accentuated by the attempt to dispel whatever suspicions might have resulted from religious differences. Fidelity to the king existed, furthermore, within the margins of an occupational, social, and confessional framework. The Lacger and their fellow Huguenot magistrates formed a solid professional and bureaucratic corps with collective social and cultural practices. The bonds of friendship and reciprocal obligation that united the Lacger and families of the Castrais had their basis in professional affiliation, associations of blood and marriage, intellectual formation, and religious affinity.

Talent, ability, and drive among the Lacger were indisputable. Family members first distinguished themselves as eloquent and polished magistrates of the local judiciary, the Parlement of Toulouse, and the *chambre de l'Edit* of Languedoc. They later became decorated ranking officers in the royal army. Yet such ambition had its boundaries. During the sixteenth century, several men in the family sought new opportunities for brides and offices at Toulouse, an important judicial and economic hub of southern France. Others subsequently pursued similar objectives within the expanding bureaucratic milieu of Paris. But the attempt to move beyond the family's regional base proved abortive, at best short-lived. Migration, especially to the emerging national capital, offered a chance for financial gain and professional improvement, the more so for those whose fortunes were tied to legal careers. Paris also held the promise of increased political patronage, a better marriage market, and a thriving intellectual and literary life. On the other hand, families always balanced these matters against regional associations, kinship ties, and confessional position. Even affiliations with other families tended to be localized. Regional bonds inevitably reasserted themselves. When Samuel de Lacger died at Paris in 1652, the family sold his office there to Paul Pellisson Fontanier, the poet whose association with the Lacger dated from his early years at Castres. Ultimately, the provincial focus of the Lacger's economic, political, and social interests as well as the declining fortunes of French Protestantism were crucial in hampering their ventures outside the Castrais.

Economic and political achievement was undoubtedly indispensable to the Lacger's initial rise. Long-term survival, however, must be attributed to the strength of kinship bonds and confessional identity. The family of the European past, as described by David Herlihy, was in its basic context a "moral unit and a moral universe."[2] The intense interaction among kin protected and promoted, consoled and encouraged, aided and nurtured, all members of the family. They engaged in joint support, collaborated for the achievement of common goals, and actively participated in the communal rituals that bound them together.

Reproduction was the crux, as it were, of family functions, and as we have observed, the failure to procreate could lead to irretrievable disaster, at least in the view of the concerned parties. Intimately associated with notions of maternity and paternity was the socializing process. Parents—above all, mothers—bore a heavy responsibility for the rearing and early training of their children. As children grew older and entered the municipal *collège* or university, the father took a more active role.

Family strategies came into play at every moment. When should a son or daughter be sent to another community for education, employment, or marriage? What were the most pressing considerations in arranging for the marriage of a child or the settling of an inheritance? How might a noble house advantageously marshal and add to its material assets, thus providing for its descendants and their future? Again, these concerns were never purely economic or political, but arose within the wide spectrum of human mores, collective customs, and communal rituals. The interaction made for the powerful dynamics of the early modern family.

Pecuniary sobriety and fiscal discipline indelibly marked the logic of marriage contracts as well as last will and testaments. At the same time, larger strategic objectives were at stake. Developed notions of the patrimony led, for example, to the favoring of the eldest son, a constant invocation of the principle of masculinity, and the tendency to exclude daughters from the inheritance. Likewise in their approach to education, families kept sight of well-defined goals. Protestant nobles and bourgeois, for professional necessity and spiritual satisfaction, had long valued literacy and education. These same Huguenot families, who watched the constriction of their political and military horizons after 1629, responded by concentrating even greater effort on scholarship and literary expression.

Longevity, too, had its place in this process. Members of the Lacger house frequently enjoyed lengthy and constructive adult lives. Some were remarkable, particularly when viewed against the backdrop of the demographic destructiveness that haunted this preindustrial world. Many Lacger men and women lived into their seventies, eighties, and nineties. This basic biological endurance imparted enormous stability and continuity to the lineage. It allowed the measured and deliberate transmission of wealth from one generation to the next, guaranteed the perpetuation of encompassing patriarchal authority, and offered a secure family structure for the salutary design, arrangement, and accomplishment of descendants' childhood training, youthful marriages, and mature careers.

The process of decision making within the family was largely subject to patriarchal domination. At first glance, the male head of house appears to have imposed his decisions on the other members. However, other family members, especially wives, did participate. They were frequently consulted, and a family, in many ways, shared its most important tasks. A woman, for example, shouldered a major portion of the responsibility for rearing and educating offspring. She took charge of the routine family affairs when a husband died leaving her with minor children. Moreover, among the Huguenots of France, women were an important conduit for conveying religious traditions from one generation to the next. Although they may have been less active publicly than their husbands, wives were never entirely confined to a private sphere.[3]

The bonds of obedience, deference, and responsibility, instilled under the influence of the family patriarch, held the family together. The fundamental solidarity and essential cohesiveness of the family was a virtual necessity. Parents, spouses, brothers and sisters, cousins, and aunts and uncles stood ever ready to extend aid and solicitude. They protected each other's dignity and, in conjunction with conventional perceptions of family continuity, provided one another with a sense of place and purpose. Relatives in a system of kin patronage conferred economic support in life and after death with gifts, professional preferments, and legacies. Family proved vital in securing both administrative offices and military positions. Kin also assisted in marriage arrangements and contributed toward dowries and inheritances.

Family solidarity among the Lacger rarely disintegrated during the ancien régime. To be sure, sons occasionally migrated elsewhere. Some went to nearby communities such as Toulouse or Castelnaudary. The distant magnet of Paris attracted others. Nonetheless, they retained real ties with parents, brothers, and sisters at Castres, the undisputed locus of the lineage. By the same token, the Lacger appear to have been able to minimize the sort of family hostility and friction that occasionally plagued and even split other houses. Divisive arguments and feuds between Lacger blood relatives were rare. Why? The answer seems to lie in economic necessity, a deep respect for patriarchal authority, a strong feeling of filial devotion, and the exigencies imposed by confessional duress. Family members repeatedly demonstrated affection for each other. Family solidarity, suffused by bonds of reciprocal dependency and sentiments of attachment, became a source of cultural satisfaction, psychological consolation, and spiritual encouragement.

The Lacger survived, in large part, through the creation of a close network of kinfolk. A strict allocation of resources, patriarchal control, and protective solidarity were recognized mechanisms for family survival.[4] To these must be added the principle of selectivity. It was another key in the process of adaptation. The family was both a custodian of tradition and an agent of change. Accordingly, it selected those aspects of the culture that were most useful in coping with new conditions and adapted them to new needs. In this regard, the family's role as protector and nurturer of religious views and customs was paramount.

The Lacger's Protestantism and the accompanying pressure, if not outright persecution, by the Catholic majority imbued the lineage with strength and vitality. Like many Huguenot *hobereaux,* these lesser and often financially strapped nobles from the provinces dared not hope to gain access to the brilliant world of Versailles or, after 1685, even the regional capitals. Instead, for them, fidelity to the ancestral religion substituted as a form of fidelity to noble honor and aristocratic bloodlines.

While many Protestant families of the high nobility converted and joined the Catholic church over the course of the seventeenth century, these provincial nobles remained devoted to Protestantism.[5] The issue of Protestantism and the determination that it imparted to those who practiced it goes still further. Philippe Joutard and others have argued that but for the Revocation, the Protestant minority would have been slowly and progressively absorbed into the Catholic majority. Persecution, far from destroying the Protestant community of France, reinvigorated it.[6] The Lacger and their coreligionists took special pride in perpetuating the Protestant tradition. In addition, the psychology of the minority, the condition of every French Protestant, generated a fierce and stubborn resolve that went beyond the basics of respect and devotion.

Adherence to the Reformed faith unquestionably and inevitably acted as a barrier, placing a ceiling on family aspirations. For the most part, however, the Lacger refused to abandon it. Their experience suggests that the lesser Protestant nobility was more resistant to religious pressure after 1685 than is sometimes supposed.[7] A few notable and ambiguous exceptions occurred during the eighteenth century. For younger and often financially disadvantaged sons, conversion to Catholicism sometimes opened economic and marital horizons. Witness the several military officers or the cadet half brother who publicly abjured Protestantism in the late 1600s. Even so, religion was never permitted to damage or adversely affect kinship relationships. Relatives at every level refused to be put off by religious differences. Brothers may have varied in their religious choices during the sixteenth century; nonetheless, they collaborated resolutely toward the attainment of agreed family objectives. Almost two centuries later, newly converted Catholic men were attentive to the welfare of both Protestant and Catholic nieces and nephews. Similarly, Catholic and Protestant half brothers invited each other to serve as godparents for their newborn children and generally cooperated for the greater benefit of the entire family.

Protestantism and the minority position to which it was relegated in France undoubtedly strengthened the kinship bonds. Internal obligations assumed greater urgency as Protestant families, under constant assault from an exterior Catholic enemy, struggled to endure. The matter transcended aspirations to higher economic or social position. Younger siblings, male and female, deserved respectable status and adequate resources.

Otherwise, they might—as a few occasionally did—find themselves compelled to forsake the Reformed religion, and their descendants might eventually drift dangerously far from the lineage. Thus younger children within these Protestant houses shared in the inheritance and were provided marriages in a pattern somewhat more egalitarian than that practiced among the Catholic nobility of southern France.

The same focused determination is evident in the external alliances that the Lacger forged. Their associations, constructed on the basis of marriage, professional connections, and political interest, were, by the mid-seventeenth century, mostly confined to a finite group of Protestant families in the Castrais. They and others like them practiced an explicit confessional endogamy or, better yet, an endogamy of conscience. These families shared economic and professional aspirations, arranged marriages between their children, and partook of a common faith. Not surprisingly, basic religious rituals, such as baptism and the choice of godparents, or marriage and the selection of spouses, served as a means to validate existing social relationships. These were the ties that bound tighter.

Even so densely Protestant a world as Castres and its immediate surroundings could not wholly avert the confusion and strife that accompanied events such as the sixteenth-century Wars of Religion or the uprisings of the 1620s. The Huguenots maintained independent views and different, sometimes divisive, strategies on the religious question and related violence. They sought diverse objectives and proposed differing tactics. After 1685, however, most of the bickering dissolved in the face of the enormous external threat and was replaced by an understandable moral unity and interior strength.

In the final analysis, the provincial world of the Lacger was clearly less brilliant than life among the great aristocrats at the power centers of Paris and Versailles. Though these lesser lineages, Protestant and provincial, suffered repeatedly from the turbulence of war and persecution, family structure and religious identity provided an essential stability and ongoing equilibrium.

The Lacger were and are an established Protestant family whose history is remarkably illuminated by exceptionally rich documentation. Not unlike other petty noble families from the relatively cohesive and homogeneous Protestant community of southern France, they were ambitious, long-lived, and deeply reliant upon one another. The Lacger shared a cluster of traits common to elite families of the period. They rose rapidly in the sixteenth century, utilized royal officeholding as the essential means for their ennoblement, and constructed a patrimony based on land, *rentes*, and posts in both the judiciary and the military. The family pursued marriages with an eye to their decisive effect upon economic and social advancement, and emphasized the strategic value of agnatic inheritance. Some family members enjoyed considerable political and intellectual accomplishment, and all exercised broad local influence. Permeating these developments was an encompassing network of kin. And the Lacger's Protestantism, while it set them apart and imposed restrictions, immeasurably assisted in their survival to the present. For this family and others like it, blood kinship and confessional identity made common cause. The abiding symbiosis of blood and belief, cooperatively sustaining and reinforcing, empowered the Lacger for generation upon generation.

List of Abbreviations

Notes

Chapter One

1. Marc-Antoine was, at christening, named for his father. To avoid confusion, it seems best to refer to them as Marc-Antoine I and Marc-Antoine II.

2. C. Barrière-Flavy, "La seigneurie de Navès: Etude historique sur une terre noble du pays de Castres (1244–1750)," 113–34, 280–91.

3. Roger Doucet, *Les institutions de la France au XVIe siècle*, 2:485–86. Marcel Marion, *Dictionnaire des institutions de la France aux XVIIe et XVIIIe siècles,* 244.

4. The *recherche*, the most complete for southern France during the ancien régime, was part of a near kingdom-wide investigation initiated at the command of Colbert. At Castres and in the surrounding region, it was conducted under the auspices of Claude Bazin, sieur de Bezons, intendant of Languedoc. He confirmed Lacger claims with a *jugement de noblesse* of 15 January 1671. AL, copie des actes, vol. 5, fols. 140–41v. See, in general: Claude Bazin, sieur de Bezons, *Jugements sur la noblesse de Languedoc, Généralité de Toulouse,* vol. 2 of *Pièces fugitives pour servir à l'histoire de France.*

5. James B. Wood, *The Nobility of the Election of Bayeux, 1463–1666: Continuity through Change,* 3–42.

6. The principal categories of documents gathered and copied by Jean-Jacques-Joseph de Lacger were: (1) legal records such as contracts for the sale or purchase of land, last will and testaments, inventories after death, marriage contracts, and documents associated with legal suits; (2) private records, including cadastral surveys as well as receipts for various payments and debts; (3) accounts for harvests, sales of grain and animals, and households expenditures; and (4) correspondence, mainly letters received, which included business as well as personal letters and instructions from various governmental authorities. Unfortunately, there are very few copies of letters sent. Except for a handful of records necessary for the *recherches de noblesse,* the originals were subsequently destroyed.

7. Compare it, for example, to the much shorter (approximately 150 pages) and more businesslike seventeenth-century *livre de mémoires* kept by Jacques de Ranchin, a Protestant magistrate whose situation resembled that of the Lacger. AD, Haute-Garonne, E 700.

8. Very few family portraits survive. Besides a later (1804) miniature of Jean-Jacques-Joseph, there are oil paintings of Jacques, a seventeenth-century judge, and two eighteenth-century military officers, François and Jean-Louis.

9. AL, copie des actes, vol. 5, fol. 1.

10. Natalie Z. Davis, "Ghosts, Kin, and Progeny: Some Features of Family Life in Early Modern France," 96–100. For an extended discussion of the notion of race and the qualities thought to be transmitted by blood, see Arlette Jouanna, *L'idée de race en France au XVIe siècle et au début du XVIIe*, especially 1:51–103. Ellery Schalk, *From Valor to Pedigree: Ideas of Nobility in France in the Sixteenth and Seventeenth Centuries*, underscores the increasing stress upon heredity, birth, and blood among the French nobility by the early seventeenth century.

11. The brief, twenty-four page *Généalogie historique de la maison de Lacger, de la ville de Castres, Haut-Languedoc* was presented to the family on 30 June 1775.

12. Regarding the value of such papers, see the remarks of Monique Cubells, "A propos des usurpations de noblesse en Provence, sous l'Ancien Régime," especially 300–301.

13. Jonathan K. Powis, *Aristocracy*, 14–19.

14. A recent study of the Verneys, a prominent English family, makes this very point. Miriam Slater, *Family Life in the Seventeenth Century: The Verneys of Claydon House*.

15. The literature on the early modern French nobility is immense. Among the more helpful recent studies are: Davis Bitton, *The French Nobility in Crisis, 1560–1640*; Guy Chaussinand-Nogaret, *The French Nobility in the Eighteenth Century: From Feudalism to Enlightenment*; Jean-Marie Constant, *Nobles et paysans en Beauce aux XVIème et XVIIème siècles*, and idem, *La vie quotidienne de la noblesse française aux XVIe–XVIIe siècles*; Jonathan Dewald, *The Formation of a Provincial Nobility: The Magistrates of the Parlement of Rouen, 1499–1610*, and idem, *Pont-St-Pierre, 1398–1789: Lordship, Community, and Capitalism in Early Modern France*; Barbara B. Diefendorf, *Paris City Councillors in the Sixteenth Century: The Politics of Patrimony*; Robert Forster, *The Nobility of Toulouse in the Eighteenth Century: A Social and Economic Study*, and idem, *The House of Saulx-Tavanes: Versailles and Burgundy, 1700–1830*; Robert R. Harding, *Anatomy of a Power Elite: The Provincial Governors of Early Modern France*; George Huppert, *Les Bourgeois Gentilshommes: An Essay on the Definition of Elites in Renaissance France*; Jouanna, *L'idée de race*; Sharon Kettering, *Patrons, Brokers, and Clients in Seventeenth-Century France*; Jean-Pierre Labatut, *Les ducs et pairs de France au XVIIe siècle*; Jean Meyer, *La noblesse bretonne au XVIIIe siècle*; Kristen B. Neuschel, *Word of Honor:*

Interpreting Noble Culture in Sixteenth-Century France; Schalk, *From Valor to Pedigree;* William W. Weary, "The House of La Trémoille, Fifteenth through Eighteenth Centuries: Change and Adaptation in a French Noble Family," on demand article. James B. Wood's *The Nobility of the Election of Bayeux* is something of an exception in that it considers the broad spectrum of the nobility in an essentially rural environment.

16. Several recent works on the Revocation include Janine Garrisson, *L'Edit de Nantes et sa révocation: Histoire d'une intolérance;* Elisabeth Labrousse, *"Une foi, une loi, un roi?" Essai sur la révocation de l'Edit de Nantes,* and idem, "Understanding the Revocation of the Edict of Nantes from the Perspective of the French Court," in Richard M. Golden, ed., *The Huguenot Connection: The Edict of Nantes, Its Revocation, and Early French Migration to South Carolina,* 49–62; Jean Quéniart, *La Révocation de l'Edit de Nantes: Protestants et catholiques français de 1598 à 1685.* Solange Deyon, *Du loyalisme au refus: Les protestants français et leur député général entre la Fronde et la Révocation,* traces the deterioration of the Huguenot political position in the decades prior to the Revocation.

17. For a recent study, see Neuschel, *Word of Honor,* an examination of the more prominent warrior nobility in the region of Picardy.

18. Cf., for example, the seigneurial fortresses of Auvergne described by Pierre Charbonnier, *Une autre France: La seigneurie rurale en Basse-Auvergne du XIVe au XVIe siècle,* 2:1144–48.

19. The wide differences and often bewildering absence of unity among the French nobility is aptly pointed up by David Bien, "Manufacturing Nobles: The Chancelleries in France to 1789," 484.

20. Nearly a century later, for instance, in November 1757, royal tax officials challenged, albeit unsuccessfully, the *"noblesse"* of Marc-Antoine II de Lacger. AD, Herault, C 1640.

21. Elisabeth Labrousse, "Calvinism in France, 1598–1685," in Menna Prestwich, ed., *International Calvinism, 1541–1715,* 285–86. Quéniart, *La Révocation de l'Edit de Nantes,* 25.

22. Jouanna, *L'idée de race,* 1:323–408 and 2:455–69.

23. There were important legal distinctions in the preferential treatment of the children of nobles as opposed to those of commoners. Much depended on whether the property in question was a seigneurial fief that, in noble succession, was meant to pass intact to the eldest son. See Ralph E. Giesey, "Rules of Inheritance and Strategies of Mobility in Prerevolutionary France," 276–77.

24. André Corvisier, *L'armée française de la fin du XVIIe siècle au ministère de Choiseul: Le soldat,* 1:290–91.

25. Janine Garrisson-Estèbe [Garrisson], *Protestants du Midi, 1559–1598,* 159–224. For the general context of these Protestant political assemblies, see: Léonce Anquez,

Histoire des assemblées politiques des réformées de France (1573–1622); Gordon Griffiths, *Representative Government in Western Europe in the Sixteenth Century,* 254–97; J. Russell Major, *Representative Government in Renaissance France,* 205–58.

26. For the wider background to this sort of political and household clientage among the great aristocratic families, see: Harding, *Anatomy of a Power Elite,* 26–29.

27. AD, Tarn-et-Garonne, 1 Mi 1, extraits du chartrier de Scorbiac. Janine Garrisson-Estèbe [Garrisson], *L'homme protestant,* 54–61. Eugène Haag and Emile Haag, *La France protestante, ou vies des protestants français* 6:65–74.

28. On the subject of Ferrier, see: P. Koch, "Jérémie Ferrier, pasteur de Nîmes (1601–1613)," 9–21, 152–63, 237–61, 341–70; Joël Poivre, *Jérémie Ferrier (1576–1626): Du protestantisme à la raison d'état.*

29. For further discussion of these and other Protestant reactions to the revocation of the Edict of Nantes, see: Philippe Joutard, "The Revocation of the Edict of Nantes: End or Renewal of Protestantism?" in Prestwich, *International Calvinism,* 339–68.

30. G. Dumons, "La famille de Nautonier de Castelfranc," 385–402. Marc Vène, *Guillaume le Nautonier, seigneur de Castelfranc.* Bezons, *Jugements sur la noblesse, Généralité de Toulouse,* vol. 2 of *Pièces fugitives,* 99. Jacques Gaches, *Mémoires sur les guerres de religion,* 125, 140, 473.

31. On the subject of lay involvement in French Protestantism, particularly by the middle social groups and lesser nobility of southern France, see: Raymond A. Mentzer, Jr., "Ecclesiastical Discipline and Communal Reorganization among the Protestants of Southern France," 165–85.

32. Gaston Mercier, "La maison de Calvairac: Comment ils ont tenu," 73 (1924): 313–23; 74 (1925): 21–30, 141–48, 261–74, 453–63. On the question of Protestants and Catholic testaments, see the brief remarks of Garrisson-Estèbe, *L'homme protestant,* 76.

33. See, for example, Emile-G. Léonard, *Mon village sous Louis XV, d'après les mémoires d'un paysan,* 239–40.

34. Jean-François Bouyssou, "La composition sociale des révoltes de Rohan à Castres (1610–1629)," 149–50.

35. Edgard de Balincourt, "Les d'Espérandieu d'Uzès et de Castres (1360–1866)," 181–244. Bezons, *Jugements sur la noblesse, Généralité de Toulouse,* vol. 2 of *Pièces fugitives,* 58.

36. Martin Wolfe, *The Fiscal System of Renaissance France,* is very helpful on these matters.

37. Robert Sauzet, *Contre-réforme et réforme catholique en Bas-Languedoc: Le diocèse de Nîmes au XVIIe siècle,* 190–210.

38. AM, Nîmes, RR 60, fols. 22–22v, 29v. Bezons, *Jugements sur la noblesse, Généralité de Montpellier,* vol. 1, pt. 2 of *Pièces fugitives,* 311. Sauzet, *Contre-réforme et*

réforme catholique, 267, 305–10, 314, 452. And above all, Prosper Falgairolle, *Une famille de l'ancienne France: Les Baudan à Nîmes et à Montpellier pendant quatre siècles.*

39. In addition to the families mentioned here, there are other examples of family survival among the petty Protestant nobility. Studies include: André Joubert, *Une famille de seigneurs calvinistes du Haut-Anjou: Les Chivré, marquis de la Barre de Bierné (XVIᵉ–XVIIIᵉ siècles);* and for bourgeois families: H. de Bellecombe, *Les Denis: Une famille bourgeoise de l'Agenais du XVIIᵉ au XVIIIᵉ siècle;* Louis Malzac, *Les Pourtalès: Histoire d'une famille huguenote des Cévennes, 1500–1860;* Elisée de Robert-Garlis, *Monographie d'une famille et d'un village: La famille de Robert et les gentilshommes verriers de Gabre;* Louis Soubeyran, *Essai historique et généalogique sur les Soubeyran ou Soubeiran cévenols.*

40. See, for example, the comments of Marc Bloch, *Les caractères originaux de l'histoire rurale française,* 129–31.

Chapter Two

1. Several confused genealogical claims predate 1523, most notably the alleged testament of a certain Antoine de Lacger dated 10 January 1518. Though it was cited for the *recherche de noblesse* of 15 January 1671, no copy of the document survives, and it seems unlikely that a copy existed in the seventeenth century. Moreover, the precise place of the alleged testator within the family remains unclear. AD, Hérault, C 1640. AL, copie des actes, vol. 1, fol. 1. Bibliothèque, SHPF, MS. Baron de Cazals, généalogie de la famille de Lacger. *Généalogie historique de la maison de Lacger,* 1.

2. Godefroy E. de Falguerolles, "Les paroissiens de l'Eglise Réformée à Puylaurens (1630–1650)," 89–108. Charles Pradel, *Notes historiques sur la ville de Puylaurens,* 3–30, 83–84.

3. Lucie Larochelle, "Le vocabulaire social et les contours de la noblesse urbaine provençale à la fin du moyen âge: L'exemple aixois," 163–73, offers a succinct discussion of these various terms.

4. See the fundamental work of Jean-Richard Bloch, *L'anoblissement en France au temps de François Iᵉʳ,* especially 27–36. Constant, *Nobles et paysans en Beauce,* 45–73, describes ennoblement in that region. On the subject of usurpation of nobility in the neighboring region of Provence: Cubells, "A propos des usurpations de noblesse," 224–301.

5. The name of this obscure holding also appears in Occitan as Laguno and occasionally in French as Lagune. AL, copie des actes, vol. 1, fol. 1; dossiers généalogiques, vol. 1, mémoire prepared by Jean-Jacques-Joseph de Lacger in 1788–89. Gaches, *Mémoires,* 193n.1.

6. AL, copie des actes, vol. 1, fols. 111v–12, 281; vol. 4, fols. 557v–58. AM, Castres, GG 34, fol. 560v. Georges Duby and Armand Wallon, eds., *Histoire de la*

France rurale, vol. 2, *L'âge classique des paysans, 1340–1789,* ed. Hugues Neveux, Jean Jacquart, and Emmanuel Le Roy Ladurie, 127–31. Germain Sicard, *Le métayage dans le Midi toulousain à la fin du moyen âge, Mémoires de l'Académie de Législation,* examines the medieval background of sharecropping in southern France. For a useful discussion of the meaning of *métairie* and *borderie,* see the remarks of Louis Merle, *La métairie et l'évolution agraire de la Gâtine poitevine de la fin du moyen âge à la Révolution,* 99–102. See also Philip T. Hoffman, "The Economic Theory of Sharecropping in Early Modern France," 309–19; and Peter H. Amann, "French Sharecropping Revisited: The Case of the Lauragais," 341–68, for the modern period. For sharecropping in the Nivernais region of central France, see: John W. Shaffer, *Family and Farm: Agrarian Change and Household Organization in the Loire Valley, 1500–1900,* especially 49–52.

7. ". . . nobilis vir Petrus Lacger dominum de Lagune(?) habitator Podio Laurenci . . ." Of the three *métairies* at Labarthe, Saint-Jacme, and Soual, the last was the largest and richest. AL, copie des actes, vol. 1, fols. 1–3v, 40, 142v–43; dossiers généalogiques, vol. 1, testament de noble Pierre de Lacger du 20 mars 1523. *Généalogie historique de la maison de Lacger,* 1.

8. AL, copie des actes, vol. 1, fols. 1v–3v. Pradel, *Notes historiques,* 58–70.

9. A paucity of surviving records coupled with the demographic dislocations and fluctuations associated with the recurrent religious warfare and numerous sieges as well as the endemic famines and plagues makes it difficult to estimate the sixteenth-century population of Castres. Mathieu Estadieu, *Annales du pays castrais depuis les temps les plus reculés jusqu'à nos jours,* 302, advances the improbable and conflicting population figures of 6,500 for 1564 and 9,500 for 1566. Georges Frêche, "La population de Castres et du Tarn de 1665 à 1968," 191–213, expresses confidence in an estimate of 10,500 inhabitants for 1695. He feels less comfortable with the tentative figure of 6,900 for 1665. The latter number results from a census commissioned by Henri d'Aguesseau, the intendant of Languedoc during the middle years of Louis XIV's reign (ca. 1665). AN, TT 247, dossier 16. Paul Gachon, *Quelques préliminaires de la révocation de l'Edit de Nantes en Languedoc (1661–1685),* xxix–xlv, has published the figures for all of Languedoc. For a general discussion of these and related questions, see: Philip Benedict, "La population réformée française de 1600 à 1685," 1433–65. During the Middle Ages, Castres's pre–Black Death population may have reached 9,500; the number subsequently fell to about 4,200. Philippe Wolff, "Trois études de démographie médiévale en France méridionale," in *Studi in onore di Armando Sapori,* 1:498–500.

10. By the end of the seventeenth century, the industry had collapsed under the weight of over-regulation, stiff competition, and the disruption of religious persecution. O. Granat, "L'industrie de la draperie à Castres au dix-septième siècle et les 'ordonnances' de Colbert," 10 (1898): 446–57 and 11 (1899): 56–67.

11. Agricultural holdings in the Castrais were traditionally small. In the eighteenth century, 85 percent were less than ten hectares. Georges Frêche, *Toulouse et la région Midi-Pyrénées au siècle des lumières (vers 1670–1789)*, 170–71.

12. AD, Tarn, E 1404, fols. 157v–58v; H 204, fol. 89v; H 205, fols. 169–70, 244v–45v; H 216, fols. 285v–86v. AL, copie des actes, vol. 1, fols. 2v–3, 9–10v, 206v–7, 219v; vol. 4, fols. 79–86v; dossiers généalogiques, vol. 1, contrat de mariage du 22 septembre 1531. Charles Portal, *Les anciennes mesures agraires du Tarn*, 3–4 and 19–20.

13. AL, copie des actes, vol. 1, fols. 5–5v, 30v–31, 50v–51; vol. 4, fols. 539–43v; vol. 5, fols. 37–38. Doucet, *Institutions* 2:515–16. Gustave Dupont-Ferrier, *Les officiers royaux des bailliages et sénéchaussées et les institutions monarchiques locales en France à la fin du moyen âge*, 400–401. Maurice Greslé-Bouignol, *Guide des Archives du Tarn*, 76–77.

14. These arrangements originated in the attempts to circumvent the prohibitions on usury. Dewald, *Provincial Nobility*, 116–22, 231–40. Giesey, "Rules of Inheritance," 278–81. Huppert, *Bourgeois Gentilshommes*, 141–44. Paul Ourliac and J. de Malafosse, *Histoire du droit privé*, vol. 2, *Les biens*, 34–35, 412–16. Wolfe, *Fiscal System*, 91–93.

15. AL, copie des actes, vol. 4, fol. 427v; dossiers généalogiques, vol. 1, mémoire. AD, Tarn, E 231.

16. Land, offices, and *rentes* were the classic elements of noble wealth, what one historian has termed proprietary wealth. All entailed few risks and provided high stability, even if offering a low return. George V. Taylor, "Noncapitalist Wealth and the Origins of the French Revolution," 469–96.

17. AL, copie des actes, vol. 1, fols. 12v–13, 20v–30, 207v. Fleury Vindry, *Les parlementaires français au XVI* siècle, vol. 2, pt. 2: 215–16.

18. AL, copie des actes, vol. 1, fols. 14, 16v, 37, 163.

19. AL, copie des actes, vol. 1, fols. 30v–31; vol. 5, fols. 140–41v; dossiers généalogiques, vol. 3, provisions de l'office du 30 avril 1560. *Généalogie historique de la maison de Lacger*, 2, and pièces justificatives, i–ii. Bibliothèque, SHPF, MS. Cazals, généalogie.

20. AL, copie des actes, vol. 1, fols. 18v, 38v–39, 43–44, 118v, 123v, 145–46v, 158v–59. Gilles Caster, *Le commerce du pastel et de l'épicerie à Toulouse, 1450–1561*, remains the principal study of the woad trade.

21. AL, copie des actes, vol. 1, fols. 8v–44. Estadieu, *Annales*, 431–33.

22. AL, copie des actes, vol. 1, fol. 194v; vol. 2, fols. 103–7v; vol. 4, fols. 79–86v.

23. AL, copie des actes, vol. 1, fols. 46v, 48v–49, 201–4, 219v, 253v–54.

24. Persons of lesser social and economic status, especially men, tended to remarry very quickly when widowed. For them, the family was a basic economic

unit whose disruption spelled disaster. Martine Segalen, *Historical Anthropology of the Family*, 33.

25. Gabrielle de Marion, or de Ruffiac, had a son, Charles Gairal, by her first husband, Giscard Gairal. AL, copie des actes, vol. 1, fols. 36, 40–40v, 145–46v. Vindry, *Parlementaires français*, vol. 2, pt. 2:216.

26. AL, copie des actes, vol. 1, fols. 39–40; dossiers généalogiques, vol. 1, mémoire. Gaches, *Mémoires*, 24. *Histoire ecclésiastique des Eglises Réformées au royaume de France*, 3:158. Jean Prouzet, *Les guerres de religion dans les pays d'Aude, 1560–1596*, 19–20.

27. On the career of Jean de Coras, see: Natalie Z. Davis, *The Return of Martin Guerre*. A. London Fell, *Origins of Legislative Sovereignty and the Legislative State*, especially 1:25–47 and 2:198–215.

28. AL, copie des actes, vol. 1, fols. 34–34v; dossiers généalogiques, vol. 1, pactes de mariage du 19 juin 1561. Doucet, *Institutions*, 1:154–59. Gaston Zeller, *Les institutions de la France au XVIe siècle*, 115–17.

29. François de Bouffard, seigneur de Fiac, who came from locally prominent Protestant aristocratic stock, perished in the plague of late 1570 or early 1571. Jean Faurin, *Journal de Faurin sur les guerres de Castres*, 58–59. Gaches, *Mémoires*, 9, 59–61, 108.

30. A widow with children could only have usufruct of the *augment*. Although the dowry was theoretically restored to a widow, as a matter of practice, when the marriage had produced children, restitution came only if she remarried or had a severe misunderstanding with the children. AL, copie des actes, vol. 1, fols. 55–55v, 209v–11; dossiers généalogiques, vol. 1, pactes de mariage du 25 mai 1576. André Gouron, "Pour une géographie de l'augment de dot," 113–30. Jean Hilaire, "L'évolution des régimes matrimoniaux dans la région de Montpellier aux XVIIe et XVIIIe siècles," 153–55, 183–86. Gabriel Lepointe, *Droit romain et ancien droit français: Régimes matrimoniaux, liberalités, successions*, 231–33. Paul Ourliac and J. de Malafosse, *Histoire du droit privé*, vol. 3, *Le droit familial*, 281–85. Adolphe Tardif, *Le droit privé au XIIIe siècle d'après les coutumes de Toulouse et de Montpellier*, 82–84.

31. Susan D. Amussen, *An Ordered Society: Gender and Class in Early Modern England*, 74–75, offers some seventeenth-century English examples of the economic advantages of serial marriage.

32. See, for example, the comments of Diefendorf, *Paris City Councillors*, 268–70.

33. AL, copie des actes, vol. 1, fols. 194v, 201–4, 219v–22v; vol. 4, fols. 543–58v; dossiers généalogiques, vol. 1, mémoire. Bibliothèque, SHPF, MS. G, dossier Romane-Musculus, no. 64. Yves Castan, *Honnêteté et relations sociales en Languedoc, 1715–1780*, 208–11. Jack Goody, "Inheritance, Property and Women: Some Comparative Considerations," in J. Goody, J. Thirsk, and E. P. Thompson, eds., *Family and Inheritance: Rural Society in Western Europe, 1200–1800*, 15–18 and 26–27.

Emmanuel Le Roy Ladurie, "Système de la coutume: Structures familiales et coutume d'héritage en France au XVIᵉ siècle," 825–46. Ourliac and Malafosse, *Histoire du droit privé*, 3:494. Jean Yver, *Egalité entre héritiers et exclusion des enfants dotés: Essai de géographie coutumière*, 155–59.

34. Antoine II had acquired, in his son's name, the land near Toulouse through his first wife, Jeanne de Coras. He, at this point, exchanged it and thereby consolidated his family's holdings. AL, copie des actes, vol. 1, fols. 38v–39, 43–45, 65v–66, 73v, 123v, 145v–46v, 158v–59, 338v–42v.

35. AL, copie des actes, vol. 1, fols. 43–44. Faurin, *Journal*, 69–70. Gaches, *Mémoires*, 151–53. Dom Claude de Vic and Dom J. Vaissète, *Histoire générale de Languedoc*, 11:573.

36. AL, copie des actes, vol. 1, fols. 45–45v.

37. AL, copie des actes, vol. 1, fols. 145v–46.

38. Antoine I de Lacger and the other unannounced Protestant jurists were witnesses to, sometimes even participants in, the many heresy trials conducted by the Parlement of Toulouse during this time. AD, Haute-Garonne, B 3424, B 3429, B 3438. Raymond A. Mentzer, Jr., *Heresy Proceedings in Languedoc, 1500–1560*.

39. For the background to this fiscal position, one which was only developing in the sixteenth century: Wolfe, *Fiscal System*, 267–68. Zeller, *Institutions*, 117.

40. Jean Dauviller, "Histoire des costumes des gens de justice dans notre ancienne France," in *Recueil de mémoires et travaux publié par la Société d'histoire du droit et des institutions des anciens pays de droit écrit*, vol. 9, *Mélanges Roger Aubenas*, 229–40.

41. AD, Haute-Garonne, B 56, fols. 249–51, 557v–58, 567; B 57, fols. 65, 70–73v; B 64, fol. 69; B 67, fols. 478v–79; E 916. AL, copie des actes, vol. 1, fols. 26, 34–34v, 207v–9v; dossiers généalogiques, vol. 1, commission de Henri de Navarre du 29 décembre 1569. Jules Cambon de Lavalette, *La chambre de l'Edit de Languedoc*, 15–16. Joan Davies, "Persecution and Protestantism: Toulouse, 1562–1575," 31–51. Janine Estèbe [Garrisson], *Tocsin pour un massacre: La saison des Saint-Barthélemy*, 152–54; and idem, "Les Saint-Barthélemy des villes du Midi," in *Actes du Colloque l'Amiral de Coligny et son temps*, 717–29. Gaches, *Mémoires*, 75 and 117–20. Mark Greengrass, "The Anatomy of a Religious Riot in Toulouse in May 1562," 367–91. Raymond A. Mentzer, Jr., "Calvinist Propaganda and the Parlement of Toulouse," 269–70. Charles Pradel, ed., "Lettres de Coras, celles de sa femme, de son fils et des ses amis," 1–56. Paul Romane-Musculus, "Les protestants de Toulouse en 1568," 69–94.

42. AL, copie des actes, vol. 1, fols. 44, 145v–46, 163. Bibliothèque, SHPF, MS. Cazals, généalogie. Gaches, *Mémoires*, 23–24, 74, and 193 n.2. *Histoire ecclésiastique* 3:157–58. Prouzet, *Guerres de religion*, 19–20.

43. Gaches, *Mémoires*, 42 and 116–17. Camille Rabaud, *Histoire du protestantisme dans l'Albigeois et le Lauragais*, 1:112–13. Concise but older summaries of the events at

Castres can be found in Pierre Cabrol, *La Réforme et les guerres de religion à Castres des origines à l'Edit de Nantes*, and Louis de Lacger, *Histoire religieuse de l'Albigeois*, 189–92.

44. On the development of the *politiques* generally, see: J. H. M. Salmon, *Society in Crisis: France in the Sixteenth Century*, 96–201. A recent and helpful critique is Christopher Bettinson, "The Politiques and the Politique Party: A Reappraisal," in Keith Cameron, ed., *From Valois to Bourbon: Dynasty, State and Society in Early Modern France*, 35–49.

45. Gaches, *Mémoires*, 193–94. Rabaud, *Protestantisme dans l'Albigeois*, 1:132–35.

46. AL, copie des actes, vol. 1, fols. 37v–38, 186. Antoine Batailler, *Mémoires de Batailler sur les guerres civiles à Castres et dans le Languedoc, 1584–1586*, 36, 39. Gaches, *Mémoires*, 298–99, 304, 308, 349–50. Rabaud, *Protestantisme dans l'Albigeois*, 1:75–77, 132–35. Vic and Vaissète, *Histoire de Languedoc*, 11:723–24, 732.

47. AL, copie des actes, vol. 2, fols. 38–40v, 51–66v, 130v, 168v, 186v–87, 295–98v, 357v; vol. 3, fol. 376v. *Généalogie historique de la maison de Lacger*, pièces justificatives, vi–ix. Jean de Bouffard-Madiane, *Mémoires de J. de Bouffard-Madiane sur les guerres civiles du duc de Rohan, 1610–1629*, 33–36, 150, 153, 169, 195, 213, 270. Bouyssou, "Révoltes de Rohan," 145–67.

48. Other families at Castres and elsewhere similarly experienced and surmounted confessional splits within their ranks. Arlette Jouanna, *Le devoir de révolte: La noblesse française et la gestion de l'état moderne (1559–1661)*, 163–65.

49. AL, copie des actes, vol. 1, fols. 50v–51, 54, 60, 61, 65v–66, 73v, 112–12v, 114, 123v, 146v, 158v–59, 163, 169v–72, 175–75v, 194v, 200v–201, 223v–24. Gaches, *Mémoires*, 193–94.

50. See, for example, the patriarchal and patrilineal family among the peasants and villagers of nearby seventeenth- and eighteenth-century Provence as described by Alain Collomp, "Alliance et filiation en Haute-Provence au XVIIIe siècle," 445–77; and generally idem, *La maison du père: Famille et village en Haute-Provence aux XVIIe et XVIIIe siècles*. For similar developments in the region around Agen to the west of Castres, see the recent study by Gregory Hanlon, *L'univers des gens de bien: Culture et comportements des élites urbaines en Agenais-Condomois au XVIIe siècle*, especially 97–106.

Chapter Three

1. See the remarks of Diefendorf, *Paris City Councillors*, 53–54, for this behavior elsewhere.

2. AL, copie des actes, vol. 1, fols. 111v–12, 194v, 239, 242, 253–54, 259v, 281; vol. 2, fols. 103–7v, 409v–11; vol. 3, fol. 153; vol. 4, fols. 389–96v.

3. AL, copie des actes, vol. 4, fols. 557v–58. Sicard, *Le métayage dans le Midi toulousain*, 59–60.

4. The absence of a consistent standard in expressing yields makes comparison difficult. The harvest is often, though not uniformly, recorded in *gerbes,* or sheaves, a unit of account used primarily for tax purposes. The *gerbe* varied from one area to another and was typically expressed as a certain number or percentage of *setiers.* Unfortunately, its relationship to the *setier* of Castres is unclear. AL, copie des actes, vol. 1, fols. 111v–12.

5. AL, copie des actes, vol. 1, fols. 229–30v, 259. The arrangements governing guardianship (*tutelle*) were normally set out in the father's testament, and Antoine II's was no exception. The mother generally acted as guardian, unless she was younger than twenty-five or if she remarried. Louis de Charrin, *Les testaments dans la région de Montpellier au moyen âge,* 118–22 and 227. Hilaire, "L'évolution des régimes matrimoniaux," 189–90. Ourliac and Malafosse, *Histoire du droit privé,* 3:115–20. Tardif, *Le droit privé,* 40–41.

6. Harvest records also survive for 1593–94 and 1631. Though far less complete, they confirm the dominance of wheat and, to a lesser extent, rye and oats. AL, copie des actes, vol. 1, fols. 239, 242, 259v; vol. 3, fol. 153.

7. AD, Tarn, H 204, fol. 89v; H 205, fols. 169–70; H 216, fols. 285v–86v. AL, copie des actes, vol. 1, fols. 2v–3, 219v, 281, 338v–42v; dossiers généalogiques, vol. 1, contrat de mariage du 22 septembre 1531.

8. AL, copie des actes, vol. 4, fols. 79–86v.

9. Mills were an important, established feature of many seigneurial estates. See, for example, the comments of Charbonnier, *Une autre France,* 1:255–59.

10. The Lacger were technically coseigneurs of Navès. AL, dossiers généalogiques, vol. 2, aveu et dénombrement de la terre et seigneurie de Navès du 14 juillet 1784; actes de partage du 18 avril 1786 et du 2 mars 1787. AD, Tarn, G 260; G 297; G 300, fol. 268. Barrière-Flavy, "La seigneurie de Navès," 123–25 and 288–91.

11. Irregular income is by its very nature a shadowy matter. See the discussions in Maurice H. Keen, *The Laws of War in the Late Middle Ages,* 137–55; Lee Kennett, *The French Armies in the Seven Years' War: A Study in Military Organization and Administration,* 88–98; Fritz Redlich, *The German Military Enterpriser and His Work Force: A Study in European Economic and Social History,* 1:331–70, 2:56–64.

12. AL, dossiers généalogiques, vol. 1, testament de François de Lacger du 30 octobre 1757.

13. Barrière-Flavy, "La seigneurie de Navès," 114.

14. The *métairies* at Burlats were Mas del Mines and Falguies. AL, copie des actes, vol. 1, fol. 219v.

15. The *métairies* of La Mellie and Soual had an assessed value of 5,300 and 7,000 livres in 1591. AL, copie des actes, vol. 1, fol. 219v.

16. AL, copie des actes, vol. 1, fol. 219v; vol. 2, fols. 136v–37v, 213v, 239.

17. The street was subsequently renamed rue de l'Hôtel de Ville.

18. AL, copie des actes, vol. 1, fols. 2v–3, 55–55v, 219v; vol. 4, fols. 543v–58v; vol. 5, fols. 127–31v; dossiers généalogiques, vol. 1, contrat de mariage du 22 septembre 1531; contrat de mariage du 25 mai 1576. Pierre de Lacger seems to have owned another house in town near the Porta Nova. It may have originally belonged to the family of his grandmother, Jeanne de Carles. AD, Tarn, E 1404, fols. 157v–58v; H 204, fol. 127v; H 206, fols 49v–51v.

19. AL, copie des actes, vol. 1, fol. 1; dossiers généalogiques, vol. 1, inventaire des biens de Marie de Barrau du 7 mars 1781, testament de Marc-Antoine II de Lacger, avril 1785; vol. 2, conventions de mariage entre Marc-Antoine II de Lacger et Marie de Barrau du 20 décembre 1725. AD, Tarn, G 300, fol. 268.

20. AM, Castres, BB 28, fols. 523v–35. Maurice de Poitevin, "Les offices municipaux à Castres (1690–1766)," in Gaillac et pays tarnais, Actes du XXXIe congrès de la Fédération des sociétés académiques et savantes, Languedoc-Pyrénées-Gascogne, 379–86.

21. AL, dossiers généalogiques, vol. 1, plan de la ville de Castres du 22 décembre 1773. AM, Castres, GG 24, pt. 2, fols. 118, 123–24. Estadieu, Annales, 247–49.

22. AL, dossiers généalogiques, vol. 1, testament de Jean-Jacques de Lacger du 16 juillet 1746. AM, Castres, GG 23, pt. 1, fols. 321–22. Bibliothèque, SHPF, MS. Cazals, généalogie. Généalogie historique de la maison de Lacger, 5.

23. Marion, Dictionnaire des institutions, 336.

24. On the subject of royal manufactories in Languedoc, see: William Beik, Absolutism and Society in Seventeenth-Century France: State Power and Provincial Aristocracy in Languedoc, 287–97.

25. AL, dossiers généalogiques, vol. 1, mémoire; vol. 2, plan du 5 germinal II. AM, Castres, BB 32. Bibliothèque, SHPF, MS. Cazals, généalogie. Généalogie historique de la maison de Lacger, 6–7.

26. See, for instance, the comments of Harding, Anatomy of a Power Elite, 141.

27. On the complex subject of rentes, see: Charles Lefebvre, Observations sur les rentes perpétuelles dans l'ancien droit français; and Bernard Schnapper, Les rentes au XVIe siècle: Histoire d'un instrument de crédit. James D. Tracy, A Financial Revolution in the Habsburg Netherlands: Renten and Renteniers in the County of Holland, 1515–1565, 7–27, offers a recent concise survey of the various forms of public debt throughout Europe at the close of the Middle Ages.

28. AL, copie des actes, vol. 1, fols. 40–41v, 109–9v.

29. The magistrates of Rouen also tended to loan money to "members of their immediate social group." Dewald, Provincial Nobility, 117–22.

30. AL, copie des actes, vol. 4, fols. 427v, 558; dossiers généalogiques, vol. 1, mémoire.

31. AD, Tarn, E 231. AL, dossiers généalogiques, vol. 1, mémoire.

32. AL, dossiers généalogiques, vol. 1, mémoire.

33. J.-R. Bloch, *L'anoblissement*, 76–96. Giesey, "Rules of Inheritance," 284–85. Christopher Stocker, "Office as Maintenance in Renaissance France," 21–43. For the honor and respect accorded subalternate magistrates: André Viala, *Le Parlement de Toulouse et l'administration royale laïque, 1420–1525 environ*, 1:227–33.

34. For an overview of the complex and frequently confusing system of ennoblement, see: Constant, *La noblesse française*, 104–31; Jouanna, *L'idée de race*, 1:166–75; and with specific reference to southern France, Cubells, "A propos des usurpations de noblesse," 224–301.

35. Giesey, "Rules of Inheritance," 281–85.

36. For the history of the *paulette*, see: Paul Louis-Lucas, *Etude sur la vénalité des charges et fonctions publiques*, 2:5–73; and Roland Mousnier, *La vénalité des offices sous Henri IV et Louis XIII*.

37. AD, Haute-Garonne, 3 B 1 (2), fols. 62–63v. AL, copie des actes, vol. 1, fols. 5, 8v, 30v–31, 50v–51, 175–75v, 219v–22v, 330; vol. 4, fols. 539–43v, 558v; vol. 5, fols. 37–38, 61, 67, 107v, 110, 140–41v; dossiers généalogiques, vol. 3, provisions de l'office de juge d'appeaux en faveur du Mr. Antoine de Lacger du 30 avril 1560.

38. The chamber for Languedoc is the best studied. Cambon de Lavalette, *La chambre de l'Edit*. Raymond A. Mentzer, Jr., "The Formation of the *chambre de l'Edit* of Languedoc," 47–56, and idem, "Bipartisan Justice and the Pacification of Late Sixteenth-Century Languedoc," in Jerome Friedman, ed., *Regnum, Religio et Ratio: Essays Presented to Robert M. Kingdon*, 125–32. The tribunals for Bordeaux and Grenoble have been examined by Emile Brives-Cazès, *La chambre de justice de Guyenne en 1583–84*, and Justin Brun-Durand, *Essai historique sur la chambre de l'Edit de Grenoble*. For the Parlement of Paris, see: Diane C. Margolf, "The Edict of Nantes' Amnesty: Appeals to the *chambre de l'Edit*, 1600–1610," 49–55.

39. AD, Haute-Garonne, B 1030, fols. 93–93v. Madeleine Brenac, "Toulouse, centre de lutte contre le protestantisme au XVIIe siècle," 31–36 and 43–45. Arie Theodorus Van Deursen, *Professions et métiers interdits: Un aspect de l'histoire de la Révocation de l'Edit de Nantes*, 172–74.

40. Maurice Virieux, "Une enquête sur le Parlement de Toulouse en 1718," 45.

41. AD, Haute-Garonne, B 1925, fols. 1–1v; 3 B 1 (2), fols. 62–63v; 3 B 1 (4), fols. 98v–100; 3 B 3, fols. 33–35. AD, Tarn, H 216, fols. 285v–86v. AL, copie des actes, vol. 2, fols. 311–13; vol. 4, fols. 403–5v; dossiers généalogiques, vol. 1, mémoire. AF, *Généalogie de la famille de Falguerolles* (provided through the kindness of the late Godefroy de Falguerolles, Château de Ladevèze, Lempaut).

42. At the end of the seventeenth century, the price of an office of *conseiller aux requêtes* was between fifteen and twenty-five thousand livres, an office of *conseiller à la grand'chambre* between thirty and sixty thousand livres. Jean-Claude Paulhet, "Les parlementaires toulousains à la fin du dix-septième siècle," 192.

43. AL, copie des actes, vol. 1, fols. 12v–13, 50v, 60, 207v–9v; 227v, 329v; vol. 2, fols. 196v, 202v; dossiers généalogiques, vol. 1, mémoire. David Bien, "The *Secrétaires du Roi*: Absolutism, Corps, and Privilege under the Ancien Régime," in Albert Cremer, ed., *De l'Ancien Régime à la Révolution française: Recherches et perspectives*, 153–68, and idem, "Manufacturing Nobles," 445–86. J.-R. Bloch, *L'anoblissement*, 82–87. Marion, *Dictionnaire des institutions*, 505–6.

44. Roger Chartier, Dominique Julia, and Marie-Madeleine Compère, *L'éducation en France du XVIe au XVIIIe siècle*, 168–71.

45. Guy's brother, the canon Jean, had taken a law degree at Toulouse, too. AL, copie des actes, vol. 1, fols. 6v–7, 15v.

46. AL, copie des actes, vol. 1, fols. 8v, 12v–13. Vindry, *Les parlementaires français*, vol. 2, pt. 2:215–16.

47. AL, copie des actes, vol. 1, fols. 139v–40, 149–49v, 190, 193, 199v, 215.

48. Daniel Bourchenin, *Etude sur les académies protestantes en France au XVIe et au XVIIe siècle*, 97–107. Marie-Madeleine Compère and Dominique Julia, *Les collèges français, 16e–18e siècles*, vol. 1, *Répertoire, France du Midi*, 490–96. Solange Deyon, "Les académies protestantes en France," 77–85. Jules Gaufrès, "Les collèges protestants: Nîmes," 23 (1874): 289–304, 337–48, 385–95; 24 (1875): 4–20, 193–208.

49. Bourchenin, *Etude sur les académies*, 129–37. Compère and Julia, *Les collèges français*, 1:446–50.

50. AL, copie des actes, vol. 1, fols. 200v, 225, 252v–53, 261–63v, 266–67, 276, 278, 279, 289, 290, 307v, 317, 326, 329v, 330, 333v; vol. 2, fols. 15, 48, 34, 196v, 202v, 236; vol. 4, fols. 374–85; dossiers généalogiques, vol. 1, mémoire.

51. Bouffard-Madiane, *Mémoires*, 33.

52. AL, copie des actes, vol. 2, fols. 173, 186v–87. Bibliothèque, SHPF, MS. 66, état-civil des protestants à Paris, fol. 94. Anquez, *Histoire des assemblées politiques*, 264–75. Bouyssou, "Révoltes de Rohan," 150. Gaches, *Suite des mémoires*, 3–5, 15–16. Charles Pradel, "Fragments de lettres de la cour sous les règnes de Henri IV et Louis XIII," 139–41. For a succinct summary of the La Trémoille and their place within a system of royal patronage reaching into the provincial world, see: Kettering, *Patrons, Brokers, and Clients*, 144–47.

53. AL, copie des actes, vol. 2, fols. 38–40v, 51–66v, 130v, 168v, 173, 186v–87, 295–98v, 386–98, 427–35. *Généalogie historique de la maison de Lacger*, pièces justificatives, iv–xiii.

54. The notion of the monarch as the preeminent patron is developed by J. Russell Major, "The Crown and Aristocracy in Renaissance France," 631–45.

55. Pradel, "Fragments de lettres," 147.

56. AD, Tarn, G 265, pp. 216–23. Bouyssou, "Révoltes de Rohan," 155.

57. ". . . en partie en caractères grecs et barbares" (Bouffard-Madiane, *Mémoires*, 35n.3).

58. Ibid., 33–36. AD, Tarn, fonds Passelac, 67, notaire Michel Rozier, année 1621, fols. 215v–16. AL, copie des actes, vol. 2, fols. 239ff.; dossiers généalogiques, vol. 1, mémoire. Bouyssou, "Révoltes de Rohan," 154–58. Gaches, *Suite des mémoires,* 24 n. 1. For a representative sample of Jacques's letters from Paris, see: Pradel, "Fragments de lettres," 129–47.

59. Bouffard-Madiane, *Mémoires,* 167. Bouyssou, "Révoltes de Rohan," 159–67.

60. AL, copie des actes, vol. 2, fol. 357v. Bouffard-Madiane, *Mémoires,* pièces annexées, 277–316. *Généalogie historique de la maison de Lacger,* iv–xiii.

61. AL, copie des actes, vol. 2, fols. 311–13, 351v–52, 354. Bouffard-Madiane, *Mémoires,* 195n.3.

62. Giesey, "Rules of Inheritance," 287–88, elaborates the notion of a "dynastic officialdom" that linked "family honor and public service." Cf. the comments of Dewald, *Pont-St-Pierre,* 178–89, for the ambiguous views of the Norman nobility on the developing absolutist state.

63. The Huguenot officeholder's intense, though often conflicting, "attachment to his faith and attachment to his king" was common throughout the seventeenth century. See, for example, the case of the marquis de Ruvigny described by Deyon, *Du loyalisme au refus,* especially 122–23.

64. Louis André, *Michel Le Tellier et l'organisation de l'armée monarchique,* 136. Albert Babeau, *La vie militaire sous l'Ancien Régime,* 2:304–6. André Dussauge, *Etudes sur la Guerre de Sept Ans: Le ministère de Belle-Isle: Krefeld et Lütterberg (1758),* 162–63. Kennett, *The French Armies,* 37. M. Lamy, *Précis historique sur le Régiment d'Auvergne,* 16. Sieur de Montandre-Lonchamps, ed., *Etat militaire de France pour l'année 1758,* 128. René-Louis de Roussel, *Essais historiques sur les régimens d'infanterie, cavalerie et dragons,* 10:21–34.

65. André Corvisier, *Les contrôles de troupes de l'Ancien Régime,* 2:218–19, and idem, *L'armée française,* 1:290–91, 2:770–71; Henry Lehr, *Les protestants d'autrefois: Vie et institutions militaires,* 249.

66. *Généalogie historique de la maison de Lacger,* 3–7. Lamy, *Précis historique,* 24–25, 30–37. Alexandre Mazas, *Histoire de l'ordre royal et militaire de Saint-Louis depuis son institution en 1693 jusqu'en 1830,* 1:647–48, 657–58; 2:383, 464; 3:14. Pinard, *Chronologie historique-militaire,* 8:287–88. Roussel, *Essais historiques,* 10:21–22, 34.

67. André Corvisier, *Armies and Societies in Europe, 1494–1789,* 100, 150–51, 163–64. Maxime Weygand, *Histoire de l'armée française,* 174. Charles J. Wrong, "The *Officiers de Fortune* in the French Infantry," 402–3.

68. Pierre de Briquet, ed., *Code militaire, ou compilation des ordonnances des roys de France concernant les gens de guerre,* 1:444–45. Corvisier, *Armies and Societies,* 150–51, 163–64; and idem, *L'armée française,* 1:789. Kennett, *The French Armies,* 58. Lucien Mouillard, *Les régiments sous Louis XV: Constitution de tous les corps de troupes à la solde de France pendant les Guerres de Succession à l'Empire et de Sept Ans,* 4–5, 13–14.

69. Babeau, *La vie militaire*, 2:100–142. Corvisier, *Armies and Societies*, 150–51. Kennett, *The French Armies*, 54–58. Mazas, *Histoire de l'ordre royal*, 1:647–48, 657–58. Mouillard, *Les régiments sous Louis XV*, 3–5. Roussel, *Essais historiques*, 10:21–22, 34.

70. André Corvisier, *Louvois*, 336–37. Pinard, *Chronologie historique-militaire*, 8:287–88. Redlich, *The German Military Enterpriser*, 2:133.

71. Babeau, *La vie militaire*, 2:113–14. Corvisier, *Armies and Societies*, 153, and idem, *L'armée française*, 1:289–95; 2:872–73, 962–63. Mazas, *Histoire de l'ordre royal*, 1:647–48, 657–58; 2:383, 464; 3:14.

72. A distinction between Huguenot and Protestant might usefully be made here. Alsatian (i.e., Lutheran) and foreign Protestant soldiers continued to serve in the royal regiments even after the Revocation. Henry Lehr, "Les soldats huguenots dans les armées de Louis XV," 412.

73. Bibliothèque, SHPF, MS. Cazals, généalogie. Emile-G. Léonard, "L'Institution du Mérite Militaire," 297–301.

74. Léonard, "L'Institution du Mérite Militaire," 299–301. Van Deursen, *Professions et métiers interdits*, 308–12.

75. AM, Castres, GG 21, pt. 2, fols. 79–80; GG 23, pt. 1, fols. 109–10, 321–22; GG 24, pt. 2, fols. 118, 123–24 and pt. 3, fols. 56–58.

76. AL, dossiers généalogiques, vol. 1, mémoire.

77. Babeau, *La vie militaire*, 2:312. Mouillard, *Les régiments sous Louis XV*, 34. Redlich, *The German Military Enterpriser*, 2:56–64, 221, 252.

78. François de Lacger's various royal pensions were paltry when compared to the tens of thousands of livres received by high nobles. Cf. the royal pensions of Henri-Charles, comte de Tavanes, for 1754. Forster, *House of Saulx-Tavanes*, 19. AL, dossiers généalogiques, vol. 1, mémoire. AM, Castres, BB 28, fols. 532v–35. Labrousse, *La révocation*, 159–63. Marion, *Dictionnaire des institutions*, 438–39. Mazas, *Histoire de l'ordre royal*, 1:647. Jean Orcibal, *Louis XIV et les protestants*, 44–79.

Chapter Four

1. AL, copie des actes, vol. 2, fols. 111–12.

2. AL, copie des actes, vol. 1, fols. 342v–44. Bibliothèque, SHPF, MS. Cazals, généalogie. Paul Romane-Musculus, "Généalogie des Toulouse-Lautrec, branche protestante de Saint-Germier (XVIᵉ et XVIIᵉ siècles)," 99–107.

3. Carolyn C. Lougee, *Le Paradis des Femmes: Women, Salons, and Social Stratification in Seventeenth-Century France*, especially chap. 10.

4. AD, Haute-Garonne, 3 B 1 (5), fols. 94–94v. Bezons, *Jugements sur la noblesse, Généralité de Montpellier*, vol. 1, pt. 2 of *Pièces fugitives*, 90–91, 260–63. Pierre Burlats-Brun, "La famille de Clausel," 919. Cambon de Lavalette, *La chambre de l'Edit*, 183–84. B. de Charnisay, "Les chiffres de M. l'Abbé Rouquette: Etude sur les fugitifs

du Languedoc (Uzès)," 136–49. Vindry, *Les parlementaires français,* vol. 2, pt. 2: 258–59. Gachon, *Quelques préliminaires,* xcvii.

5. AD, Haute-Garonne, 3 B 1 (2), fols. 62–63v. AL, copie des actes, vol. 5, fols. 107v, 143v–45v. Bouyssou, "Révoltes de Rohan," 160. *Généalogie historique de la maison de Lacger,* 4–5. Rabaud, *Protestantisme dans l'Albigeois,* 1:245–47. For the strength of these relationships, especially the political bonds, among the nobility of Languedoc in general, see: Mark Greengrass, "Noble Affinities in Early Modern France: The Case of Henri I de Montmorency, Constable of France," 275–311. Roger Mettam, *Power and Faction in Louis XIV's France,* suggests that family groups functioned at all administrative levels in seventeenth-century France.

6. AL, copie des actes, vol. 2, fols. 1–3. AF, généalogie de la famille de Falguerolles.

7. AL, copie des actes, vol. 1, fols. 342v–44; vol. 2, fols. 449–49v. Bibliothèque, SHPF, MS. G, dossier Romane-Musculus, no. 64.

8. AL, dossiers généalogiques, vol. 1, mémoire. Gaches, *Mémoires,* 466–67.

9. AL, copie des actes, vol. 2, fols. 136v–37v; vol. 3, fols. 424v–25v; vol. 4, fols. 111v, 493–95v, 511v, 513–14v; vol. 5, fols. 143v–45v, 156v. AM, Castres, GG 18, pt. 6, fol. 48.

10. Cf. the geographically limited "familial nebula" created through intermarriage among the nobility of Artois. Robert Muchembled, "Famille, amour et mariage: Mentalité et comportements des nobles artésiens à l'époque de Philippe II," 233–61.

11. See the comments of Forster, *The Nobility of Toulouse,* 131.

12. Although never completely closed to outsiders and "mixed marriages," the Protestant community throughout the region seems to have been marked by a strong cohesiveness. See the studies of Aubais, a village near Nîmes: Léonard, *Mon village sous Louis XV;* Robert Pic, "Les protestants d'Aubais de la Révocation à la Révolution," 53–108.

13. AL, dossiers généalogiques, vol. 1, mémoire; vol. 2, dossier François de Lacger, dossier Marc-Antoine II de Lacger; vol. 3, dossier Marc-Antoine I de Lacger. AM, Castres, GG 21, pt. 1, p. 215 and pt. 2, pp. 79–80; GG 23, pt. 1, fols. 109–10, 391–92; GG 24, pt. 3, fols. 56–58; GG 34, fols. 358–58v. Bibliothèque, SHPF, MS. Cazals, généalogie. *Généalogie historique de la maison de Lacger,* 4–7.

14. The bent toward endogamy went deep. It marked the marriage patterns of the Parisian elite and the Bayeux nobility. Diefendorf, *Paris City Councillors,* 202. Wood, *The Nobility of the Election of Bayeux,* 104–9 and 117–19. See generally, Castan, *Honnêteté et relations sociales,* 376–79; Jean-Marie Gouesse, "Parenté, famille et mariage en Normandie aux XVIIe et XVIIIe siècles: Présentation d'une source et d'une enquête," 1142. For similar trends among the peasants of Provence: Collomp, *La maison du père,* 211–14.

15. Revel, another strongly Protestant town, is less than thirty kilometers south-west of Castres. Several Lacger *métairies* lay in the general direction.

16. Rabaud, *Protestantisme dans l'Albigeois*, 2:248, 254, 570–72, 584.

17. Donna Bohanan, "Matrimonial Strategies among Nobles of Seventeenth-Century Aix-en-Provence," 505–6. Forster, *The Nobility of Toulouse*, 125–30. The chances for marriage among the legitimate children of the sixteenth-century French provincial governors was "only slightly better than 50-50." Harding, *Anatomy of a Power Elite*, 160. See also, Lawrence Stone, *The Family, Sex and Marriage in England 1500–1800*, 380–86.

18. AL, copie des actes, vol. 1, fols. 261–61v; vol. 2, fols. 196v–97; vol. 4, fols. 181, 213v; dossiers généalogiques, vol. 1, mémoire. AM, Castres, GG 28; GG 35, fols. 193v–94.

19. See the remarks of Diefendorf, *Paris City Councillors*, 150–51, for the nuances of younger sons' ecclesiastical and military careers during the sixteenth and seventeenth centuries.

20. By contrast, only 56 percent of the adult males of noble families of Toulouse studied by Forster married. The survey encompasses four generations from 1670 to 1790. Forster, *The Nobility of Toulouse*, 128.

21. Davis, "Ghosts, Kin, and Progeny," 107–8. Sarah Hanley, "Engendering the State: Family Formation and State Building in Early Modern France," 6–15. François A. Isambert et al., eds., *Recueil général des anciens lois français depuis l'an 420 jusqu'à la Révolution de 1789*, 13:469–71.

22. AL, copie des actes, vol. 1, fols. 34–34v, 314v–15; vol. 2, fols. 136v–37v. For details of the Perrin house, see: Bezons, *Jugements sur la noblesse, Généralité de Toulouse*, vol. 2 of *Pièces fugitives*, 107–8.

23. AL, copie des actes, vol. 1, fols. 34–34v, 55–55v; vol. 3, fols. 424v–25v.

24. AL, copie des actes, vol. 1, fols. 201–4, 314v–15, 342v–44; vol. 2, fols. 449–49v.

25. AL, copie des actes, vol. 1, fols. 342v–44; vol. 2, fols. 136v–37v; vol. 4, fols. 493–95v; vol. 5, fols. 143v–45; dossiers généalogiques, vol. 2, dossier François de Lacger; vol. 3, dossier Marc-Antoine I de Lacger.

26. Jean de Lacger, the sole child of this marriage, later shared in the estate of his maternal grandfather, Jean de Coras, after the older man's assassination in 1572. Coras's inheritance was the subject of a protracted legal battle involving Catholic officials at Toulouse; his second wife, Jacqueline de Bussy, and her heirs; his son Jacques de Coras; and his son-in-law Antoine II de Lacger. AL, copie des actes, vol. 1, fols. 41v–42v, 44, 56–59v, 67v–68v, 211v–14, 338v–42v.

27. AL, copie des actes, vol. 1, fols. 23v, 34–34v, 55–55v, 145v–46; dossiers généalogiques, vol. 1, mémoire.

28. AL, copie des actes, vol. 1, fols. 342v–44; vol. 2, fols. 1–3.

29. AL, copie des actes, vol. 3, fols. 424v–25v; vol. 5, fols. 143v–45v; dossiers généalogiques, vol. 1, mémoire; vol. 2, dossier François de Lacger; vol. 3, dossier Marc-Antoine I de Lacger.

30. Bohanan, "Matrimonial Strategies," 505–8. Harding, *Anatomy of a Power Elite,* 112–15. Sharon Kettering, *Judicial Politics and Urban Revolt in Seventeenth-Century France: The Parlement of Aix, 1629–1659,* 232–33. Labatut, *Les ducs et pairs,* 114–15, 144–48, 252–54. Paulhet, "Les parlementaires toulousains," 200. Dewald, *Provincial Nobility,* 262–69, offers some figures on the evolution of dowries among *parlementaires* at Rouen during the sixteenth century.

31. AL, copie des actes, vol. 1, fols. 201–4; vol. 2, fols. 136v–37v, 233–34; vol. 4, fols. 493–95v; dossiers généalogiques, vol. 1, mémoire; vol. 2, dossier Marc-Antoine I de Lacger. Burlats-Brun, "La famille de Clausel," 919.

32. AL, dossiers généalogiques, vol. 1, mémoire; vol. 2, dossier Marc-Antoine II de Lacger.

33. Robert Wheaton, "Recent Trends in the Historical Study of the French Family," in Robert Wheaton and Tamara K. Hareven, eds., *Family and Sexuality in French History,* 14–15.

34. Barbara B. Diefendorf, "Widowhood and Remarriage in Sixteenth-Century Paris," 379–95, offers an illuminating analysis of the condition of widows in northern France.

35. Marriage contracts often mentioned a husband's gift of "clothes, rings and jewelry." AL, copie des actes, vol. 1, fols. 136v–37v, 342v–44.

36. AL, copie des actes, vol. 1, fols. 55–55v; vol. 3, fols. 424v–25v; vol. 4, fols. 493–95v.

37. Hilaire, "L'évolution des régimes matrimoniaux," 153–55. Lepointe, *Droit romain et ancien droit français,* 230–34. Ourliac and Malafosse, *Histoire du droit privé,* 3:279–92. Tardif, *Droit privé,* 81–84.

38. Diefendorf, *Paris City Councillors,* 179–81, for example, found a difference of about ten years in the average age of marriage for men and women of the sixteenth-century Parisian civic elite.

39. AM, Castres, GG 21, pt. 1, p. 215. Bibliothèque, SHPF, MS. 66, état-civil des protestants à Paris.

40. AL, copie des actes, vol. 1, fols. 342v–44; vol. 2, fols. 136v–37v; vol. 4, fols. 513–14v; dossiers généalogiques, vol. 1, mémoire. Tardif, *Droit privé,* 81–83. For similar practices among the eighteenth-century nobility at Toulouse, see: Forster, *The Nobility of Toulouse,* 121–22.

41. See Dewald, *Provincial Nobility,* 290–92, for noble families' "eagerness to have children."

42. "Feda jova e marro vielh an lèu format le tropèl." It is a nineteenth-century folk saying quoted in Martine Segalen, "Le mariage et la femme dans les proverbes du

sud de la France," 275, and idem, *Love and Power in the Peasant Family: Rural France in the Nineteenth Century*, 58.

43. AL, copie des actes, vol. 1, fols. 60, 248v; vol. 2, fols. 1–3. Diefendorf, *Paris City Councillors*, 181–84.

44. AL, copie des actes, vol. 1, fols. 280v–81; vol. 2, fols. 1–3, 218, 219v–20v, 239; vol. 3, fols. 370v–80; dossiers généalogiques, vol. 1, mémoire.

45. The youngest of the female children died in infancy. AL, copie des actes, vol. 3, fols. 358, 424v–25v; vol. 4, fols. 161, 213v; vol. 5, fol. 241.

46. "L'espine suit la roze et ceux qui sont contans ne le sont pas longtemps." AL, copie des actes, vol. 3, fols. 370–71v.

47. Hilaire, "L'évolution des régimes matrimoniaux," 151–53. Lepointe, *Droit romain et ancien droit français*, 233. Tardif, *Droit privé*, 82–83.

48. AL, copie des actes, vol. 3, fol. 375v.

49. AL, copie des actes, vol. 3, fols. 370–80, 414–15, 418, 465, 540v; vol. 5, fol. 273.

50. Mark Motley, *Becoming an Aristocrat: The Education of the Court Nobility, 1580–1715*, chap. 1.

51. At the time of his death in 1523, Pierre de Lacger had two servants, a man and a woman. AL, dossiers généalogiques, vol. 1, mémoire. The parlementary magistrate Jacques and his wife had, in 1685, a household consisting of themselves and their four youngest children, two adult female relatives, a law clerk, and two domestic servants. AF, généalogie de la famille de Falguerolles. Samuel, living at Paris during the first half of the seventeenth century, also had two household servants. AL, dossiers généalogiques, vol. 1, mémoire. When Jean-Jacques, the chevalier de Lacger, died at Castres in 1746, he employed two servants, a man and a woman. AL, dossiers généalogiques, vol. 1, mémoire; vol. 2, dossier Jean-Jacques de Lacger. Cf. the substantially larger number of attendants and servants in the great noble's household: Forster, *House of Saulx-Tavanes*, 122–23; Kettering, *Patrons, Brokers, and Clients*, 214–21; Neuschel, *Word of Honor*, 162–63.

52. For the role of wives in the administration of business affairs: Dewald, *Provincial Nobility*, 281–82; Diefendorf, *Paris City Councillors*, 176–77; and generally, James B. Collins, "The Economic Role of Women in Seventeenth-Century France," 436–70. Regarding the religious sphere, see the findings of Elisabeth Labrousse for Mauvezin after 1685: "Les mariages bigarrés: Unions mixtes en France au XVIIIe siècle," in Léon Poliakov, ed., *Le couple interdit: Entretiens sur le racisme*, 167–70; idem, "Conversion dans les deux sens," 167–68; idem, "Calvinism in France," in Prestwich, *International Calvinism*, 294. Women in English Puritan households seem to have had a crucial role in children's religious education, too: Margo Todd, "Humanists, Puritans and the Spiritualized Household," 25–28. Merry E. Wiesner, "Nuns, Wives, and

Mothers: Women and the Reformation in Germany," in Sherrin Marshall, ed., *Women in Reformation and Counter-Reformation Europe: Public and Private Worlds,* 8–28, discusses, among other things, the domestic religious activities of Protestant women.

53. AL, copie des actes, vol. 1, fols. 139–140, 333v. Pradel, "Fragments de lettres," 130.

54. AL, copie des actes, vol. 3, fol. 91v; dossiers généalogiques, vol. 1, mémoire. Charrin, *Testaments,* 118–22. Christian Chêne, "Testaments, fortunes et religions: La pratique testamentaire à Ganges de la fin du XVIe siècle au debut du XVIIIe siècle," 192. Hilaire, "L'évolution des régimes matrimoniaux," 189–90. Lepointe, *Droit romain et ancien droit français,* 428–33. Ourliac and Malafosse, *Histoire du droit privé,* 3:115–20. Tardif, *Droit privé,* 40–42. For a discussion of practice at Paris, see: Diefendorf, *Paris City Councillors,* 279–88.

55. AL, copie des actes, vol. 1, fols. 201–4, 229–30v, 239, 242, 253v–54, 259, 262v.

56. AL, copie des actes, vol. 2, fol. 236; vol. 3, fols. 228v–32.

57. AD, Haute-Garonne, 3 B 3, fols. 33–35. AL, copie des actes, vol. 4, fols. 128, 207, 215, 402v, 433–33v, 511v, 513–14v; dossiers généalogiques, vol. 1, mémoire.

Chapter Five

1. Inheritance practices possessed considerable nuance and were more flexible than is suggested by an isolated reading of customary law. Bernard Derouet, "Pratiques successorales et rapport à la terre: Les sociétés paysannes d'Ancien Régime," 173–206. Gregory Hanlon and Elspeth Carruthers, "Wills, Inheritance and the Moral Order in the Seventeenth-Century Agenais," especially 151–52.

2. Nicole Castan, "La criminalité familiale dans le ressort du Parlement de Toulouse (1690–1730)," in *Crimes et criminalité en France sous l'Ancien Régime, 17e–18e siècles,* 98. Yves Castan, "Pères et fils en Languedoc à l'époque classique," 31–43, crisply describes paternal authority and summarizes the relationship between father and eldest son (and heir). If the eldest son was a failure or obviously prodigal, a father might designate a younger son as heir. Jean-Marie Augustin, *Famille et société: Les substitutions fidéicommissaires à Toulouse et en Haut-Languedoc au XVIIIe siècle,* 86.

3. Goody, "Inheritance, Property and Women," *Family and Inheritance,* 15–18, 26–27.

4. Davis, "Ghosts, Kin, and Progeny," 89–92. Diefendorf, *Paris City Councillors,* 268–70. Giesey, "Rules of Inheritance," 276. Hilaire, "L'évolution des régimes matrimoniaux," 175–83. Charles Lefebvre, *L'ancien droit des successions,* 1:122–47 and

2:9–19. Le Roy Ladurie, "Système de la coutume," 825–46. Ourliac and Malafosse, *Histoire du droit privé*, 3:392–94, 401–4, 432–37, 493–96. James F. Traer, *Marriage and the Family in Eighteenth-Century France*, 41–43. Yver, *Egalité entre héritiers*, 155–59. For an examination of inheritance in the French southwest during the Middle Ages, see: Jacques Poumarède, *Les successions dans le sud-ouest de la France au moyen âge;* among the nobility of eighteenth-century Brittany and Burgundy: Meyer, *La noblesse bretonne*, 1:103–34 and Forster, *House of Saulx-Tavanes*, 4–7. On the matter of entail (*substitution*), a helpful summary of French practice is J. P. Cooper, "Patterns of Inheritance and Settlement by Great Landowners from the Fifteenth to the Eighteenth Centuries," in J. Goody, J. Thirsk, and E. P. Thompson, eds., *Family and Inheritance: Rural Society in Western Europe, 1200–1800,* 252–76. General discussion of the issues related to noble inheritance in France can be found in Roland Mousnier, *Les institutions de la France sous la monarchie absolue,* 1:47–69.

5. For similar practices at Aix-en-Provence: Bohanan, "Matrimonial Strategies," 505; and to the west at Bordeaux: Robert Wheaton, "Affinity and Descent in Seventeenth-Century Bordeaux," in R. Wheaton and T. K. Hareven, eds., *Family and Sexuality in French History,* 111–34. In the late sixteenth century, Gaspard de Saulx's equal division of his estate between two sons, for example, was regarded as lethal to the family's best interests. Forster, *House of Saulx-Tavanes,* 4–5.

6. Chêne, "Testaments, fortunes et religions," 186–90. Agnès Fine, "Le prix de l'exclusion: Dot et héritage dans le Sud-Ouest occitan," in *La dot: La valeur des femmes,* 31–51. Jean Hilaire, "Vie en commun: Famille et esprit communautaire," 20. Lepointe, *Droit romain et ancien droit français,* 330–37 and 464–68. Jean Maillet, "De l'exclusion coutumière des filles dotées à la renonciation à succession future dans les coutumes de Toulouse et Bordeaux," 514–45. Ourliac and Malafosse, *Histoire du droit privé,* 3:372, 374, 380, 468–73, 490–91, 515–26.

7. A. N. Galpern, *The Religions of the People in Sixteenth-Century Champagne,* 20–29, offers an illuminating discussion of late medieval testamentary piety and funeral practices.

8. AL, dossiers généalogiques, vol. 1, mémoire. Tardif, *Droit privé,* 65–67.

9. Chêne, "Testaments, fortunes et religions," 208–14.

10. AL, copie des actes, vol. 1, fols. 201–4, 219v–22v.

11. AL, copie des actes, vol. 4, fols. 494, 543–58v; dossiers généalogiques, vol. 1, mémoire. Although the prohibition weakened considerably during and after the sixteenth century, according to the customary law of Toulouse a dowered and married daughter received no *légitime,* for she was not entitled to a share in the inheritance of her father and mother. Tardif, *Droit privé,* 68–69.

12. AL, dossiers généalogiques, vol. 1, mémoire. Jean de Catellan, *Arrests remarquables du Parlement de Toulouse,* 2:66. Giesey, "Rules of Inheritance," 276–77. Ourliac and Malafosse, *Histoire du droit privé,* 3:481–87.

13. AL, copie des actes, vol. 2, fols. 136v–37v; vol. 4, fols. 493–95v; vol. 5, fols. 143v–45; dossiers généalogiques, vol. 2, dossier Marc-Antoine I and dossier Marc-Antoine II.

14. AL, copie des actes, vol. 5, fols. 113v–16, 127–31v; dossiers généalogiques, vol. 1, mémoire.

15. AL, copie des actes, vol. 4, fol. 435; dossiers généalogiques, vol. 1, mémoire. The *Coutume de Toulouse,* much as customary law elsewhere in the Midi, established an order of inheritance for intestate succession. Lepointe, *Droit romain et ancien droit français,* 332, 465–66. Tardif, *Droit privé,* 62–65. See also the comments of Pierre-Clément Timbal, "La dévolution successorale *ab intestat* dans la coutume de Toulouse," 51–82.

16. AL, dossiers généalogiques, vol. 1, mémoire.

17. René Filhol, "Protestantisme et droit d'aînesse au XVIe siècle," 195–205.

18. AL, dossiers généalogiques, vol. 1, mémoire. AF, généalogie de la famille de Falguerolles.

19. Ourliac and Malafosse, *Histoire du droit privé,* 3:371.

20. Forster, *The Nobility of Toulouse,* 126, notes, for example, that within Catholic Caulet family at Toulouse, it was customary for a *chevalier de Malte* to leave his modest inheritance to a cadet nephew to pay for his reception into the same order. See also Collomp, *La maison du père,* 164–65.

21. AD, Tarn, I 3 (13 et 20 septembre 1673); I 4, fol. 10.

22. AL, copie des actes, vol. 4, fols. 374–85, 427v; dossiers généalogiques, vol. 1, mémoire. Bibliothèque, SHPF, MS. 66, état-civil des protestants à Paris, fol. 245.

23. The ambiguities of Protestant and crypto-Protestant or "new Catholic" wills in the region of Provence after 1685 is discussed in Michel Vovelle, "Jalons pour une histoire du silence: Les testaments réformés dans le sud-est de la France du XVIIIe siècle," in M. Vovelle, *De la cave au grenier,* 387–404. See also: Garrisson-Estèbe, *L'homme protestant,* 76; and for Catholic practice: Germain Sicard, "Pratiques testamentaires et attitudes religieuses à Toulouse à la fin de l'Ancien Régime," 271–87.

24. AL, dossiers généalogiques, vol. 1, mémoire; vol. 2, dossier Jean-Jacques de Lacger.

25. AL, dossiers généalogiques, vol. 1, mémoire; vol. 3, donation de la terre de Navès du 23 septembre 1757. AD, Tarn, E 231. Lefebvre, *Droit des successions,* 1:202–22. Tardif, *Droit privé,* 70–72.

26. AL, dossiers généalogiques, vol. 3, brevet de confirmation de donation du 10 décembre 1757.

27. Chaussinand-Nogaret, *The French Nobility in the Eighteenth Century,* 50–64, offers an informative treatment of economic stratification among the eighteenth-century French nobility; see also his "Capital et structure sociale sous l'Ancien Régime," 463–76.

28. AL, dossiers généalogiques, vol. 1, mémoire; vol. 3, brevet de confirmation de donation du 10 décembre 1757.

29. Chaussinand-Nogaret, "Capital et structure sociale," 475–76.

30. AL, dossiers généalogiques, vol. 1, mémoire; vol. 2, dossier Marc-Antoine II and dossier François de Lacger. Giesey, "Rules of Inheritance," 275. Ourliac and Malafosse, *Histoire du droit privé,* 3:508–12.

31. AL, dossiers généalogiques, vol. 1, mémoire.

32. AL, dossiers généalogiques, vol. 2, dossier Marc-Antoine II.

33. Bibliothèque, SHPF, MS. Cazals, généalogie.

34. AL, copie des actes, vol. 1, fols. 38v, 41v–42v, 43–45, 56–59v, 67v–68v, 118v, 123v, 145v–46v, 338v–42v; vol. 3, fols. 370v–80; vol. 5, fol. 273.

35. Cf. the remarks of Forster, *The Nobility of Toulouse,* 151, that at Toulouse "the burden of the family settlement was met in a businesslike manner."

Chapter Six

1. For a discussion of the nuances of education and intellectual formation within the highest aristocratic circles of early modern France, see Motley, *Becoming an Aristocrat,* especially chap. 2. For a general introduction to the European educational traditions, Paul F. Grendler, "Schooling in Western Europe," 775–87.

2. Chartier, Julia, and Compère, *L'éducation en France,* 168–71.

3. Schalk, *From Valor to Pedigree,* 69–72, 86, 174–81, outlines the essential argument.

4. Henri Meylan, "Collèges et académies protestantes en France au XVIᵉ siècle," *Actes du 95ᵉ Congrès National des Sociétés Savantes, Reims, 1970,* vol. 1, *Enseignement intellectuel (IXᵉ–XVIᵉ siècle),* 301–9.

5. Compère and Julia, *Les collèges français,* 1:206–9. A. Poux, *Histoire de collège de Castres depuis les origines jusqu'à nos jours,* 9, 49–128. Rabaud, *Protestantisme dans l'Albigeois,* 1:143–44.

6. Rulman had been appointed *régent* already in 1580. Albert Puech, *Une ville au temps jadis ou Nîmes en 1592,* 351.

7. AL, copie des actes, vol. 1, fols. 200v, 225–25v, 232, 251v–53, 266–67, 276, 278, 289–90v, 326, 333v; vol. 2, fols. 15, 48; vol. 5, fol. 61. Pradel, "Fragments de lettres," 130.

8. Bourchenin, *Etude sur les académies protestantes,* 97–107. Jules Gaufrès, "Les collèges protestants," 200–208.

9. Davis, *The Return of Martin Guerre,* 110.

10. The question of women's public role, to include education, is succinctly sum-

marized by Merry E. Wiesner, "Women's Defense of Their Public Role," in Mary Beth Rose, ed., *Women in the Middle Ages and the Renaissance*, 1–27. See also: Natalie Z. Davis, "City Women and Religious Change," in N. Z. Davis, *Society and Culture in Early Modern France: Eight Essays*, 82–86. Wendy Gibson, *Women in Seventeenth-Century France*, 17–40. Stone, *Family, Sex and Marriage*, 202–6, 343–60.

11. The number of forms varied in the sixteenth century. The Protestant colleges at Castres and Saint-Lô had five, while those of Die, Montauban, and Nîmes had seven.

12. Frank Delteil, "Le collège protestant de Millau," in *La Réforme et l'éducation*, 19–34. Deyon, "Les académies protestantes," 77–81. George Huppert, *Public Schools in Renaissance France*, 48–51, 53–54, 79. "Les lois et règlements de l'Académie de Montauban, dressés l'an 1600, au mois d'octobre et publiés au grand Temple," 398–408. Meylan, "Collèges et académies protestantes," 1:302–4, and idem, "Professeurs et étudiants, questions d'horaires et de leçons," in *La Réforme et l'éducation*, 67–85. Poux, *Histoire du collège de Castres*, 56. Michel Reulos, "L'organisation, le fonctionnement et les programmes du Collège protestant de Saint-Lô (1563)," in *La Réforme et l'éducation*, 143–51.

13. AL, copie des actes, vol. 1, fols. 273v–75.

14. These features also characterize the Protestant libraries analyzed by Philip Benedict, "Bibliothèques protestantes et catholiques à Metz au XVIIe siècle," 343–70.

15. For the possibilities and difficulties in working with such lists, see the discussion by Joan Davies, "The Libraries of Some Protestants of Toulouse in 1572: Cultural Influences and Calvinism," 555–66.

16. Pierre de Lacger, judge of Castres, also had a personal library. It was inventoried "en sept feuillets et une page papier" in November 1635. Unfortunately, neither the list nor any indication of the titles and the number of volumes has survived. AL, copie des actes, vol. 1, fol. 174v; vol. 4, fols. 375v–85, 547v; vol. 5, fols. 124–24v.

17. Labatut, *Les ducs et pairs*, 231–38. Meyer, *La noblesse bretonne*, 2:1156–77.

18. Described as *Institute Theophile rouge aurale et fillets*, it was the *Institutiones* of Justinian, compiled by Tribonius, Theophilus, and Dorotheus. There were many editions throughout the sixteenth century.

19. Georges Louët, *Recueil d'aucuns notables arrests donnez en la cour de Parlement de Paris, pris des Mémoires de feu M. Maistre Georges Louët* (first published at Paris in 1602 with many subsequent editions). Pierre Guenois, *La conference des ordonnances royaux* (Paris, 1620), or an earlier edition. Jean Coras, *Ioannis Corasii . . . in titulum Pandectarum de Iustitia et Iure, ac sequentes legum iuris, magistratuúmq* (Lyon, 1560). Samuel d'Escorbiac, *Recueil general des edicts, declarations, arrests et reglemens notables entre les baillifs, seneschaux, magistrats presidiaux, viguiers, chastellains, et juges, et tous autres officiers inferieurs du ressort du Parlement de Tolose, pour les droicts, rang, seance, exer-*

cice, fonction, prérogatives, et attributions de leurs charges, avec plusieurs Edicts de leur establissement (Paris, 1638).

20. *Le code du Roy Henry III . . . Redigé en ordre par Messire B. Brisson . . .* (Paris, 1593). There were subsequent editions.

21. Henri-Jean Martin, *Livres, pouvoirs et sociétés à Paris au XVIIᵉ siècle (1598–1701)*, 1:503–6.

22. Listed as *Catule, Tibule, Properce comante par Scaliger et Muret*, the edition was probably *Catulli, Tibulli, Propertii, noua editio. Iosephus Scaliger recensuit. Ejusdem in eosdem Castigationum liber*, etc. (*M. Antonii Mureti Commentarius in Catullum. Eiusdem Scholia in Tibullum, et Propertium.*) (Antwerp, 1582), or an earlier edition.

23. Listed as *Epistole Lipsiy*, the volume was probably an edition of *J. Lipsii Epistolarum*.

24. Aldo Pio Manuzio [1449–1515], *Aldi Manutii Grammaticae*. There were many editions during the sixteenth century, including a *Grammatica Aldi* (Lyon, 15?).

25. Ambrosius Calepinus (Ambrigio Calepino), *Dictionarium septem linguarum*. There were many editions, most published at Lyon. Better known was Calepinus's dictionary in eight or even eleven rather than seven languages. Louis Le Roy, dit Regius, *Le Timée de Platon, traittant de la nature du monde et de l'homme et de ce qui concerne universellement tant l'âme que le corps des deux, translaté de grec en françois, avec l'exposition des lieux plus obscurs et difficiles, pars Loys Le Roy, dit Regius* (Paris, several late sixteenth-century editions).

26. Martin, *Livres à Paris*, 1:510–14.

27. Enrico Caterino Davila, *Histoire des guerres civiles de France* (many editions). Bernard de Girard, sieur du Haillan, probably *Histoire générale des roys de France, contenant les choses mémorables advenues tant au royaume de France qu'ès provinces étrangères sous la domination des François* (Paris, several early seventeenth-century editions). Etienne Pasquier, *Les recherches de la France* (Paris, several early seventeenth-century editions).

28. Louis Maimbourg, *Histoire de la décadence de l'empire après Charlemagne*, 2 vols. (Paris, several editions during the 1670s and thereafter); *Histoire des croisades pour la délivrance de la Terre Sainte*, 4 vols. (Paris, 1680 and other editions).

29. Probably Gilbert Saulnier, sieur du Verdier, *Le Romant des Romans*, 7 pts. (Paris, 1626–29).

30. *Histoire des Juifs, écrite par Flavius Joseph, sous le titre de Antiquitez judaïques traduite sur l'original grec reveu sur divers manuscrits, par Monsieur Arnaud d'Andilly*, 5 vols. (Paris, 1672). The brief catalogue of Jacques de Lacger's library mentions only four volumes specifically.

31. Dewald, *Pont-St-Pierre*, 189–92. Martin, *Livres à Paris*, 1:477–81.

32. Martin, *Livres à Paris*, 1:493–503.

33. John Calvin, *Commentaire de M. Jean Calvin, sur les cinq livres de Moyse* (Geneva,

1564), and idem, *Leçons de M. Jean Calvin sur le livre des propheties de Daniel* (Geneva, 1562), or subsequent editions thereof.

34. Philippe de Mornay, sieur du Plessis-Marly, *Traité de la verité de la religion chrestienne: Contre les Athées, Epicuriens, Payens, Juifs, Mahumedists et autres infideles* (several editions: Antwerp, 1581; Paris, 1582; Geneva, 1583). Michel Le Faucheur, *Traitté de la Cène du Seigneur . . . avec la Réfutation des instances et oppositions du cardinal Du Perron . . . par Michel Le Faucheur* (Geneva, 1635).

35. See Ralph E. Giesey, "The Monarchomach Triumvirs: Hotman, Beza and Mornay," 41–56.

36. Edme Aubertine, *L'Eucharistie de l'ancienne eglise; ou, Traitté auquel il est monstré quelle a esté durant les six premiers siecles depuis l'institution de l'Eucharistie* (Geneva: P. Aubert, 1633).

37. Jean Daillé, *Replique aux deux livres que messieurs Adam et Cottiby ont publiez contre luy*, 2 vols. (Geneva: J. Antoine et S. de Tournes, 1662), and subsequent editions.

38. AL, copie des actes, vol. 4, fols. 128, 207, 215.

39. *Recueil de pièces galantes en prose et en vers, de Mme. la comtesse de La Suze et de M. Pellisson* (Paris, 1664).

40. Antoine Adam, *Histoire de la littérature française au XVIIe siècle*, vol. 2, *L'époque de Pascal*, 14–15. Gédéon Tallemant des Réaux, *Historiettes*, 2:105–13, 1004–11. Lougee, *Le Paradis des Femmes*, explores the role of women in salon society.

41. "Ce Lacger est un grand coquin . . ." and, elsewhere, "c'est un gros tout rond, qui n'est nullement honneste homme . . ." Tallemant des Réaux, *Historiettes*, 2:109, 430.

42. Frédéric Lachèvre, *Le livre d'amour d'Hercule de Lacger. Vers pour Iris (Henriette de Coligny, comtesse de La Suze). Publiés sur le manuscrit original inédit avec une notice* (Paris: Sansot, 1910). These verses and others can be found in the Bibliothèque Nationale, manuscrits français 12680 and 19145, as well as Charles de Sercy, ed., *Poésies choisies*, 5 pts. (Paris, 1653–60). Note that Lachèvre and, indeed, all modern editors confuse Jacques de Lacger with his cousin Hercule. Raymond A. Mentzer, Jr., "The Misidentification of the Poet Lacger," 18–19.

43. Lachèvre, *Vers pour Iris*, 22–25. Tallemant des Réaux, *Historiettes*, 2:108–9, 430, 1007–8.

44. Lachèvre, *Vers pour Iris*, 26–36. Tallemant des Réaux, *Historiettes*, 2:430–31, 1274–76. On the issue of dueling, see: François Billaçois, *Le duel dans la société française des XVIe–XVIIe siècles: Essai de psychosociologie historique*; V. G. Kiernan, *The Duel in European History*. Harding, *Anatomy of a Power Elite*, 77–79, describes dueling in the sixteenth century. Dueling was, of course, a salient trait of nobility: Schalk, *From Valor to Pedigree*, 162–73.

45. See the recent and helpful Jeanette Lee Atkinson, "Queen Christina of Sweden: Sovereign between Throne and Altar," in Katharina M. Wilson and Frank J. Warnke, eds., *Women Writers of the Seventeenth Century*, 405–27.

46. Joyce G. Simpson, *Le Tasse et la littérature et l'art baroques en France*.

47. AL, copie des actes, vol. 4, fols. 342–42v, 345v, 348–49, 397–97v, 399v. AM, Castres, II 9, fols. 106, 137, 140. Jean-Louis Guez, sieur de Balzac, *Les oeuvres de Monsieur de Balzac*, 1:1023–27. François Le Métal de Boisrobert, *Epistres en vers*, 2:79–83. Gunnar Castrén, "Beys och Lacger: Två av drottning Kristinas franska ballettförfattare," *Studier tillägnade Arvid Hultin*, 53–57. Lachèvre, *Vers pour Iris*, 41–56.

48. AL, copie des actes, vol. 4, fols. 374–75v, 388v, 402v–5v, 433–33v, 435, 558v; vol. 5, fol. 155v; dossiers généalogiques, vol. 1, mémoire.

49. AL, copie des actes, vol. 4, fols. 513–14v. Bibliothèque, SHPF, MS. G, dossier Romane-Musculus, no. 64.

50. Pierre Chabbert, "L'Académie de Castres," 271–87. O. Granat, "Une académie de province au XVIIᵉ siècle," 183, 185–86. Magloire Nayral, *Biographie castraise*, 2:348–50. Daniel Roche, *Le siècle des lumières en province: Académies et académiciens provinciaux, 1680–1789*, 1:20. Several of the other academies also saw themselves as a common meeting ground for the two religious cultures. See Emile-G. Léonard, *Histoire générale du protestantisme*, vol. 2, *L'établissement*, 333–35.

51. AM, Castres, II 9, fols. 101v, 102–2v. AM, Castres, II 9 and II 10 are the two-volume proceedings of the Academy. Louis Barbaza, *L'Académie de Castres et la société de Mlle de Scudéry, 1648–1670*, has published extensive excerpts. Chabbert, "L'Académie de Castres," 274. Granat, "Une académie de province," 182–85. Charles Pradel, "Notice sur la vie du poète Ranchin (1616–1692)," 408–10.

52. AD, Haute-Garonne, 3 B 1 (3), fols. 69–72; 3 B 1 (4), fols. 133–34v; 3 B 1 (5), fols. 94–94v, 108; 3 B 3, fols. 12v–13v, 33–35. Balincourt, "Les d'Espérandieu," 207–9. Bezons, *Jugements sur la noblesse, Généralité de Toulouse*, vol. 2 of *Pièces fugitives*, 76, 107. Eugène Haag and Emile Haag, *La France protestante, ou vies des protestants français*, 1st ed., 6:21 and 9:66; and 2nd ed., 6:104–6.

53. AD, Tarn, I 2, fols. 381–82.

54. AD, Haute-Garonne, 3 B 1 (2), fols. 79–80, 114–14v; 3 B 1 (5), fol. 108; 3 B 3, fols. 12v–13v; E 700, fol. 1. Adam, *Histoire de la littérature*, 2:40–46. *Biographie toulousaine*, 2:234–37. Bezons, *Jugements sur la noblesse, Généralité de Montpellier*, vol. 1, pt. 2 of *Pièces fugitives*, 244–45. Alexandre Cioranescu, *Bibliographie de la littérature française du dix-septième siècle*, 3:1719. Granat, "Une académie de province," 188. Greengrass, "Noble Affinities," 284–85. Haag and Haag, *La France protestante*, 1st ed., 8:377–78. Nayral, *Biographie castraise*, 3:259–74. Pradel, "La vie du poète Ranchin," 402–28. Tallemant des Réaux, *Historiettes*, 1:180, 866; 2:1220.

55. Adam, *Histoire de la littérature* 2:42–43. Cioranescu, *Bibliographie*, 2:1061.

Nayral, *Biographie castraise,* 2:298–311. Tallemant des Réaux, *Historiettes,* 2:449, 1324–25.

56. AL, copie des actes, vol. 4, fol. 427v.

57. On the relationship between Pellisson and Scudéry, see: Alain Niderst, *Madeleine de Scudéry, Paul Pellisson et leur monde.*

58. Paul Pellisson Fontanier, *Discours au Roy, par un de ses fidèles sujets, ou première défense de M. Fouquet* (n.p., 1661), in-quarto, 59 pp.; *Seconde défense de M. Fouquet* (n.p., 1661), in-quarto, 70 pp.; *Considérations sommaires sur le procès de M. Fouquet* (n.p., n.d.), in-quarto.

59. The sincerity of Pellisson Fontanier's conversion is open to question. Although interpretations vary, on his deathbed at Versailles in 1693, he did not receive the last sacraments. Labrousse, *La révocation,* 161.

60. AD, Haute-Garonne, E 700, livre de raison de Jacques de Ranchin, fols. 22–22v.

61. It was officially known as the *Caisse des Economats.* O. Douen, "Le fondateur de la caisse des conversions," 145–60. Labrousse, "Calvinism in France," in Prestwich, *International Calvinism,* 306–7, and idem, *La révocation,* 159–63. Garrisson, *L'Edit de Nantes,* 136–39. Orcibal, *Louis XIV,* 44–79.

62. AD, Haute-Garonne, 3 B 1 (3), fols. 69–72; 3 B 1 (4), fols. 133–34v; E 700, fols. 22–22v. Adam, *Histoire de la littérature,* 2:98–104. Cioranescu, *Bibliographie,* 3:1601–02. Granat, "Une académie de province," 186–87. Haag and Haag, *La France protestante,* 1st ed., 8:172–80. Nayral, *Biographie castraise,* 3:55–116. Rabaud, *Protestantisme dans l'Albigeois,* 1:322–34, 360–72; 2:23–24.

63. Granat, "Une académie de province," 187. Haag and Haag, *La France protestante,* 1st ed., 8:171–72. Nayral, *Biographie castraise,* 3:50–54.

64. Adam, *Histoire de la littérature,* 2:153. Cioranescu, *Bibliographie,* 1:401–2. Pierre Chabbert, "Pierre Borel (1620?–1671)," 303–43. Haag and Haag, *La France protestante,* 2nd ed., 2:893–903. Emile Jolibus, "Pierre Borel," 132–33. Nayral, *Biographie castraise,* 1:168–79. M.-L. Puech-Milhau, "Pierre Borel, 1620(?)–1671," 278–80.

65. *Traitté des usurpations des roys d'Espagne sur la couronne de France, depuis Charles VIII* (Paris, 1625 and several subsequent editions); *La justice des armes du Roy très-chrestien contre le Roy d'Espagne* (Paris, 1647). Haag and Haag, *La France protestante,* 2nd ed., 1:736–39. Nayral, *Biographie castraise,* 1:122–29.

66. AM, Castres, II 9, fol. 164v; II 10, fols. 18, 31.

67. AM, II 9, fol. 135. Nayral, *Biographie castraise,* 2:350.

68. Pierre Borel, *Trésor de recherches et antiquitez gauloises et françoises réduites en ordre alphabétique et enrichies de beaucoup d'origines, épitaphes et autres choses rares et curieuses* (Paris, 1655), in-quarto, 611 pp.

69. Pierre Saporta, *Traicté de la mesure des eaux courantes de Benoist Castelli, . . .*

traduit d'italien en françois, avec un Discours de la jonction des mers, adressé à messeigneurs les commissaires députez par Sa Majesté. Ensemble un Traicté du mouvement des eaux d'Evangelista Torricelli, . . . traduit du latin en françois (Castres, 1664), in-quarto, 87 pp. There is also a 1665 edition.

70. AM, Castres, II 9, fols. 106, 137, 141; II 10, fol. 36v. Granat, "Une académie de province," 188–92. Georges Mongrédien, "Le tricentenaire de l'Académie de Castres," 89–91.

71. Note, for example, the preponderance of classical, legal, and historical texts in the libraries of eighteenth-century Parisian *parlementaires*. François Bluche, *Les magistrats du Parlement de Paris au XVIIIe siècle (1715–1771)*, 289–96. For the provinces west of Paris: Jean Quéniart, *Culture et société urbaines dans la France de l'ouest au XVIIIe siècle*, 308–36.

Chapter Seven

1. The views expressed here owe much to the discussion in Gary W. McDonogh, *Good Families of Barcelona: A Social History of Power in the Industrial Era*, especially 202–3. Useful examination of the historical definition of frequently confusing terms such as family, household, house, lineage, and kin can be found in Jean-Louis Flandrin, *Familles: Parenté, maison, sexualité dans l'ancienne société*, 7–53; and Stone, *Family, Sex and Marriage*, 21–30.

2. The recent literature of the early modern European family is enormous. Several basic studies include: Flandrin, *Familles;* Jack Goody, *The Development of the Family and Marriage in Europe;* Michael Mitterauer and Reinhard Sieder, *The European Family: Patriarchy to Partnership from the Middle Ages to the Present;* Steven Ozment, *When Fathers Ruled: Family Life in the Reformation;* Stone, *Family, Sex and Marriage*. For a succinct summary and helpful overview of current scholarship, see Tamara K. Hareven, "The History of the Family and the Complexity of Social Change," 95–124.

3. Flandrin, *Familles*, 117–20. Stone, *Family, Sex and Marriage*, 85–91 and 150–59. On the relationship between family and state, see the recent and imaginative discussion by Hanley, "Engendering the State," 4–27.

4. At Montauban, a major Protestant stronghold to the northwest of Castres, the city magistrates imprisoned a man in 1596 for "harshly beating" and "injuring" his spouse. The Reformed consistory also chastised the man for what was clearly regarded as an outrageous case of wife-beating. AD, Tarn-et-Garonne, I, 1, fol. 153v.

5. N. Castan, "La criminalité familiale," 93. Davis, "Ghosts, Kin, and Progeny," 87–92. Flandrin, *Familles*, 120–28. Gibson, *Women in Seventeenth-Century France*, 61–62. Hanlon, *L'univers des gens de bien*, 99–100. Ourliac and Malafosse, *Histoire du*

droit privé, 3:132–52. Stone, *Family, Sex and Marriage*, 195–202. Tardif, *Droit privé*, 30, 81–83. See, concerning the physical abuse of women during an earlier period, the remarks of Emmanuel Le Roy Ladurie, *Montaillou, village occitan de 1294 à 1324*, 279–83.

6. Flandrin, *Familles*, 128–38. Stone, *Family, Sex and Marriage*, 161–95.

7. Eph. 5:22–6:9 and Exod. 20:12.

8. Janine Garrisson, *Les protestants au XVIᵉ siècle*, 37–39, 88–91. Hanlon, *L'univers des gens de bien*, 219. Raymond A. Mentzer, Jr., "*Disciplina nervus ecclesiae*: The Calvinist Reform of Morals at Nîmes," 109–11. Samuel Mours, *Le protestantisme en France au XVIIᵉ siècle (1598–1685)*, 123–26. Amanda Porterfield, "Women's Attraction to Puritanism," 205. Stone, *Family, Sex and Marriage*, 135–42. Wheaton, "Recent Trends," 4, 14–15.

9. Davis, "City Women and Religious Change," in her *Society and Culture*, 86–87. Labrousse, "Les mariages bigarrés," 167–70. Idem, "Conversion dans les deux sens," 167–68.

10. Among recent studies of historical naming patterns are Louis Perouas et al., *Léonard, Marie, Jean et les autres: Les prénoms en Limousin depuis un millénaire;* and Agnès Fine, "L'héritage du nom de baptême," 853–77.

11. Galpern, *Religions of the People*, 43–46. Goody, *Development of the Family*, 201.

12. Philip Benedict, *Rouen during the Wars of Religion*, 104–6, 256–60. Garrisson, *Les protestants*, 47–48.

13. Bibliothèque, SHPF, MS. 66, état-civil des protestants à Paris, fol. 94.

14. This particular Jacques was the son of Jean, judge of Castelnaudary, and nephew of Antoine II. Bibliothèque, SHPF, MS. Cazals, généalogie.

15. AL, copie des actes, vol. 1, fols. 291–91v. Bibliothéque, SHPF, MS. 66, fol. 94. Gaches, *Mémoires*, 417–18.

16. AM, Castres, GG 23, pt. 1, fol. 454. Bibliothèque, SHPF, MS. Cazals, généalogie. AF, généalogie de la famille de Falguerolles.

17. Bibliothèque, SHPF, MS. Cazals, généalogie. Romane-Musculus, "Généalogie des Toulouse-Lautrec," 103–5.

18. AD, Haute-Garonne, 3 B 3, fol. 68. AM, Castres, GG 20, pt. 2, fol. 52. GG 24, pt. 3, fol. 111. AF, généalogie de la famille de Falguerolles.

19. The findings of Hanlon and Carruthers, "Wills, Inheritance and the Moral Order," 152–53, indicate that, on the whole, testamentary bequests from godparents to godchildren were fewer than commonly supposed.

20. John Bossy, "Blood and Baptism: Kinship, Community and Christianity in Western Europe from the Fourteenth to the Seventeenth Centuries," in Derek Baker, ed., *Sanctity and Secularity: The Church and the World*, 129–43, and idem, "Godparenthood: The Fortunes of a Social Institution in Early Modern Christianity," in

Kaspar von Greyerz, ed., *Religion and Society in Early Modern Europe, 1500–1800*, 194–201. Flandrin, *Familles*, 35–36. Galpern, *Religions of the People*, 45. Motley, *Becoming an Aristocrat*, 32–35. Wheaton, "Affinity and Descent," 117. For an appreciation of the popular strength of baptismal bonds within the pre-Reformation world, see: Louis Haas, "Boccaccio, Baptismal Kinship, and Spiritual Incest," 343–56; and in general, Sidney W. Mintz and Eric R. Wolf, "An Analysis of Ritual Co-parenthood (Compadrazgo)," 341–68.

21. Garrisson, *Les protestants*, 46–47. François Méjan, *Discipline de l'Eglise Réformée de France annotée et précédée d'une introduction historique*, 262–74.

22. AL, copie des actes, vol. 1, fols. 291–91v; vol. 4, fol. 181; vol. 5, fol. 153v. AM, Castres, GG 16, fol. 345; GG 23, pt. 1, fol. 454; GG 23, pt. 2, fols. 23–24, 185–86; GG 24, pt. 1, fols. 44, 332; GG 24, pt. 3, fols. 111, 265–66; GG 34, fols. 15–15v, 427–27v; GG 35, fols. 228, 354v; GG 53, fols. 134, 148, 174, 199v, 207, 251v. Bibliothèque, SHPF, MS. 66, état-civil des protestants à Paris, fols. 90, 96. AF, généalogie de la famille de Falguerolles.

23. Witness, for instance, the whirl of family connections and patronage associated with the Montmorency household. Joan Davies, "Family Service and Family Strategies: The Household of Henri, duc de Montmorency, ca. 1590–1610," 27–43. Greengrass, "Noble Affinities," 275–311. For a description of the rhetoric that marked this patronage system, see Neuschel, *Word of Honor*, 69–78.

24. Bibliothèque, SHPF, MS. 66, état-civil des protestants de Paris, fol. 94. Pradel, "Fragments de lettres," 140.

25. AM, Castres, GG 32 (18 février 1698); GG 33, fols. 87, 167, 409; GG 34, fol. 560v; GG 35, fol. 76v.

26. Sharon Kettering, "Patronage and Kinship in Early Modern France," 408–35, and idem, "The Patronage Power of Early Modern French Noblewomen," 817–41; and generally, idem, *Patrons, Brokers, and Clients*. Wheaton, "Affinity and Descent," 117.

27. Muchembled, "Famille, amour et mariage," 237–38, 251–55. David Sabean, "Aspects of Kinship Behavior and Property in Rural Western Europe before 1800," in Jack Goody, Joan Thirsk, and E. P. Thompson, eds., *Family and Inheritance: Rural Society in Western Europe, 1200–1800*, 96–111.

28. AL, copie des actes, vol. 4, fols. 374–75v, 388v, 402v–5v, 427v, 433–33v, 435, 558–58v; vol. 5, fols. 127–31v, 155v; dossiers généalogiques, vol. 1, mémoire.

29. AL, dossiers généalogiques, vol. 1, mémoire.

30. AL, dossiers généalogiques, vol. 1, mémoire. AM, Castres, GG 23, pt. 1, fols. 391–92. Roussel, *Essais historiques*, 10:34.

31. AL, dossiers généalogiques, vol. 1, mémoire. AF généalogie de la famille de Falguerolles.

32. AL, copie des actes, vol. 1, introduction; vol. 2, fols. 136v–37v; vol. 4, fols. 493–95v; dossiers généalogiques, vol. 1, mémoire.

33. Bibliothèque, SHPF, MS. Cazals, généalogie. AF, généalogie de la famille de Falguerolles.

34. See, for example, the remarks of Stone, *Family, Sex and Marriage,* 115–16.

35. Forster, *The Nobility of Toulouse,* 127.

36. Davis, "Ghosts, Kin, and Progeny," 97.

37. For these and other examples of cross-confessional godparenthood within the Lacger house, see: AM, Castres, GG 23, pt. 2, fols. 185–86; GG 34, fols. 15–15v; GG 35, fols. 228, 354v; GG 53, fol. 174.

38. See, for example, the remarks of Stone, *Family, Sex and Marriage,* 90–91.

39. Cf. the kinship system among the bourgeoisie: Flandrin, *Familles,* 28–38.

40. Davis, "Ghosts, Kin, and Progeny," 98.

41. Modern family tradition finds this the portrait of a homely man.

42. Davis, "Ghosts, Kin, and Progeny," 92, 105.

43. Longevity continues to favor the Lacger. François de Lacger, who first introduced this author to his family's archives, lived ninety-two years. His sister Antoinette enjoyed an even longer life.

44. Bibliothèque, SHPF, MS. Cazals, généalogie; MS. G, dossier Romane-Musculus, no. 64. *Généalogie historique de la maison de Lacger.* AF, généalogie de la famille de Falguerolles.

Chapter Eight

1. AD, Tarn, I 2, fols. 27, 43–44; I 4, fols. 3–4.

2. AD, Tarn, I 4, fols. 20, 325.

3. See AD, Tarn, I 1, I 2, I 3, I 4, I 5, I 6, délibérations du consistoire de Castres (1645–84), for the annual elections of the elders.

4. The church at nearby Montauban sometimes employed the phrase *corps d'Eglise* to denote a general assembly of the local church. Thus in June 1596, the members of the consistory were joined by the city consuls, several judges from the court of the seneschal, and numerous professionals, merchants, and craftsmen to debate the ticklish issue of pastors' salaries. About a year later, this same *corps* discussed the excommunication of people who leased Catholic ecclesiastical benefices as well as a critical shortage of pastors at Montauban. On other occasions, however, the church at Montauban seems to have applied the term *corps d'Eglise* in specific reference to the consistory. AD, Tarn-et-Garonne, I 1, fols. 45–50v, 72–72v, 144, 160v–62, 172–72v, 248–49, 250v.

5. Membership on Castres's governing consulate had been *mi-partie* since the 1630s. There were two Catholic and two Protestant consuls. Rabaud, *Protestantisme dans l'Albigeois,* 1:275–76.

6. AD, Tarn, I 1, fols. 30–31, 322–23, 337–38, 340–41, 911, 913, 914, 926.

7. AD, Tarn, I 1, fols. 154–55, 183–84, 192–93, 262, 270–72, 503, 527, 1005, 1013–15, 1220–21; I 2, fols. 99, 103, 146, 148, 149, 299–300, 410–11.

8. AL, copie des actes, vol. 2, fols. 38–40v, 51–66v, 130v, 168v, 173, 186v–87, 295–98v, 386–98, 427–35. *Généalogie historique de la maison de Lacger*, pièces justificatives, iv–xiii. Gaches, *Suite des mémoires*, 15–16.

9. Gaches, *Mémoires*, 440–51. Rabaud, *Protestantisme dans l'Albigeois*, 1:182–87, 472–75.

10. Raymond A. Mentzer, Jr., "Le consistoire et la pacification du monde rural," 373–89, idem, *"Disciplina nervus ecclesiae,"* 89–115, and idem, "Ecclesiastical Discipline and Communal Reorganization," 165–85.

11. This was the "branche de Puget," founded by the son of Jean de Lacger, sixteenth-century judge of Castelnaudary. Bibliothèque, SHPF, MS. Cazals, généalogie. The presence and position of illegitimate children within French noble households appears to have varied from one region to another. Constant, *La noblesse française*, 233.

12. AD, Haute-Garonne, B 1030, fols. 93–93v; B 1087 (le 14 juillet 1685); E 700, livre de raison de Jacques de Ranchin, fols. 22–22v, 59–59v. Brenac, "Toulouse, centre de lutte," 31–45. Cambon de Lavalette, *La chambre de l'Edit*, 143–46, 180–81. The Protestant *président* and *conseillers* represent slightly less than 10 percent of the parlement's 111 members at the end of the seventeenth century. Paulhet, "Les parlementaires toulousains," 190–91, 198.

13. Members of the Escorbiac house continued to serve on the high court at Toulouse well into the eighteenth century. AD, Haute-Garonne, B 1121, fols. 189–89v, 190–91v; B 1334 (juin 1714); B 1707, fol. 726; B 1708, fol. 241; B 1809, fol. 405; B 1924, fols. 117v–18, 118v, 121v–22v. AN, TT 434, II, III, VII, VIII. Garrisson-Estèbe, *L'homme protestant*, 58–61.

14. Garrisson-Estèbe, *L'homme protestant*, 58–61.

15. Labrousse, "Conversion dans les deux sens," 167–68, and idem, "Les mariages bigarrés," 167–70.

16. AD, Haute-Garonne, B 1884, fol. 216. Bibliothèque, SHPF, MS. G, dossier Romane-Musculus, no. 64. AF, généalogie de la famille de Falguerolles.

17. Crypto-Protestants at Montauban, another strongly Huguenot town, found it difficult to obtain *certificats de baptême* as well as *certificats de catholicité* and therefore were frequently excluded from royal offices. Daniel Ligou, "La Cour des Aides de Montauban à la fin du XVIIIᵉ siècle," 314–15.

18. AD, Tarn, H 216, fols. 285v–86v.

19. AD, Haute-Garonne, B 1925, fols. 1–1v. AL, dossiers généalogiques, vol. 1, mémoire. AF, généalogie de la famille de Falguerolles.

20. AD, Haute-Garonne, B 1227, fol. 284. AF, généalogie de la famille de

Falguerolles. The comments of Gibson, *Women in Seventeenth-Century France,* 232–35, attest to the widespread modern perception of women as "pillars of Protestant resistance."

21. Barbara B. Diefendorf, "Houses Divided: Religious Schism in Sixteenth-Century Parisian Families," in S. Zimmerman and R. Weissman, eds., *Urban Life in the Renaissance,* 80–99.

22. AD, Haute-Garonne, 3 B 1 (1), fol. 12; 3 B 1 (2), fols. 70–71v, 78–80; 3 B 1 (4), fols. 91v–93, 104v–5v; 3 B 1 (5), fols. 54v–55v, 59–60; 3 B 3, fol. 164v; 3 B 5, fols. 54–55v. Cambon de Lavalette, *La chambre de l'Edit,* 174–81. Vindry, *Les parlementaires français,* vol. 2, pt. 2:249.

23. AD, Haute-Garonne, 3 B 1 (2), fols. 62–63v, 106v–9; 3 B 1 (4), fols. 98v–100, 133–34v; 3 B 3, fols. 33–35. Bezons, *Jugements sur la noblesse, Généralité de Montpellier,* vol. 1, pt. 2 of *Pièces fugitives,* 159. Cambon de Lavalette, *La chambre de l'Edit,* 174–81.

24. Rabaud, *Protestantisme dans l'Albigeois,* 1:281–82.

25. See the comments of Labatut, *Les ducs et pairs,* 217–19 and 432, regarding conversion among the high nobility.

26. The Intendancy of Languedoc, for example, reported François de Lacger among the "new Catholics" who attended Easter mass in 1701. AD, Hérault, C 274. I am indebted to Margaret Sumner for this reference.

27. AM, Castres, GG 21, pt. 2, fols. 79–80; GG 23, pt. 1, fols. 109–10, 321–22; GG 24, pt. 2, fols. 118, 123–24; pt. 3, fols. 56–58. Bibliothèque, SHPF, MS. Cazals, généalogie. Léonard, "L'Institution du Mérite Militaire," 297–301.

28. Cf. the inner obstinacy revealed in the *nouveaux convertis* testamentary formulae examined by Vovelle, "Jalons pour une histoire du silence," 387–404, and various other acts of discreet defiance described by Joutard, "The Revocation of the Edict of Nantes," in Prestwich, *International Calvinism,* 358–60.

29. AL, dossiers généalogiques, vol. 1, mémoire.

30. Léonard, *Mon village sous Louis XV,* 239–45, offers the example of the "new convert" Charles de Baschi, marquis of Aubais, who became the protector of Protestants in the region immediately surrounding his estates.

31. Bibliothèque, SHPF, MS. Cazals, généalogie.

32. AM, Castres, GG 23, pt. 2, fols. 185–86; GG 34, fols. 15–15v; GG 35, fols. 228, 354v; GG 53, fol. 174.

33. See, by way of background: Philippe Joutard, *Les Camisards;* idem, *La légende des Camisards: Une sensibilité au passé;* and idem, "The Revocation of the Edict of Nantes," in Prestwich, *International Calvinism,* 339–68. Religious resistance at the town of Le Mas-d'Azil to the west in the foothills of the Pyrenees is described by Alice Wemyss, *Les protestants du Mas-d'Azil: Histoire d'une résistance, 1680–1830.*

34. Georges Frêche, "Contre-Réforme et dragonnades (1640–1789): Pour une

orientation statistique de l'histoire du Protestantisme," 364–66. Rabaud, *Protestantisme dans l'Albigeois,* 2:186–88, 215–18.

35. The wife of a carder at Aubais (near Nîmes) contemptuously informed two soldiers "that she will not go to mass because she doesn't believe in it." Pic, "Les protestants d'Aubais," 63.

36. Emile Appolis, "Les Protestants dans le diocèse de Lodève de la Révocation de l'Edit de Nantes à la Révolution," 299–301. Joutard, "The Revocation of the Edict of Nantes," in Prestwich, *International Calvinism,* 341.

37. B. Faucher, "Les registres de l'état civil protestant en France depuis le XVIe siècle jusqu'à nos jours," 307–18.

38. A clandestine Protestant synod for Languedoc and the mountainous Cévennes region, for instance, acknowledged in 1718 the validity of baptisms performed by the Roman church, though in subsequent decades Protestant pastors discouraged parents from such action. Faucher, "Les registres de l'état civil protestant," 329. Wemyss, *Les protestants du Mas-d'Azil,* 140.

39. Labrousse, "Les mariages bigarrés," 159–60. Malzac, *Les Pourtalès,* 63–64. Pic, "Les protestants d'Aubais," 76–79.

40. Daniel Ligou and Janine Garrisson-Estèbe [Garrisson], "La bourgeoisie réformée montalbanaise à la fin de l'Ancien Régime," 397.

41. AM, Castres, GG 32 (18 février 1698); GG 33, fols. 87, 167, 409; GG 34, fol. 560v; GG 35, fol. 76v.

42. David Bien, "Catholic Magistrates and Protestant Marriage in the French Enlightenment," 409–29, summarizes the legal difficulties and subsequent changes during the eighteenth century.

43. See the comments of Pic, "Les protestants d'Aubais," 79–81.

44. Ligou and Garrisson-Estèbe, "La bourgeoisie réformée montalbanaise," 395.

45. AL, dossiers généalogiques, vol. 1, dossier Marc-Antoine II de Lacger. AM, Castres, GG 21, pt. 1, p. 215. Emile-G. Léonard, "Le problème du mariage civil et les protestants français au XVIIIe siècle," 254–57.

46. AM, Castres, GG 32 (le 7 février 1694); GG 34, fols. 358–58v. Faucher, "Les registres de l'état civil protestant," 329.

47. Léonard, "Le problème du mariage," 257–62.

48. Some 80 percent of the Protestant bourgeoisie at Montauban, for example, married in the Catholic church and had their children baptized there, too, rather than risk an "irregular situation." Ligou and Garrisson-Estèbe, "La bourgeoisie réformée montalbanaise," 395–96.

49. Léonard, "Le problème du mariage," 296–99; and idem, *Histoire générale du protestantisme,* vol. 3, *Déclin et renouveau,* 27–29. Faucher, "Les registres de l'état civil protestant," 332–35. Traer, *Marriage and the Family,* 64–65, 68–70, 90.

50. Labrousse, "Les mariages bigarrés," 160–61. Malzac, *Les Pourtalès,* 63–64. Pic, "Les protestants d'Aubais," 81–82. Wemyss, *Les protestants du Mas-d'Azil,* 98.

51. AM, Castres, GG 20, pt. 2, fol. 52; GG 34, fol. 118v.

52. AL, papiers concernant la religion.

53. Appolis, "Les protestants dans le diocèse de Lodève," 310. *Déclaration du roy, concernant la forme de tenir des baptesmes, mariages, sepultures, vestures, noviciats et professions, et des extraits qui en doivent estre delivrez,* 7. Faucher, "Les registres de l'état civil protestant," 326–28.

54. AL, dossiers généalogiques, vol. 2. AM, Castres, GG 19, pt. 1, fol. 295; GG 20, pt. 2, fol. 52; GG 34, fol. 118v; GG 54, fols. 206v–7v, 267v–68v.

55. AM, Castres, GG 53, fols. 134, 148, 156v, 174, 199v, 207, 251v. Pic, "Les protestants d'Aubais," 83.

56. In contrast, Pic, "Les protestants d'Aubais," 75–76, emphasizes the comfort of the larger social circle—the religious community at the village level, for example. He is less certain of the benefit provided by "narrowly limited" family groupings.

Chapter Nine

1. Weary, "The House of La Trémoille," on demand article.

2. David Herlihy, "Family," 1–16.

3. The ambiguity of "women's role in marriage and household" in light of the Reformation is ably described for the German world by Lyndal Roper, *The Holy Household: Women and Morals in Reformation Augsburg.*

4. Cf. Slater, *Family Life,* 29.

5. S. Deyon, *Du loyalisme au refus,* 161–62.

6. Joutard, "The Révocation of the Edict of Nantes," in Prestwich, *International Calvinism,* 339–41, 366–68.

7. Cf. the remarks of Wemyss, *Les protestants du Mas-d'Azil,* 185–87.

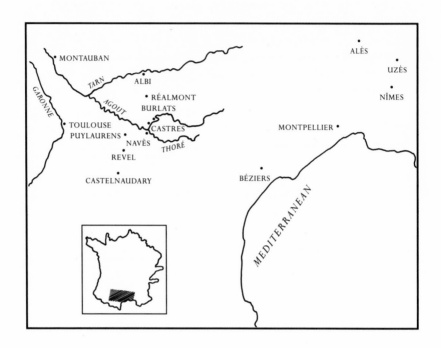

Lacger Family Genealogy

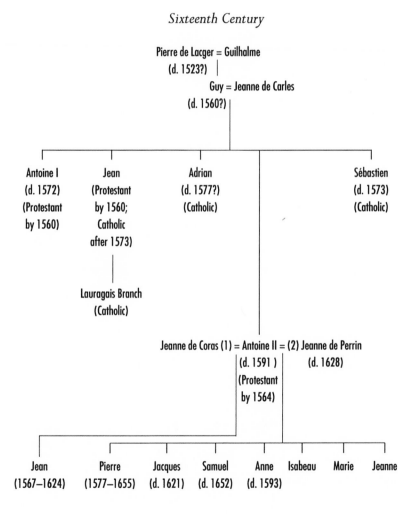

Sixteenth Century

Pierre de Lacger = Guilhalme
(d. 1523?)

Guy = Jeanne de Carles
(d. 1560?)

Antoine I
(d. 1572)
(Protestant
by 1560)

Jean
(Protestant
by 1560;
Catholic
after 1573)

Adrian
(d. 1577?)
(Catholic)

Sébastien
(d. 1573)
(Catholic)

Lauragais Branch
(Catholic)

Jeanne de Coras (1) = Antoine II = (2) Jeanne de Perrin
(d. 1591)
(Protestant
by 1564)
(d. 1628)

Jean
(1567–1624)

Pierre
(1577–1655)

Jacques
(d. 1621)

Samuel
(d. 1652)

Anne
(d. 1593)

Isabeau

Marie

Jeanne

Descendants of Antoine II de Lacger

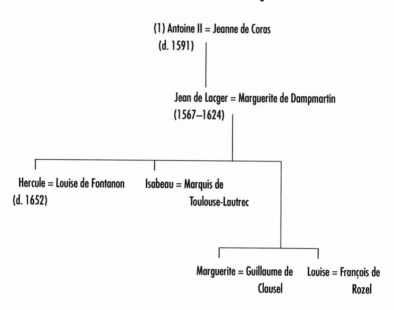

(1) Antoine II = Jeanne de Coras
(d. 1591)

Jean de Lacger = Marguerite de Dampmartin
(1567–1624)

Hercule = Louise de Fontanon
(d. 1652)

Isabeau = Marquis de
Toulouse-Lautrec

Marguerite = Guillaume de
Clausel

Louise = François de
Rozel

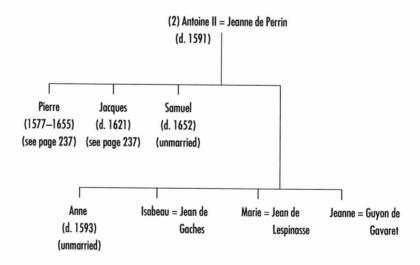

(2) Antoine II = Jeanne de Perrin
(d. 1591)

Pierre
(1577–1655)
(see page 237)

Jacques
(d. 1621)
(see page 237)

Samuel
(d. 1652)
(unmarried)

Anne
(d. 1593)
(unmarried)

Isabeau = Jean de
Gaches

Marie = Jean de
Lespinasse

Jeanne = Guyon de
Gavaret

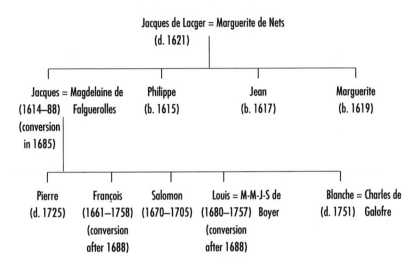

Descendants of Jacques de Lacger
(second son of Antoine II and Jeanne de Perrin)

Jacques de Lacger = Marguerite de Nets
(d. 1621)

Jacques = Magdelaine de   Philippe   Jean   Marguerite
(1614–88)   Falguerolles   (b. 1615)   (b. 1617)   (b. 1619)
(conversion
in 1685)

Pierre   François   Salomon   Louis = M-M-J-S de   Blanche = Charles de
(d. 1725)   (1661–1758) (1670–1705)   (1680–1757) Boyer   (d. 1751)   Galofre
            (conversion   (conversion
            after 1688)   after 1688)

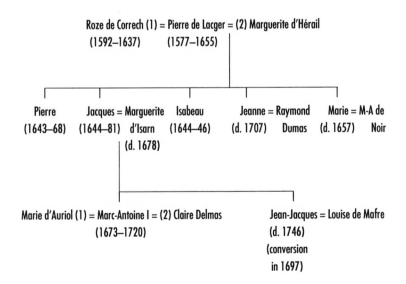

Descendants of Pierre de Lacger
(eldest son of Antoine II and Jeanne de Perrin)

Roze de Correch (1) = Pierre de Lacger = (2) Marguerite d'Hérail
(1592–1637)   (1577–1655)

Pierre   Jacques = Marguerite   Isabeau   Jeanne = Raymond   Marie = M-A de
(1643–68)   (1644–81) d'Isarn   (1644–46)   (d. 1707) Dumas   (d. 1657)   Noir
                       (d. 1678)

Marie d'Auriol (1) = Marc-Antoine I = (2) Claire Delmas   Jean-Jacques = Louise de Mafre
                    (1673–1720)   (d. 1746)
                                                             (conversion
                                                             in 1697)

Descendants of Marc-Antoine I de Lacger
(eldest son of Jacques and Marguerite d'Isarn)

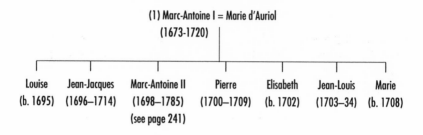

(1) Marc-Antoine I = Marie d'Auriol
(1673-1720)

Louise	Jean-Jacques	Marc-Antoine II	Pierre	Elisabeth	Jean-Louis	Marie
(b. 1695)	(1696–1714)	(1698–1785)	(1700–1709)	(b. 1702)	(1703–34)	(b. 1708)
		(see page 241)				

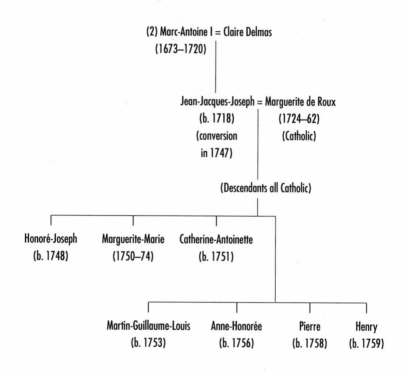

(2) Marc-Antoine I = Claire Delmas
(1673–1720)

Jean-Jacques-Joseph = Marguerite de Roux
(b. 1718)　　　　　　(1724–62)
(conversion　　　　　(Catholic)
in 1747)

(Descendants all Catholic)

Honoré-Joseph	Marguerite-Marie	Catherine-Antoinette
(b. 1748)	(1750–74)	(b. 1751)

Martin-Guillaume-Louis	Anne-Honorée	Pierre	Henry
(b. 1753)	(b. 1756)	(b. 1758)	(b. 1759)

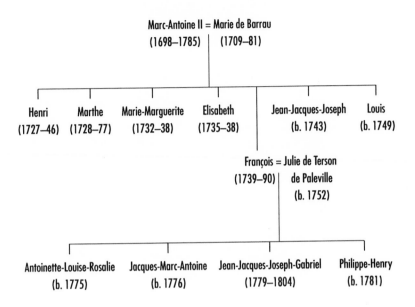

Descendants of Marc-Antoine II de Lacger
(son of Marc-Antoine I and Marie d'Auriol)

Marc-Antoine II = Marie de Barrau
(1698–1785) | (1709–81)

Henri (1727–46) Marthe (1728–77) Marie-Marguerite (1732–38) Elisabeth (1735–38) Jean-Jacques-Joseph (b. 1743) Louis (b. 1749)

François = Julie de Terson
(1739–90) | de Paleville
(b. 1752)

Antoinette-Louise-Rosalie (b. 1775) Jacques-Marc-Antoine (b. 1776) Jean-Jacques-Joseph-Gabriel (1779–1804) Philippe-Henry (b. 1781)

Bibliography

Manuscript Sources

Archives de la famille de Falguerolles. Château de Ladevèze, Lempaut.
  Généalogie de la famille de Falguerolles.
Archives de la famille de Lacger. Château de Navès, Castres.
  Copie des actes de la famille de M. de Lacger. 5 vols. (1518–1675).
  Dossiers généalogiques. 3 vols. (sixteenth through nineteenth centuries).
  Papiers concernant la religion.
Archives départementales. Haute-Garonne.
  B 56, 57, 64, 67, 1030, 1087, 1121, 1227, 1287, 1334, 1707, 1708, 1809,
  1884, 1924, 1924 bis, 1925, 1929, 1937, 3424, 3429, 3438.
  3 B 1 (1-5), 3 B 3, 3 B 4, 3 B 5.
  E 700, 916.
Archives départementales. Hérault.
  C 274, C 285, C 290, C 311, C 1640, C 1647.
Archives départementales. Tarn.
  E 231, 1404, 1409.
  G 260, 265, 297, 300.
  H 204, 205, 206, 216.
  I 1-6. Registres du consistoire de Castres (1645–84).
  Fonds Passelac, 67.
Archives départementales. Tarn-et-Garonne.
  I, 1. Registre du consistoire de Montauban (1595–98).
  1 Mi 1. Extraits du chartrier de Scorbiac.
Archives historiques. Service historique de l'armée de terre. Paris.
  Revues d'inspection. Rôles des officiers. Gratifications.
Archives municipales. Castres.
  AA 3.

BB 28, 32.

GG 16, 18, 19, 20, 21, 23, 24, 32, 33, 34, 35, 46, 53, 54.

II, 9-10.

Archives municipales. Nîmes.

RR 60.

Archives nationales. Paris.

TT 247, 437, 430, 433, 434, 440, 441, 442.

Bibliothèque de la Société de l'histoire du protestantisme français. Paris.

Baron de Cazals. Généalogie de la famille de Lacger.

MS. G. Dossier Romane-Musculus, no. 64.

MS. 66. Etat-civil des protestants à Paris.

Printed Sources

Balzac, Jean-Louis Guez, sieur de. *Les oeuvres de Monsieur de Balzac.* 2 vols. Paris, 1665. Reprint. Geneva: Slatkine, 1971.

Batailler, Antoine. *Mémoires de Batailler sur les guerres civiles à Castres et dans le Languedoc, 1584–1586.* Edited by Charles Pradel. Fasc. 2 of *Archives historiques de l'Albigeois.* Albi: G.-M. Nouguiès, 1894.

Bezons, Claude Bazin, sieur de. *Jugements sur la noblesse de Languedoc.* In *Pièces fugitives pour servir à l'histoire de France.* Vol. 1, pt. 2, *Généralité de Montpellier.* Vol. 2, *Généralité de Toulouse.* Paris: Chaubert et Hernissant, 1759.

Boisrobert, François Le Métal de. *Epistres en vers.* Edited by Maurice Cauchie. 2 vols. Paris: Hachette, 1927.

Bouffard-Madiane, Jean de. *Mémoires de J. de Bouffard-Madiane sur les guerres civiles du duc de Rohan, 1610–1629.* Edited by Charles Pradel. Paris, Toulouse, and Albi: Picard, Privat and Nouguiès, 1897.

Briquet, Pierre de, ed. *Code militaire, ou compilation des ordonnances des roys de France concernant les gens de guerre.* 4 vols. Paris: Imprimerie royale, 1728.

Déclaration du roy, concernant la forme de tenir des baptesmes, mariages, sepultures, vestures, noviciats et professions, et des extraits qui en doivent estre delivrez. Paris: Imprimerie royale, 1736.

Faurin, Jean. *Journal de Faurin sur les guerres de Castres.* Edited by Charles Pradel. In *Piéces fugitives pour servir à l'histoire de France,* edited by Ménard and D'Aubais. 2nd ed. Montpellier: M. de La Pijardière, 1878. Reprint. Marseilles: Lafitte, 1981.

Gaches, Jacques. *Mémoires sur les guerres de religion à Castres et dans le Languedoc*

(1555–1610) and *Suite des mémoires (1610–1612)*. Edited by Charles Pradel. Paris, 1879–94. Reprint. Geneva: Slatkine, 1970.

Généalogie historique de la maison de Lacger, de la ville de Castres, Haut-Languedoc. N.p., n.d.

Histoire ecclésiastique des Eglises Réformées au royaume de France. Edited by G. Baum, Ed. Cunitz, and R. Reuss. 3 vols. Paris, 1883–89.

Lachèvre, Frédéric, ed. *Le livre d'amour d'Hercule de Lacger. Vers pour Iris (Henriette de Coligny, comtesse de La Suze).* Paris: Sansot, 1910.

Lamy, M. *Précis historique sur le Régiment d'Auvergne.* Clostercamp, 1783.

"Les lois et règlements de l'Académie de Montauban, dressés l'an 1600, au mois d'octobre et publiés au grand Temple." *BSHPF* 9 (1860): 398–408.

Méjan, François. *Discipline de l'Eglise Réformée de France annotée et précédée d'une introduction historique.* Paris: Editions 'Je Sers,' 1947.

Montandre-Lonchamps, le sieur de, ed. *Etat militaire de France pour l'année 1758.* Paris: Guillyn, 1758.

Pinard. *Chronologie historique-militaire.* 8 vols. Paris: Claude Herrissant, 1760–78.

Pradel, Charles, ed. "Lettres de Coras, celles de sa femme, de son fils et de ses amis." *Revue historique, scientifique et littéraire du départment du Tarn* 3 (1880): 1–56.

———. "Fragments de lettres de la cour sous les règnes de Henri IV et Louis XIII." *Mémoires de l'Académie des sciences, inscriptions et belles-lettres de Toulouse,* 8ème série, 5 (1883): 129–47.

Quincy, Charles Sévin, marquis de. *Histoire militaire du règne de Louis le Grand, roy de France, où l'on trouve un détail de toutes les batailles, sièges, combats particuliers, et généralement de toutes les actions de guerre qui se sont passées pendant le cours de son règne, tant sur terre que sur mer.* 7 vols. Paris: Mariette, 1726.

Roussel, René-Louis de. *Essais historiques sur les régimens d'infanterie, cavalerie et dragons.* 10 vols. Paris: Guillyn, 1765–67.

Secondary Sources

Adam, Antoine. *Histoire de la littérature française au XVIIe siècle.* Vol. 2, *L'époque de Pascal* (1951). Paris: Editions Mondiales, 1949–56.

Amann, Peter H. "French Sharecropping Revisited: The Case of the Lauragais." *European History Quarterly* 20 (1990): 341–68.

Amussen, Susan D. "Gender, Family and Social Order, 1560–1725." In *Order and Disorder in Early Modern England,* edited by A. J. Fletcher and J. Stevenson, 196–217. Cambridge: Cambridge University Press, 1985.

Amussen, Susan D. *An Ordered Society: Gender and Class in Early Modern England.* Oxford: Basil Blackwell, 1988.

Anderson, Michael. *Approaches to the History of the Western Family, 1500–1914.* London: Macmillan, 1980.

André, Louis. *Michel Le Tellier et l'organisation de l'armée monarchique.* Paris: Félix Alcan, 1906.

Anquez, Léonce. *Histoire des assemblées politiques des réformées de France (1573–1622).* Paris, 1859. Reprint. Geneva: Slatkine, 1970.

Appolis, Emile. "Les protestants dans le diocèse de Lodève de la Révocation de l'Edit de Nantes à la Révolution." *Bulletin philologique et historique (jusqu'à 1715) du Comité des travaux historiques et scientifiques* (1957): 295–349.

Artigaut, René. *Grands jours de Castres.* 2nd ed. Castres: Société Culturelle du Pays Castrais, 1984.

————. *Les protestants de Castres et l'Edit de Nantes, 1598–1685.* Castres: Société Culturelle du Pays Castrais, 1985.

Atkinson, Jeanette Lee. "Queen Christina of Sweden: Sovereign between Throne and Altar." In *Women Writers of the Seventeenth Century*, edited by Katharina M. Wilson and Frank J. Warnke, 405–27. Athens: University of Georgia Press, 1989.

Augustin, Jean-Marie. *Famille et société: Les substitutions fidéicommissaires à Toulouse et en Haut-Languedoc au XVIIIe siècle.* Paris: Presses Universitaires de France, 1980.

Avenel, Georges d'. *Richelieu et la monarchie absolue.* 2nd ed. 4 vols. Paris: Plon, 1895.

Babeau, Albert. *La vie militaire sous l'Ancien Régime.* 2 vols. Paris: Firmin-Didot, 1889–90.

Balincourt, Edgard de. "Les d'Espérandieu d'Uzès et de Castres (1360–1866)." *Mémoires de l'Académie de Nîmes*, 7ème série, 24 (1901): 181–244.

Barbaza, Louis. *L'Académie de Castres et la société de Mlle de Scudéry, 1648–1670.* Castres: Abeilhou, 1890.

Barrière-Flavy, C. "La seigneurie de Navès: Etude historique sur une terre noble du pays de Castres (1244–1750)." *Revue historique, scientifique et littéraire du département du Tarn* 17 (1892): 113–34 and 280–91.

Beik, William. *Absolutism and Society in Seventeenth-Century France: State Power and Provincial Aristocracy in Languedoc.* Cambridge: Cambridge University Press, 1985.

Bellecombe, H. de. *Les Denis: Une famille bourgeoise de l'Agenais du XVIIe au XVIIIe siècle.* Paris: Fischbacher, 1894.

Benedict, Philip. "Bibliothèques protestantes et catholiques à Metz au XVIIe siècle." *Annales: e.s.c.* 40 (1985): 343–70.

―――. *The Huguenot Population of France, 1600–1685: The Demographic Fate and Customs of a Religious Minority.* Transactions of the American Philosophical Society. Vol. 81, pt. 5. Philadelphia, 1991.

―――. "La population réformée française de 1600 à 1685." *Annales: e.s.c.* 42 (1987): 1433–65.

―――. *Rouen during the Wars of Religion.* Cambridge: Cambridge University Press, 1981.

Bettinson, Christopher. "The Politiques and the Politique Party: A Reappraisal." In *From Valois to Bourbon: Dynasty, State and Society in Early Modern France,* edited by Keith Cameron, 35–49. Exeter Studies in History no. 24. Exeter: University of Exeter, 1989.

Bien, David. "Catholic Magistrates and Protestant Marriage in the French Enlightenment." *French Historical Studies* 2 (1962): 409–29.

―――. "Manufacturing Nobles: The Chancelleries in France to 1789." *Journal of Modern History* 61 (1989): 445–86.

―――. "The *Secrétaires du Roi:* Absolutism, Corps, and Privilege under the Ancien Régime." In *De l'Ancien Régime à la Révolution française: Recherches et perspectives,* edited by Albert Cremer, 153–68. Göttingen: Vandenhoeck und Ruprecht, 1978.

Billaçois, François. *Le duel dans la société française des XVIe–XVIIe siècles: Essai de psychosociologie historique.* Paris: Ecole des Hautes Etudes en Sciences Sociales, 1986.

Biographie toulousaine. 2 vols. Paris: L. G. Michaud, 1823.

Bitton, Davis. *The French Nobility in Crisis, 1560–1640.* Stanford: Stanford University Press, 1969.

Bloch, Jean-Richard. *L'anoblissement en France au temps de François Ier.* Paris: Félix Alcan, 1934.

Bloch, Marc. *Les caractères originaux de l'histoire rurale française.* Paris: Armand Colin, 1960.

Bluche, François. *Les magistrats du parlement de Paris au XVIIIe siècle (1715–1771).* Paris: Belles Lettres, 1960.

Bohanan, Donna. "Matrimonial Strategies among Nobles of Seventeenth-Century Aix-en-Provence." *Journal of Social History* 19 (1986): 503–10.

Bossy, John. "Blood and Baptism: Kinship, Community and Christianity in Western Europe from the Fourteenth to the Seventeenth Centuries." In *Sanctity and Secularity: The Church and the World,* edited by Derek Baker. Studies in Church History, vol. 10. New York: Harper and Row, 1973, 129–43.

―――. "Godparenthood: The Fortunes of a Social Institution in Early Modern

Christianity." In *Religion and Society in Early Modern Europe, 1500–1800,* edited by Kaspar von Greyerz, 194–201. London: Allen and Unwin, 1984.

Boudet, Jacques, ed. *Histoire universelle des armées.* 4 vols. Paris: Robert Laffont, 1966.

Bourchenin, Daniel. *Etude sur les académies protestantes en France au XVIe et au XVIIe siècle.* Paris: Grassart, 1882.

Boutaric, Edgard. *Institutions militaires de la France avant les armées permanentes.* Paris: Plon, 1863.

Bouyssou, Jean-François. "Aspects de la société protestante à Castres au début du XVIIe siècle." *Castres et le pays tarnais. Actes du XXVIe Congrès d'études de la Fédération des Sociétés académiques et savantes de Languedoc-Pyrénées-Gascogne,* 247–70. Albi: Editions de la "Revue du Tarn," 1972.

———. "La composition sociale des révoltes de Rohan à Castres (1610–1629)." *Revue du Tarn* (1970): 145–67.

Brenac, Madeleine. "Toulouse, centre de lutte contre le protestantisme au XVIIe siècle." *Annales du Midi* 77 (1965): 31–45.

Brives-Cazès, Emile. *La chambre de justice de Guyenne en 1583–84.* Bordeaux: Gounouilhon, 1874.

Brun-Durand, Justin. *Essai historique sur la chambre de l'Edit de Grenoble.* Valence: Chenevier et Chauvet, 1873.

Burlats-Brun, Pierre. "La famille de Clausel." *Cahiers du Centre de Généalogie Protestante* 17, 1er trimestre (1987): 913–26.

Cabrol, Pierre. *La Réforme et les guerres de religion à Castres des origines à l'Edit de Nantes.* Thèse de Baccalauréat en Théologie, Faculté de théologie protestante de Montauban. Montauban: Orphelins Imprimeurs, 1906.

Cambon de Lavalette, Jules. *La chambre de l'Edit de Languedoc.* Paris: Sandoz et Fischbacher, 1879.

Castan, Nicole. "La criminalité familiale dans le ressort du Parlement de Toulouse (1690–1730)." In *Crimes et criminalité en France sous l'Ancien Régime, 17e–18e siècles,* 91–107. Cahiers des Annales, no. 33. Paris: Librairie Armand Colin, 1971.

Castan, Yves. *Honnêteté et relations sociales en Languedoc, 1715–1780.* Paris: Plon, 1974.

———. "Pères et fils en Languedoc à l'époque classique." *XVIIe siècle,* no. 102–3 (1974): 31–43.

Caster, Gilles. *Le commerce du pastel et de l'épicerie à Toulouse, 1450–1561.* Toulouse: Privat, 1962.

Castrén, Gunnar. "Beys och Lacger: Två av drottning Kristinas franska ballett-författare." *Studier tillägnade Arvid Hultin.* Helsinki: J. S. Arvingar, 1915, 53–57.

Catellan, Jean de. *Arrests remarquables du Parlement de Toulouse.* 2 vols. Toulouse: Caranove, 1730.

Chabbert, Pierre. "L'Académie de Castres." In *Castres et le pays tarnais. Actes du XXVIe Congrès d'études de la Fédération des Sociétés académiques et savantes de Languedoc-Pyrénées-Gascogne,* 271–87. Albi: Editions de la "Revue du Tarn," 1972.

————. "Pierre Borel (1620?–1671)." *Revue d'histoire des sciences* 21 (1968): 303–43.

Charbonnier, Pierre. *Une autre France: La seigneurie rurale en Basse-Auvergne du XIVe au XVIe siècle.* 2 vols. Clermont-Ferrand: Institut d'Etudes du Massif Central, 1980.

Charnisay, B. de. "Les chiffres de M. l'Abbé Rouquette: Etude sur les fugitifs du Languedoc (Uzès)." *BSHPF* 62 (1913): 136–49.

Charrin, Louis de. *Les testaments dans la région de Montpellier au moyen âge.* Ambilly: Presses de Savoie, 1961.

Chartier, Roger, Dominique Julia, and Marie-Madeleine Compère. *L'éducation en France du XVIe au XVIIIe siècle.* Paris: Société d'Edition d'Enseignement Supérieur, 1976.

Chaussinand-Nogaret, Guy. "Capital et structure sociale sous l'Ancien Régime." *Annales: e.s.c.* 25 (1970): 463–76.

————. *The French Nobility in the Eighteenth Century: From Feudalism to Enlightenment.* Translated by W. Doyle. Cambridge: Cambridge University Press, 1985.

Chêne, Christian. "Testaments, fortunes et religions: La pratique testamentaire à Ganges de la fin du XVIe siècle au début du XVIIIe siècle." In *Confluence des droits savants et des pratiques juridiques. Actes du Colloque de Montpellier* (1977), 181–220. Milan: Guiffrè, 1979.

Chrisman, Miriam U. "Family and Religion in Two Noble Families: French Catholic and English Puritan." *Journal of Family History* 8 (Summer 1983): 190–210.

Cioranescu, Alexandre. *Bibliographie de la littérature française du dix-septième siècle.* 3 vols. Paris: CNRS, 1965–67.

Collins, James B. "The Economic Role of Women in Seventeenth-Century France." *French Historical Studies* 16, no. 2 (1989): 436–70.

————. *Fiscal Limits of Absolutism: Direct Taxation in Early Seventeenth-Century France.* Berkeley, Los Angeles, and London: University of California Press, 1988.

Collomp, Alain. "Alliance et filiation en Haute-Provence au XVIIIe siècle." *Annales: e.s.c.* 32 (1977): 445–77.

————. "Famille nucléaire et famille élargie en Haute-Provence au XVIIIe siècle (1703–1734)." *Annales: e.s.c.* 27 (1972): 969–75.

Collomp, Alain. *La maison du père: Famille et village en Haute-Provence aux XVIIe et XVIIIe siècles*. Paris: Presses Universitaires de France, 1983.

―――. "Tensions, Dissensions, and Ruptures inside the Family in Seventeenth- and Eighteenth-Century Haute-Provence." In *Interest and Emotion: Essays on the Study of Family and Kinship*, edited by Hans Medick and David Warren Sabean, 145–70. Cambridge: Cambridge University Press, 1984.

Compère, Marie-Madeleine, and Dominique Julia. *Les collèges français, 16e–18e siècles*. Vol. 1, *Répertoire, France du Midi*. Paris: INRP-CNRS, 1984.

Constant, Jean-Marie. *Nobles et paysans en Beauce aux XVIème et XVIIème siècles*. Thèse de doctorat d'Etat, Université de Lille III, 1981.

―――. *La vie quotidienne de la noblesse française aux XVIe–XVIIe siècles*. Paris: Hachette, 1985.

Cooper, J. P. "Patterns of Inheritance and Settlement by Great Landowners from the Fifteenth to the Eighteenth Centuries." In *Family and Inheritance: Rural Society in Western Europe, 1200–1800*, edited by J. Goody, J. Thirsk, and E. P. Thompson, 192–327. Cambridge: Cambridge University Press, 1976.

Corvisier, André. *L'armée française de la fin du XVIIe siècle au ministère de Choiseul: Le soldat*. 2 vols. Paris: Presses Universitaires de France, 1964.

―――. *Armies and Societies in Europe, 1494–1789*. Translated by A. T. Siddall. Bloomington and London: Indiana University Press, 1979.

―――. *Les contrôles de troupes de l'Ancien Régime*. 4 vols. Paris: Ministère des Armées, 1968–70.

―――. *Louvois*. Paris: Fayard, 1983.

Coste, Emile. "La 'Maison de Gabriac' en Vallée Française aux XVIe et XVIIe siècle." *BSHPF* 86 (1937): 265–301.

Cubells, Monique. "A propos des usurpations de noblesse en Provence, sous l'Ancien Régime." *Provence historique* 20 (1970): 224–301.

Dauviller, Jean. "Histoire des costumes des gens de justice dans notre ancienne France." In *Recueil de mémoires et travaux publié par la Société d'histoire du droit et des institutions des anciens pays de droit écrit*, vol. 9, *Mélanges Roger Aubenas*, 229–40. Montpellier: Faculté de droit et des sciences économiques, 1974.

Davies, Joan. "Family Service and Family Strategies: The Household of Henri, duc de Montmorency, ca. 1590–1610." *Bulletin of the Society for Renaissance Studies* 3 (1985): 27–43.

―――. "The Libraries of Some Protestants of Toulouse in 1572: Cultural Influences and Calvinism." *Bibliothèque d'Humanisme et Renaissance* 41 (1979): 555–66.

————. "Persecution and Protestantism: Toulouse, 1562–1575." *Historical Journal* 22 (1979): 31–51.

————. "The Politics of the Marriage Bed: Matrimony and the Montmorency Family, 1527–1612." *French History* 6 (1992): 63–95.

Davis, Natalie Zemon. "Ghosts, Kin, and Progeny: Some Features of Family Life in Early Modern France." *Daedalus* 106, no. 2 (Spring 1977): 87–114.

————. *The Return of Martin Guerre.* Cambridge: Harvard University Press, 1983.

————. *Society and Culture in Early Modern France: Eight Essays.* Stanford: Stanford University Press, 1975.

Delumeau, Jean. *Naissance et affirmation de la réforme.* Paris: Presses Universitaires de France, 1965.

Derouet, Bernard. "Pratiques successorales et rapport à la terre: Les sociétés paysannes d'Ancien Régime." *Annales: e.s.c.* 44 (1989): 173–206.

Dewald, Jonathan. *The Formation of a Provincial Nobility: The Magistrates of the Parlement of Rouen, 1499–1610.* Princeton: Princeton University Press, 1980.

————. *Pont-St-Pierre, 1398–1789: Lordship, Community, and Capitalism in Early Modern France.* Berkeley and Los Angeles: University of California Press, 1987.

Deyon, Pierre. *Amiens, capitale provinciale: Etude sur la société urbaine au 17e siècle.* Paris and The Hague: Mouton, 1967.

————. "Mentalités populaires: Un sondage à Amiens au XVIIe siècle." *Annales: e.s.c.* 17 (1962): 448–58.

Deyon, Solange. "Les académies protestantes en France." *BSHPF* 135 (1989): 77–85.

————. *Du loyalisme au refus: Les protestants français et leur député général entre la Fronde et la Révocation.* Lille: Publications de l'Université de Lille III, 1976.

Diefendorf, Barbara B. "Houses Divided: Religious Schism in Sixteenth-Century Parisian Families." In *Urban Life in the Renaissance,* edited by S. Zimmerman and R. Weissman, 80–99. Newark: University of Delaware Press, 1989.

————. *Paris City Councillors in the Sixteenth Century: The Politics of Patrimony.* Princeton: Princeton University Press, 1983.

————. "Widowhood and Remarriage in Sixteenth-Century Paris." *Journal of Family History* 7 (1982): 379–95.

Dolan, Claire. "Géniteur ou gestionnaire? L'image du père à Aix-en-Provence au XVIe siècle." *Histoire sociale / Social History* 18, no. 35 (1985): 29–43.

————. "Solidarités familiales à Aix au XVIe siècle." *Provence historique* 32, no. 128 (1982): 145–52.

Doucet, Roger. *Les institutions de la France au XVIe siècle.* 2 vols. Paris: Picard, 1948.

Douen, O. "Le fondateur de la caisse des conversions." *BSHPF* 30 (1881): 145–60.

Duby, Georges, and Armand Wallon, eds. *Histoire de la France rurale*. 4 vols. Paris: Seuil, 1975–76.

Dumons, G. "La famille de Nautonier de Castelfranc." *BSHPF* 60 (1911): 387–402.

Dupont-Ferrier, Gustave. *Les officiers royaux des bailliages et sénéchaussées et les institutions monarchiques locales en France à la fin du moyen âge*. Paris: Bouillon, 1902.

Dussauge, André. *Etudes sur la Guerre de Sept Ans: Le ministère de Belle-Isle: Krefeld et Lütterberg (1758)*. Paris: Fournier, 1914.

Estadieu, Mathieu. *Annales du pays castrais depuis les temps les plus reculés jusqu'à nos jours*. Castres, 1893. Reprint. Marseilles: Lafitte, 1977.

———. *Notes chronologiques et statistiques pour servir à l'histoire de la ville de Castres*. Castres, 1882. Reprint. Marseilles: Lafitte, 1976.

Estèbe [Garrisson], Janine. *Tocsin pour un massacre: La saison des Saint-Barthélemy*. Paris: Centurion, 1968.

———. "Les Saint-Barthélemy des villes du Midi." In *Actes du Colloque l'Amiral de Coligny et son temps*, 717–29. Paris: SHPF, 1974.

Falgairolle, Prosper. *Une famille de l'ancienne France: Les Baudan à Nîmes et à Montpellier pendant quatre siècles*. Cavaillon: Imprimerie Mistral, 1926.

Falguerolles, Godefroy E. de. "Les paroissiens de l'Eglise Réformée à Puylaurens (1630–1650)." *BSHPF* 111 (1965): 89–108.

Faucher, B. "Les registres de l'état civil protestant en France depuis le XVIe siècle jusqu'à nos jours." *Bibliothèque de l'Ecole des Chartes* 84 (1923): 306–46.

Fell, A. London. *Origins of Legislative Sovereignty and the Legislative State*. 4 vols. to date. Cambridge, MA, and Königstein im Taunus: Oelgeschlager, Gunn and Hain, and Athenäum; and New York: Praeger, 1983–.

Filhol, René. "Protestantisme et droit d'aînesse au XVIe siècle." *Recueil de mémoires et travaux publié par la société d'histoire du droit et des institutions des anciens pays de droit écrit* 7 (1970): 195–205.

Fine, Agnès. "L'héritage du nom de baptême." *Annales: e.s.c.* 42 (1987): 853–77.

———. "Le prix de l'exclusion: Dot et héritage dans le Sud-Ouest occitan." In *La dot: La valeur des femmes*, 31–51. Toulouse: L'Université de Toulouse-Le Mirail, 1982.

Flandrin, Jean-Louis. *Familles: Parenté, maison, sexualité dans l'ancienne société*. Paris: Hachette, 1976.

Forster, Robert. *The House of Saulx-Tavanes: Versailles and Burgundy, 1700–1830*. Baltimore: Johns Hopkins University Press, 1971.

————. *The Nobility of Toulouse in the Eighteenth Century: A Social and Economic Study.* Baltimore: Johns Hopkins University Press, 1960.

————. "The Provincial Noble: A Reappraisal." *AHR* 68 (1963): 681–91.

Frêche, Georges. "Contre-Réforme et dragonnades (1640–1789): Pour une orientation statistique de l'histoire du protestantisme." *BSHPF* 119 (1973): 362–83.

————. "Dénombrement de feux et d'habitants de 2973 communautés de la région toulousaine." *Annales de démographie historique* 4 (1968): 389–421; 5 (1969): 393–471.

————. "La population de Castres et du Tarn de 1665 à 1968." *Annales du Midi* 83 (1971): 191–213.

————. *Toulouse et la région Midi-Pyrénées au siècle des lumières (vers 1670–1789).* Paris: Cujas, 1974.

Gachon, Paul. *Quelques préliminaires de la révocation de l'Edit de Nantes en Languedoc (1661–1685).* Toulouse: Privat, 1899.

Galpern, A. N. *The Religions of the People in Sixteenth-Century Champagne.* Cambridge: Harvard University Press, 1976.

Garrisson, Janine. *L'Edit de Nantes et sa révocation: Histoire d'une intolérance.* Paris: Seuil, 1985.

————. *Les Protestants au XVIe siècle.* Paris: Fayard, 1988.

Garrisson-Estèbe [Garrisson], Janine. *L'homme protestant.* Paris: Hachette, 1980.

————. *Protestants du Midi, 1559–1598.* Toulouse: Privat, 1980.

Gaufrès, Jules. "Les collèges protestants." *BSHPF* 22 (1873): 269–82, 413–23; 23 (1874): 289–304, 337–48, 385–408; 24 (1875): 4–20, 193–208; 27 (1878): 193–208.

Gibson, Wendy. *Women in Seventeenth-Century France.* New York: St. Martin's Press, 1989.

Giesey, Ralph E. "The Monarchomach triumvers: Hotman, Beza and Mornay." *Bibliothèque d'Humanisme et Renaissance* 32 (1970): 41–56.

————. "Rules of Inheritance and Strategies of Mobility in Prerevolutionary France." *AHR* 82 (1977): 271–89.

Golden, Richard M., ed. *The Huguenot Connection: The Edict of Nantes, Its Revocation, and Early French Migration to South Carolina.* Dordrecht: Kluwer Academic Publishers, 1988.

Goody, Jack. *The Development of the Family and Marriage in Europe.* Cambridge: Cambridge University Press, 1983.

————. "Inheritance, Property and Women: Some Comparative Considerations." In *Family and Inheritance: Rural Society in Western Europe, 1200–1800,* edited by

J. Goody, J. Thirsk, and E. P. Thompson, 10–36. Cambridge: Cambridge University Press, 1976.

Goubert, Pierre. "Family and Province: A Contribution to the Knowledge of Family Structures in Early Modern France." *Journal of Family History* 2/3 (1977): 179–95.

Gouesse, Jean-Marie. "Parenté, famille et mariage en Normandie aux XVIIe et XVIIIe siècles: Présentation d'une source et d'une enquête." *Annales: e.s.c.* 17 (1972): 1139–54.

Gouron, André. "Pour une géographie de l'augment de dot." *Mémoires de la Société pour l'histoire du droit et des institutions des anciens pays bourguignons, comtois et romands* 27 (1966): 113–30.

Granat, O. "Une académie de province au XVIIe siècle." *Revue des universités du Midi* 20 (1898): 181–95.

———. "L'industrie de la draperie à Castres au dix-septième siècle et les 'ordonnances' de Colbert." *Annales du Midi* 10 (1898): 446–57; 11 (1899): 56–67.

Granier, Raymond. "La peste à Cordes et dans ses alentours du XVIe au XVIIIe siècle." In *Gaillac et pays tarnais. Actes du XXXIe Congrès de la Fédération des Sociétés académiques et savantes, Languedoc-Pyrénées-Gascogne*. Albi: Ateliers Professionnels de l'Orphelinat Saint-Jean, 1977.

Greengrass, Mark. "The Anatomy of a Religious Riot in Toulouse in May 1562." *Journal of Ecclesiastical History* 34 (1983): 367–91.

———. *France in the Age of Henry IV: The Struggle for Stability.* London and New York: Longman, 1984.

———. "Noble Affinities in Early Modern France: The Case of Henri I de Montmorency, Constable of France." *European History Quarterly* 16 (1986): 275–311.

———. "Property and Politics in Sixteenth-Century France: The Landed Fortune of Constable Anne de Montmorency." *French History* 2 (1988): 371–98.

Grendler, Paul F. "Schooling in Western Europe." *Renaissance Quarterly* 43 (1990): 775–87.

Greslé-Bouignol, Maurice. *Guide des Archives du Tarn.* Albi: Archives départementales, 1978.

Griffiths, Gordon. *Representative Government in Western Europe in the Sixteenth Century.* Oxford: Oxford University Press, 1968.

Haag, Eugène, and Emile Haag. *La France protestante, ou vies des protestants français.* 1st ed. 10 vols. Paris: Cherbuliez, 1846–58.

———. *La France protestante, ou vies des protestants français.* 2nd ed. Edited by Henri Bordier. 6 vols. Paris: Sandoz et Fischbacher, 1877–88.

Haas, Louis. "Boccaccio, Baptismal Kinship, and Spiritual Incest." *Renaissance and Reformation / Renaissance et Réforme* 4 (1989): 343–56.

Hanley, Sarah. "Engendering the State: Family Formation and State Building in Early Modern France." *French Historical Studies* 16, no. 1 (1989): 4–27.

Hanlon, Gregory. *L'univers des gens de bien: Culture et comportements des élites urbaines en Agenais-Condomois au XVIIe siècle.* Talence: Presses Universitaires de Bordeaux, 1989.

Hanlon, Gregory, and Elspeth Carruthers. "Wills, Inheritance and the Moral Order in the Seventeenth-Century Agenais." *Journal of Family History* 15, no. 2 (1990): 149–61.

Hanoteau, Jean, and Emile Bonnot. *Bibliographie des historiques des régiments français.* Paris: Honoré Champion, 1913.

Harding, Robert R. *Anatomy of a Power Elite: The Provincial Governors of Early Modern France.* New Haven: Yale University Press, 1978.

Hareven, Tamara K. "The History of the Family and the Complexity of Social Change." *AHR* 96 (1991): 95–124.

Herlihy, David. "Family." *AHR* 96 (1991): 1–16.

Hilaire, Jean. "L'évolution des régimes matrimoniaux dans la région de Montpellier aux XVIIe et XVIIIe siècles." *Mémoires de la Société pour l'histoire du droit et des institutions des anciens pays bourguignons, comtois et romans* 27 (1966): 133–94.

———. *Le régime des biens entre époux dans la région de Montpellier du début du XIIIe siècle à la fin du XVIe siècle: Contribution aux études d'histoire du droit écrit.* Montpellier: Causse, Graille et Castelnau, 1957.

———. "Vie en commun: Famille et esprit communautaire." *Revue historique de droit français et étranger* 51 (1973): 8–53.

Hoffman, Philip T. "The Economic Theory of Sharecropping in Early Modern France." *Journal of Economic History* 44 (1984): 309–19.

Holt, Mack. *The Duke of Anjou and the Politique Struggle during the Wars of Religion.* Cambridge: Cambridge University Press, 1986.

Howard, Michael. *War in European History.* Oxford: Oxford University Press, 1976.

Hudson, Elizabeth K. "The Protestant Struggle for Survival in Early Bourbon France: The Case of the Huguenot Schools." *Archiv für Reformationsgeschichte* 76 (1985): 271–95.

Hughes, Diane Owen. "From Brideprice to Dowry in Mediterranean Europe." *Journal of Family History* 3 (1978): 262–96.

Hunt, David. *Parents and Children in History: The Psychology of Family Life in Early Modern France.* New York and London: Basic Books, 1970.

Huppert, George. *Les Bourgeois Gentilshommes: An Essay on the Definition of Elites in Renaissance France*. Chicago and London: University of Chicago Press, 1977.

———. "Lucullus, Crassus and Cato in Grenoble." *Historical Reflections / Réflexions historiques* 15 (1988): 271–78.

———. *Public Schools in Renaissance France*. Urbana and Chicago: University of Illinois Press, 1984.

Jolibus, Emile. "Pierre Borel." *Revue du département du Tarn* 3 (1880–81): 132–33.

Jones, Colin. "The Military Revolution and the Professionalisation of the French Army under the Ancien Régime." In *The Military Revolution and the State, 1500–1800*, edited by Michael Duffy, 29–48. Exeter Studies in History, no. 1. Exeter: University of Exeter, 1980.

Jouanna, Arlette. *Le devoir de révolte: La noblesse française et la gestion de l'état moderne (1559–1661)*. Paris: Fayard, 1989.

———. *L'idée de race en France au XVIe siècle et au début du XVIIe*. 2 vols. Montpellier: Université Paul Valéry, 1981.

———. "Recherches sur la notion d'honneur au XVIe siècle." *Revue d'histoire moderne et contemporaine* 15 (1968): 597–623.

Joubert, André. *Une famille de seigneurs calvinistes du Haut-Anjou: Les Chivré, marquis de la Barre de Bierné (XVIe–XVIIIe siècles)*. Nantes and Paris: Grimaud et Lechevalier, 1887.

Joutard, Philippe. *Les Camisards*. Paris: Gallimard, 1976.

———. *La légende des Camisards: Une sensibilité au passé*. Paris: Gallimard, 1977.

Kalas, Robert J. "The Selve Family of Limousin: Members of a New Elite in Early Modern France." *Sixteenth Century Journal* 18 (1987): 147–72.

Keen, Maurice H. *The Laws of War in the Late Middle Ages*. London and Toronto: Routledge and Kegan Paul and University of Toronto Press, 1965.

Kennett, Lee. *The French Armies in the Seven Years' War: A Study in Military Organization and Administration*. Durham, N.C.: Duke University Press, 1967.

Kettering, Sharon. *Judicial Politics and Urban Revolt in Seventeenth-Century France: The Parlement of Aix, 1629–1659*. Princeton: Princeton University Press, 1978.

———. "Patronage and Kinship in Early Modern France." *French Historical Studies* 16, no. 2 (1989): 408–35.

———. "The Patronage Power of Early Modern French Noblewomen." *Historical Journal* 32 (1989): 817–41.

———. *Patrons, Brokers, and Clients in Seventeenth-Century France*. New York and Oxford: Oxford University Press, 1986.

Kiernan, V. G. *The Duel in European History*. Oxford: Oxford University Press, 1986.

Koch, P. "Jérémie Ferrier, pasteur de Nîmes (1601–1613)." *BSHPF* 89 (1940): 9–21, 152–63, 237–61, 341–70.

Labarre, Albert. *Le livre dans la vie amiénoise du seizième siècle: L'enseignement des inventaires après décès, 1503–1576.* Paris and Louvain: Nauwelaerts, 1971.

Labatut, Jean-Pierre. *Les ducs et pairs de France au XVIIe siècle.* Paris: Presses Universitaires de France, 1972.

Labrousse, Elisabeth. "Conversion dans les deux sens." *La conversion au XVIIe siècle. Actes du XIIe Colloque de Marseille (janvier 1982),* edited by J. Solé, 161–77. Marseille, 1983.

———. "Les mariages bigarrés: Unions mixtes en France au XVIIIe siècle." *Le couple interdit: Entretiens sur le racisme,* edited by Léon Poliakov, 159–76. Paris: Mouton, 1980.

———. *"Une foi, une loi, un roi?" Essai sur la révocation de l'Edit de Nantes.* Geneva and Paris: Payot and Labor et Fides, 1985.

Lacger, Louis de. "La crise protestante en terre tarnaise: Albi, Castres et Lavaur (1517–1598)." *Bulletin de littérature ecclésiastique* 58 (1956): 3–30.

———. *Histoire religieuse de l'Albigeois.* Albi: Imprimerie Coopérative du Sud-Ouest, 1962.

Larochelle, Lucie. "Le vocabulaire social et les contours de la noblesse urbaine provençale à la fin du moyen âge: L'exemple aixois." *Annales du Midi* 104 (1992): 163–73.

Latreille, Albert. *L'oeuvre militaire de la révolution: L'armée et la nation à la fin de l'Ancien Régime: Les derniers Ministres de la Guerre de la monarchie.* Paris: Librairie Chapelot, 1914.

Lecestre, Léon. *Liste alphabétique des officiers généraux jusqu'en 1762 dont les notices biographiques se trouvent dans la Chronologie militaire de Pinard. Extrait du Biographie moderne.* Paris: Picard, 1903.

Lefebvre, Charles. *L'ancien droit des successions.* 2 vols. Paris: Recueil Sirey, 1912–18.

———. *Observations sur les rentes perpétuelles dans l'ancien droit français.* Paris: Recueil Sirey, 1914.

Lehr, Henry. *Les protestants d'autrefois: Vie et institutions militaires.* Paris: Librairie Fischbacher, 1901.

———. "Les soldats huguenots dans les armées de Louis XV." *Revue chrétienne,* 3ème série, 5 (1897): 412–24.

Léonard, Emile-G. *L'armée et ses problèmes au XVIIIe siècle.* Paris: Plon, 1958.

———. *Histoire générale du protestantisme.* 3 vols. Paris: Presses Universitaires de France, 1961–64.

Léonard, Emile-G. "L'Institution du Mérite Militaire." *BSHPF* 82 (1933): 297–320 and 456–73.

———. *Mon village sous Louis XV, d'après les mémoires d'un paysan.* Paris: Presses Universitaires de France, 1941.

———. "Le problème du mariage civil et les protestants français au XVIIIe siècle." *Revue de théologie et d'action évangélique* 2 (1942): 241–99.

———. *Le protestant français.* Paris: Presses Universitaires de France, 1955.

Lepointe, Gabriel. *Droit romain et ancien droit français: Régimes matrimoniaux, liberalités, successions.* Paris: Montchrestien, 1958.

Le Roy Ladurie, Emmanuel. "Family Structure and Inheritance Customs in Sixteenth-Century France." In *Family and Inheritance: Rural Society in Western Europe, 1200–1800,* edited by J. Goody, J. Thirsk, and E. P. Thompson, 37–72. Cambridge: Cambridge University Press, 1976.

———. *Montaillou, village occitan de 1294 à 1324.* Paris: Gallimard, 1975.

———. *Les paysans de Languedoc.* 2nd ed. 2 vols. Paris: Mouton, 1966.

———. "Système de la coutume: Structures familiales et coutume d'héritage en France au XVIe siècle." *Annales: e.s.c.* 27 (1972): 825–46.

Lick, Richard. "Les intérieurs domestiques dans la seconde moitié du XVIIIe siècle d'après les inventaires après décès de Coutances." *Annales de Normandie* 20 (1970): 293–316.

Ligou, Daniel. "La Cour des Aides de Montauban à la fin du XVIIIe siècle." *Annales du Midi* 64 (1952): 297–324.

———. "La structure sociale du protestantisme montalbanais à la fin du XVIIIe siècle." *BSHPF* 102 (1954): 93–110.

———. *Le protestantisme en France de 1598 à 1715.* Paris: SEDES, 1968.

Ligou, Daniel, and Janine Garrisson-Estèbe [Garrisson]. "La bourgeoisie réformée montalbanaise à la fin de l'Ancien Régime." *Revue d'histoire économique et sociale* 33 (1955): 377–404.

Lougee, Carolyn C. *Le Paradis des Femmes: Women, Salons, and Social Stratification in Seventeenth-Century France.* Princeton: Princeton University Press, 1976.

Louis-Lucas, Paul. *Etude sur la vénalité des charges et fonctions publiques.* 2 vols. Paris: Challamel, 1882.

Lublinskaya, A. D. *French Absolutism: The Crucial Phase, 1620–1629.* Cambridge: Cambridge University Press, 1968.

McDonogh, Gary W. *Good Families of Barcelona: A Social History of Power in the Industrial Era.* Princeton: Princeton University Press, 1986.

Maillet, Jean. "De l'exclusion coutumière des filles dotées à la renonciation à succession future dans les coutumes de Toulouse et Bordeaux." *Revue historique de droit français et étranger* 30 (1952): 514–45.

Major, J. Russell. "The Crown and Aristocracy in Renaissance France." *AHR* 69 (1964): 631–45.

———. "Noble Income, Inflation, and the Wars of Religion in France." *AHR* 86 (1981): 21–48.

———. *Representative Government in Renaissance France.* New Haven and London: Yale University Press, 1980.

Malzac, Louis. *Les Pourtalès: Histoire d'une famille huguenote des Cévennes, 1500–1860.* Paris: Hachette, 1914.

Margolf, Diane C. "The Edict of Nantes' Amnesty: Appeals to the chambre de l'Edit, 1600–1610." *Proceedings of the Annual Meeting of the Western Society for French History* 16 (1988): 49–55.

Marion, Marcel. *Dictionnaire des institutions de la France aux XVIIe et XVIIIe siècles.* Paris: A. et J. Picard, 1968.

Marshall, Sherrin, ed. *Women in Reformation and Counter-Reformation Europe: Public and Private Worlds.* Bloomington and Indianapolis: Indiana University Press, 1989.

Martin, Henri-Jean. *Livres, pouvoirs et sociétés à Paris au XVIIe siècle (1598–1701).* 2 vols. Geneva: Droz, 1969.

Marturé, B. A. *Histoire du pays castrais.* 2 vols. Castres: J. Auger, 1882.

Mazas, Alexandre. *Histoire de l'ordre royal et militaire de Saint-Louis depuis son institution en 1693 jusqu'en 1830.* 2nd ed. 3 vols. Paris: Firmin-Didot, 1860–61.

Mentzer, Raymond A., Jr. "Bipartisan Justice and the Pacification of Late Sixteenth-Century Languedoc." In *Regnum, Religio et Ratio: Essays Presented to Robert M. Kingdon,* edited by Jerome Friedman, 125–32. Kirksville, Mo.: Sixteenth Century Journal Publishers, 1987.

———. "Calvinist Propaganda and the Parlement of Toulouse." *Archiv für Reformationsgeschichte* 68 (1977): 268–83.

———. "Le consistoire et la pacification du monde rural." *BSHPF* 135 (1989): 373–89.

———. "*Disciplina nervus ecclesiae:* The Calvinist Reform of Morals at Nîmes." *Sixteenth Century Journal* 18 (1987): 89–115.

———. "Ecclesiastical Discipline and Communal Reorganization among the Protestants of Southern France." *European History Quarterly* 21 (1991): 165–85.

———. "The Formation of the *chambre de l'Edit* of Languedoc." *Proceedings of the Annual Meeting of the Western Society for French History* 8 (1980): 47–56.

———. *Heresy Proceedings in Languedoc, 1500–1560.* Transactions of the American Philosophical Society. Vol. 74, pt. 5. Philadelphia, 1984.

Mentzer, Raymond A., Jr. "The Misidentification of the Poet Lacger." *French Studies Bulletin*, no. 37 (Winter 1990/91): 18–19.

Mercier, Gaston. "La maison de Calvairac: Comment ils ont tenu." *BSHPF* 73 (1924): 313–23; 74 (1925): 21–30, 141–48, 261–74, 453–63.

Merle, Louis. *La métairie et l'évolution agraire de la Gâtine poitevine de la fin du moyen âge à la Révolution.* Paris: SEVPEN, 1958.

Mettam, Roger. *Power and Faction in Louis XIV's France.* Oxford and New York: Basil Blackwell, 1988.

Meyer, Jean. *La noblesse bretonne au XVIIIᵉ siècle.* 2 vols. Paris: SEVPEN, 1966.

Meylan, Henri. "Collèges et académies protestantes en France au XVIᵉ siècle." *Actes du 95ᵉ Congrès National des Sociétés Savantes, Reims, 1970,* vol. 1, *Enseignement intellectuel (IXᵉ–XVIᵉ siècle),* 301–9. Paris: Bibliothèque nationale, 1975.

Mintz, Sidney W., and Eric R. Wolf, "An Analysis of Ritual Co-parenthood (Compadrazgo)." *Southwestern Journal of Anthropology* 6 (1950): 341–68.

Mitterauer, Michael, and Reinhard Sieder. *The European Family: Patriarchy to Partnership from the Middle Ages to the Present.* Translated by K. Oosterveen and M. Hörzinger. Chicago: University of Chicago Press, 1982.

Mongrédien, Georges. "Le tricentenaire de l'Académie de Castres." *XVIIᵉ siècle* 88 (1970): 89–91.

Motley, Mark. *Becoming an Aristocrat: The Education of the Court Nobility, 1580–1715.* Princeton: Princeton University Press, 1990.

Mouillard, Lucien. *Les régiments sous Louis XV: Constitution de tous les corps de troupes à la solde de France pendant les Guerres de Succession à l'Empire et de Sept Ans.* Paris: Baudoin, 1882.

Mours, Samuel. *Le protestantisme en France au XVIᵉ siècle.* Paris: Librairie Protestante, 1959.

———. *Le protestantisme en France au XVIIᵉ siècle (1598–1685).* Paris: Librairie Protestante, 1967.

Mours, Samuel, and Daniel Robert. *Le protestantisme en France du XVIIIᵉ siècle à nos jours (1685–1970).* Paris: Librairie Protestante, 1972.

Mousnier, Roland. *Les institutions de la France sous la monarchie absolue.* 2 vols. Paris: Presses Universitaires de France, 1974–80.

———. *La vénalité des offices sous Henri IV et Louis XIII.* 2nd ed. Paris: Presses Universitaires de France, 1971.

Muchembled, Robert, "Famille, amour et mariage: Mentalité et comportements des nobles artésiens à l'époque de Philippe II." *Revue d'histoire moderne et contemporaine* 22 (1975): 233–61.

Nayral, Magloire. *Biographie castraise*. 4 vols. Castres: Vidal Aîné, 1833–37.

Neubert, Fritz. "Zur Problematik französischer Renaissancebriefe: Die 'lettres de Jean de Coras, celles de sa femme, de son fils et de ses amis' (1566–1573)." *Bibliothèque d'Humanisme et Renaissance* 26 (1964): 28–54.

Neuschel, Kristen B. "Noble Households in the Sixteenth Century: Material Settings and Human Communities." *French Historical Studies* 15, no. 4 (Fall 1988): 595–622.

———. *Word of Honor: Interpreting Noble Culture in Sixteenth-Century France*. Ithaca and London: Cornell University Press, 1989.

Niderst, Alain. *Madeleine de Scudéry, Paul Pellisson et leur monde*. Rouen: Publications de l'Université de Rouen, 1976.

Orcibal, Jean. *Louis XIV et les protestants*. Paris: Vrin, 1951.

Ourliac, Paul, and J. de Malafosse. *Histoire du droit privé*. 3 vols. Paris: Presses Universitaires de France, 1957–68.

Ozment, Steven. *When Fathers Ruled: Family Life in the Reformation*. Cambridge: Harvard University Press, 1983.

Parker, David. *La Rochelle and the French Monarchy: Conflict and Order in Seventeenth-Century France*. London: Royal Historical Society, 1980.

Parker, Geoffrey. *The Thirty Years' War*. London and New York: Routledge and Kegan Paul, 1987.

Paulhet, Jean-Claude. "Les parlementaires toulousains à la fin du dix-septième siècle." *Annales du Midi* 76 (1964): 189–204.

Perouas, Louis, et al. *Léonard, Marie, Jean et les autres: Les prénoms en Limousin depuis un millénaire*. Paris: CNRS, 1984.

Pic, Robert. "Les protestants d'Aubais de la Révocation à la Révolution." *BSHPF* 126 (1980): 53–108.

Poitevin, Maurice de. "Les offices municipaux à Castres (1690–1766)." In *Gaillac et pays tarnais. Actes du XXXIe congrès de la Fédération des sociétés académiques et savantes, Languedoc-Pyrénées-Gascogne*, 379–86. Albi: Ateliers Professionnels de l'Orphelinat Saint-Jean, 1977.

Poivre, Joël. *Jérémie Ferrier (1576–1626): Du Protestantisme à la raison d'état*. Geneva: Librairie Droz, 1990.

Portal, Charles. *Les anciennes mesures agraires du Tarn*. Albi: Larrieu, 1913. (Extrait de l'*Annuaire du Tarn*, 1913.)

Porterfield, Amanda. "Women's Attraction to Puritanism." *Church History* 60 (1991): 196–209.

Poumarède, Jacques. *Les successions dans le sud-ouest de la France au moyen âge*. Paris: Presses Universitaires de France, 1972.

Poux, A. *Histoire du collège de Castres depuis les origines jusqu'à nos jours.* Castres: Monsarrat, 1902.

Powis, Jonathan K. *Aristocracy.* Oxford and New York: Blackwell, 1984.

―――. "Order, Religion, and the Magistrates of a Provincial Parlement in Sixteenth-Century France." *Archiv für Reformationsgeschichte* 71 (1980): 180–97.

Pradel, Charles. *Notes historiques sur la ville de Puylaurens.* Toulouse: Privat, 1907. Reprint. Castres: Jacques Mas, 1980.

―――. "Notice sur la vie du poète Ranchin (1616–1692)." *Mémoires de l'Académie des sciences, inscriptions et belles-lettres de Toulouse* 9 (1887): 402–28.

Prestwich, Menna, ed. *International Calvinism, 1541–1715.* Oxford: Clarendon Press, 1985.

Prouzet, Jean. *Les guerres de religion dans les pays d'Aude, 1560–1596.* Toulouse: Jean Prouzet, 1975.

Puech, Albert. *Une ville au temps jadis ou Nîmes en 1592.* Nîmes: Grimaud, Gervais-Bedot, and Catelan, 1884.

Puech-Milhau, M.-L. "Pierre Borel, 1620(?)–1671." *Revue du Tarn* (1936): 278–80.

Quéniart, Jean. *Culture et société urbaines dans la France de l'ouest au XVIIIe siècle.* Paris: C. Klincksieck, 1978.

―――. *La Révocation de l'Edit de Nantes: Protestants et catholiques français de 1598 à 1685.* Paris: Desclée de Brouwer, 1985.

Rabaud, Camille. *Histoire du protestantisme dans l'Albigeois et le Lauragais.* 2 vols. Paris: Fischbacher, 1873 and 1898.

―――. "La réforme à Castres: Trois époques de l'histoire du protestantisme dans l'Albigeois et le Lauragais." *BSHPF* 22 (1873): 49–64.

Reboul, Frédéric. *La vie au dix-huitième siècle: L'armée.* Paris: Marcel Seheur, 1931.

Redlich, Fritz. *The German Military Enterpriser and His Work Force: A Study in European Economic and Social History.* 2 vols. Wiesbaden: Fritz Steiner Verlag, 1964–65.

La Réforme et l'éducation. Toulouse: Privat, 1974.

Robert, B. "La famille d'Ocagne ou Occagne au XVIIIe siècle." *BSHPF* 85 (1936): 333–35.

Robert-Garlis, Elisée de. *Monographie d'une famille et d'un village: La famille de Robert et les gentilshommes verriers de Gabre.* Toulouse: Privat, 1899.

Roche, Daniel. *Le siècle des lumières en province: Académies et académiciens provinciaux, 1680–1789.* 2 vols. Paris and The Hague: Mouton, 1978.

Romane-Musculus, Paul. "Généalogie des Toulouse-Lautrec, branche protestante de Saint-Germier (XVIe et XVIIe siècles)." *Annales du Midi* 77 (1965): 99–107.

————. "Les protestants de Toulouse en 1568." *BSHPF* 107 (1961): 69–94.

Roper, Lyndal. *The Holy Household: Women and Morals in Reformation Augsburg.* Oxford: Oxford University Press, 1989.

Sabean, David W. "Aspects of Kinship Behavior and Property in Rural Western Europe before 1800." In *Family and Inheritance: Rural Society in Western Europe, 1200–1800,* edited by J. Goody, J. Thirsk, and E. P. Thompson, 96–111. Cambridge: Cambridge University Press, 1976.

Salmon, J. H. M. *Society in Crisis: France in the Sixteenth Century.* New York: St. Martin's Press, 1975.

————. "Storm over the Noblesse." *Journal of Modern History* 53 (1981): 242–57.

Sars, R. de. *Le recrutement de l'armée permanente sous l'Ancien Régime.* Paris: Rousseau, 1920.

Sauzet, Robert. *Contre-réforme et réforme catholique en Bas-Languedoc: Le diocèse de Nîmes au XVIIᵉ siècle.* Paris and Louvain: Vander-Oyez and Nauwelaerts, 1979.

Schalk, Ellery. "Ennoblement in France from 1350 to 1660." *Journal of Social History* 16, no. 2 (Winter 1982): 100–110.

————. *From Valor to Pedigree: Ideas of Nobility in France in the Sixteenth and Seventeenth Centuries.* Princeton: Princeton University Press, 1986.

Schnapper, Bernard. *Les rentes au XVIᵉ siècle: Histoire d'un instrument de crédit.* Paris: SEVPEN, 1957.

Segalen, Martine. "'Avoir sa part': Sibling Relations in Partible Inheritance Brittany." In *Interest and Emotion: Essays on the Study of Family and Kinship,* edited by Hans Medick and David Warren Sabean, 129–44. Cambridge: Cambridge University Press, 1984.

————. *Historical Anthropology of the Family.* Translated by J. C. Whitehouse and Sarah Matthews. Cambridge: Cambridge University Press, 1986.

————. *Love and Power in the Peasant Family: Rural France in the Nineteenth Century.* Translated by S. Matthews. Chicago: University of Chicago Press, 1983.

————. "Le mariage et la femme dans les proverbes du sud de la France." *Annales du Midi* 87 (1975): 265–88.

Shaffer, John W. *Family and Farm: Agrarian Change and Household Organization in the Loire Valley, 1500–1900.* Albany: State University of New York Press, 1982.

Sicard, Germain. *Le métayage dans le Midi toulousain à la fin du moyen âge. Mémoires de l'Académie de Législation.* Toulouse: Soubiron, 1956.

————. "Pratiques testamentaires et attitudes religieuses à Toulouse à la fin de l'Ancien Régime." *Mémoires de la Société pour l'histoire du droit et des institutions des anciens pays bourguignons, comtois et romans* 31(1970–71): 271–87.

Simpson, Joyce G. *Le Tasse et la littérature et l'art baroques en France.* Paris: Nizet, 1962.

Slater, Miriam. *Family Life in the Seventeenth Century: The Verneys of Claydon House.* London: Routledge and Kegan Paul, 1984.

———. "The Weightiest Business: Marriage in an Upper-Gentry Family in Seventeenth-Century England." *Past and Present,* no. 72 (1976): 25–54.

Solé, Jacques. "Le gouvernement royal et les protestants de Languedoc à la veille de la Fronde (1633–1648) d'après la correspondance imprimée du Chancellier Seguier." *BSHPF* 114 (1968): 5–32.

Soliday, Gerald L., ed. *History of the Family and Kinship: A Select International Bibliography.* Millwood, N. Y.: Kraus International, 1980.

Soubeyran, Louis. *Essai historique et généalogique sur les Soubeyran ou Soubeiran cévenols.* Dieulefit: Chez l'auteur, 1934.

Stauffer, Richard. "Le calvinisme et les universités." *BSHPF* 126 (1980): 27–51.

Stocker, Christopher. "Office as Maintenance in Renaissance France." *Canadian Journal of History* 6 (1971): 21–43.

Stone, Lawrence. *The Family, Sex and Marriage in England 1500–1800.* New York: Harper and Row, 1977.

Susane, Louis Auguste. *Histoire de l'infanterie française.* 2nd ed. 5 vols. Paris: Dumaine, 1876.

Tallemant des Réaux, Gédéon. *Historiettes.* Edited by Antoine Adam. 2 vols. Paris: Gallimard, 1960–61.

Tardif, Adolphe. *Le droit privé au XIIIe siècle d'après les coutumes de Toulouse et de Montpellier.* Paris: Picard, 1886.

Tavernier, Félix. *La vie quotidienne à Marseille de Louis XIV à Louis-Philippe.* Paris: Librairie Hachette, 1973.

Taylor, George V. "Noncapitalist Wealth and the Origins of the French Revolution." *AHR* 72 (1967): 469–96.

Timbal, Pierre-Clément. "La dévolution successorale *ab intestat* dans la coutume de Toulouse." *Revue historique de droit français et étranger* 33 (1955): 51–82.

Todd, Margo. "Humanists, Puritans and the Spiritualized Household." *Church History* 49 (1980): 18–34.

Tracy, James D. *A Financial Revolution in the Habsburg Netherlands: Renten and Renteniers in the County of Holland, 1515–1565.* Berkeley and Los Angeles: University of California Press, 1985.

Traer, James F. *Marriage and the Family in Eighteenth-Century France.* Ithaca: Cornell University Press, 1980.

Tuety, Louis. *Les officiers sous l'ancien régime: Nobles et routiers.* Paris: Plon, 1908.

Van Deursen, Arie Theodorus. *Professions et métiers interdits: Un aspect de l'histoire de la Révocation de l'Edit de Nantes.* Groningen: J. B. Wolters, 1960.

Vène, Marc. *Guillaume le Nautonier, seigneur de Castelfranc.* Marseille: La Duraulié, 1991.

Vergnette, Hubert de. "Famille de Rozel." *Héraldique et généalogie* 21 (1989): 381–84.

Viala, André. *Le Parlement de Toulouse et l'administration royale laïque, 1420–1525 environ.* 2 vols. Albi: Orphelins-Apprentis, 1953.

Vic, Dom Claude de, and Dom. J. Vaissète. *Histoire générale de Languedoc.* 16 vols. Toulouse: Privat, 1872–1904.

Vindry, Fleury. *Les parlementaires français au XVIe siècle.* 2 vols. Paris: Honoré Champion, 1909–12.

Virieux, Maurice. "Une enquête sur le Parlement de Toulouse en 1718." *Annales du Midi* 87 (1975): 37–65.

Vovelle, Michel. "Jalons pour une histoire du silence: Les testaments réformés dans le sud-est de la France du XVIIIe siècle." In *De la cave au grenier,* edited by M. Vovelle, 387–404. Quebec: Serge Fleury, 1980.

Weary, William W. "The House of La Trémoille, Fifteenth through Eighteenth Centuries: Change and Adaptation in a French Noble Family." *Journal of Modern History* 49 (1977): on demand article.

Wemyss, Alice. *Les protestants du Mas-d'Azil: Histoire d'une résistance, 1680–1830.* Toulouse: Privat, 1961.

Weygand, Maxime. *Histoire de l'armée française.* Paris: Flammarion, 1961.

Wheaton, Robert. "Affinity and Descent in Seventeenth-Century Bordeaux." In *Family and Sexuality in French History,* edited by Robert Wheaton and Tamara K. Hareven, 111–34. Philadelphia: University of Pennsylvania Press, 1980.

———. "Recent Trends in the Historical Study of the French Family." In *Family and Sexuality in French History,* edited by Robert Wheaton and Tamara K. Hareven, 3–26. Philadelphia: University of Pennsylvania Press, 1980.

Wiesner, Merry E. "Women's Defense of Their Public Role." In *Women in the Middle Ages and the Renaissance,* edited by Mary Beth Rose, 1–27. Syracuse: Syracuse University Press, 1986.

Wolfe, Martin. *The Fiscal System of Renaissance France.* New Haven and London: Yale University Press, 1972.

Wolff, Philippe. "Trois études de démographie médiévale en France méridionale." *Studi in onore di Armando Sapori.* 2 vols. Milan: Istituto Editoriale Cisalpino, 1957, 1:493–503.

Wood, James B. *The Nobility of the Election of Bayeux, 1463–1666: Continuity through Change.* Princeton: Princeton University Press, 1980.

Wrong, Charles J. "The Officiers de Fortune in the French Infantry." *French Historical Studies* 9 (1976): 400–431.

Yver, Jean. *Egalité entre héritiers et exclusion des enfants dotés: Essai de géographie coutumière*. Paris: Editions Sirey, 1966.

Zeller, Gaston. *Les institutions de la France au XVIe siècle*. Paris: Presses Universitaires de France, 1948.

Zink, Anne. *Azereix: La vie d'une communauté à la fin du XVIIIe siècle*. Paris: SEVPEN, 1969.

Index

Fouquet, Nicolas, 136
Franc-fief, 2
Francis I, 32
Fronde, 131

Gabelle, 23
Gaches, Jean, husband of Isabeau de Lacger, 89
Gaches, pastor, 138, 165
Galèye, chaplaincy of, 34, 40
Gavaret, Guyon de, husband of Jeanne de Lacger, 96
Généalogie historique de la maison de Lacger, 3, 159
Genealogy, 159
Godparents, 148–51
 agricultural tenants and servants as, 151, 178
 at Bordeaux, 149
 child named for, 148–49
 cross-confessional, 150–51, 176
 responsibilities of, 149–50
 selection of, 150–51, 178
Gondran, Madame de, 130
Guardianship for minor children, 50–51, 84, 95, 101–2, 156
Guilhalme, wife of Pierre de Lacger, 28, 29

Henry II, 88
Henry of Navarre (Henry IV of France), 13, 19, 41, 44, 63, 65, 127
Hérail family
 Marguerite d', second wife of Pierre de Lacger: dowry of, 91, 95, 154
 Marie d', 154
Herlihy, David, 188
Huguenots
 conversion of, to Catholicism, 11, 16–22, 24–25, 55–56, 77, 133, 136–37, 158; and aid of Protestant kin, 175–76; and family strategies, 171–72; among judicial officials, 168–73; among military officers, 174–76; resistance to, by women, 170–72, 182
 as fiscal officers, 20–21, 23–24
 intellectual endeavors of, 132–41
 as judicial magistrates, 13–14, 19, 21, 23–24, 36, 172–73
 and literary circles, 128–31
 as military officers, 18, 23–24, 77–78
 as municipal officers, 19, 22–23
 and political assemblies, 9–10, 13, 15, 44, 62, 173; at Grenoble (1615), 20, 68, 166

and political patronage, 13, 19, 31–32, 173
and resistance to revocation of Edict of Nantes, 177–82

Inheritance, 7–8, 37, 104, 160
 antifeminist tendencies of, 106, 107–8
 collateral, 53, 112–13, 158–59
 customary laws and usages of, 105; in Normandy, 105; in Paris basin, 105; in southern France, 105
 and favoring of eldest son, 105–6, 117
 intestate, 93, 102
 through marriage, 84, 93–94, 97
Inter vivos donations, 105, 109–10, 115–18
Intestate succession, 111–12
Isarn family, 133, 140
 Benoît d', 134, 135, 164
 Marguerite d', wife of Jacques de Lacger, 84, 102; dowry of, 90, 92; marriage contract of, 110
 Samuel d', 128, 135–36, 137

Jointure (*douaire*), 96
Joutard, Philippe, 191
Joyeuse, vicomte de, 43
Juge d'appeaux, office at Castres, 31, 33, 61, 66, 85
Juge family, 173
 Claude de, 170, 172
Juge mage for Uzès, 19, 21
Juge ordinaire, office of, 67
 at Brassac, 32, 64, 66
 at Castelnaudary, 33, 65
 at Castres, 31, 45, 61, 67, 108, 166

Kin patronage, 152–56
 and assistance to women, 154
 and matrilineal associations, 155–56, 160–61
 within professional sphere, 154–56
 and uncles and nephews, 152–54
Kin solidarity, 66, 73, 78, 113, 156–59, 189–90
 cross-confessional, 157–58, 176–77
 and inheritance practices, 113–16, 118–19
 within Lacger family, 45–47, 158
 among siblings, 156–57

Lacaune, 97
Lacger family
 Adrian de, merchant of Toulouse, 33, 35, 38, 46, 113, 118; religious position of, 40–41; wife's dowry, 91
 Antoine, baron de Lacger, 57

Lacger family (continued)
    library of, 124–28; rentes of, 58–59;
        royal offices of, at Paris, 65, 67, 113,
        136
    Sébastien de, canon at Burlats, 33–35,
        38–40, 42, 53, 113, 118
    town houses of, 52, 53–55, 56–57, 112
    vineyards of, 51
Lacrouzette, sieur de, 43–44
La Rochelle, 21, 70
La Roque, Astruge de, 89
Last will and testament, 19, 28, 29, 37, 41,
        96, 98, 101, 105–6, 144
    and expressions of piety, 107, 113–15
    legal practices of, 106
    and testamentary gifts, 114
La Suze, Henriette de Coligny, comtesse de,
        128–31, 137
La Trémoille family, 68, 151, 155, 161, 186
    duc de La Trémoille, 69–70
La Trinque, seigneury of, 56
Lauragais, 42, 57, 158, 168
    county of, 33, 35
    seneschalsy of, 33, 65
Lausanne, 15
Lautrec, 29
    vicomté of, 31
Le Faucheur, Michel, 127–28, 163
Légitime (minimum share in inheritance),
        108–11, 117
Lenclos, Ninon de, 130
Lespinasse family, 85
Libraries of Antoine II, Samuel, and Jacques
        de Lacger, 124–28
Lisle-sur-Tarn, 63
Lombers, Baronnie of, 31
Louis XIII, 68, 70, 84
Louis XIV, 5, 11, 72, 75, 77, 136
    wars of, 10, 23, 73
Louis XV, 11
    wars of, 73
Louvois, minister of war, 75

Marion, Gabrielle de, 35
Marriage, 30, 35
    and age differences, 95, 97
    Catholic practices forced on Protestants,
        177, 179
    choice of spouse, 82, 87
    and confessional considerations, 82, 85–87
    criteria for, 35–36, 86
    au Désert, 86, 179–80
    economic motives for, 8, 84–85
    and local affiliations, 85
    parental authority over, 88–89

patterns of, 8, 82; among nobility of Aix-
        en-Provence and Toulouse, 87
    place of, in ancien régime, 81–82
    and professional alliances, 83–84, 97
    among Protestants of Castres, 82, 88, 92
    reproductive expectations for, 96, 97–98,
        100, 188
    role of family in, 89–90
    successive, 35–36
Marriage contract, 36, 89, 95–97, 109–11
Maternal authority, 102–3
Maternal responsibilities, 100–103
Métairies, 7, 29, 50–51, 97
Michelade, 22–23
Military service
    benefits of, 78–80
    careers in, 74
    decorations of, 74, 77–79, 175
    grades in, 75–77
    income from, 52, 79
    promotion in, 74–75
Millau, 41
Montagne Noire, 6
Montauban, 6, 12–14, 39, 62, 69, 166, 173,
        178
    bipartisan government of, 14
Montgomery, count of, 44
Montmorency-Damville, duc de, 19, 43–45
Montpellier, 22, 83, 85, 86, 170, 173
    chambre des comptes at, 24, 83, 135
    university at, 66, 121, 124, 135, 137
Montredon, 15
Mornay, Philippe du Plessis, 127, 163

Naming practices, 145–49
Nantes, Edict of, 6, 20, 39, 63, 113, 124
    revocation of, 5, 12, 16, 55, 64, 77, 85,
        86, 101, 112, 124, 132, 151, 158, 168,
        172, 174, 176, 179; and family strate-
        gies, 169–72; Protestant reaction to,
        182–83
Nautonier family, 15–17
Nets family, 151, 155, 161
    François de, 68
    Marguerite de, wife of Jacques de Lacger,
        90, 101–3, 128, 151
New Catholics, 16–17, 18–19, 170–71, 175,
        177, 179, 182
Nîmes, 6, 15, 19, 22–24, 39, 62, 132, 170
Nobility
    and family, 142
    of robe, 5, 36, 141
    of sword, 5
Noir, Marc-Antoine de, husband of Marie de
        Lacger, 95